I0810496

IMAGES
of America

BARRE

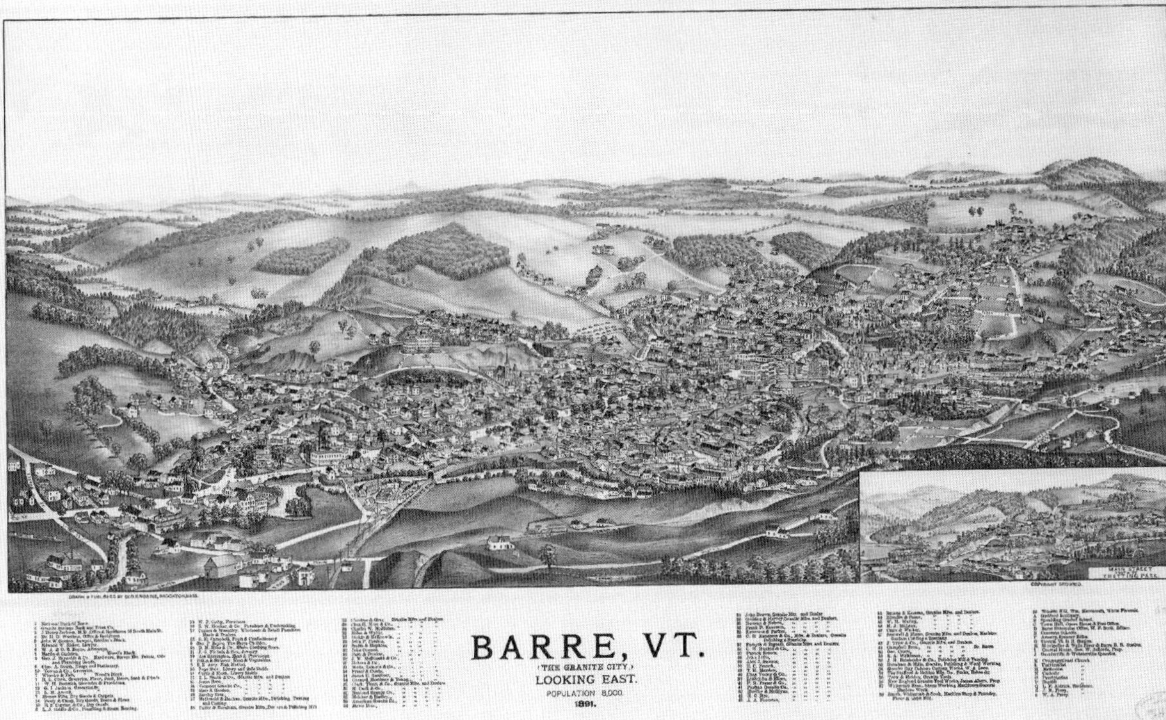

This 1891 "Barre, VT, The Granite City, Looking East" map was drawn in pencil by George E. Norris, traveling map artist, and published by "Geo. Eng. Rie, Brocton, Mass." In 1788, just a few families who came from Massachusetts made the first settlement in Barre. From 1880 to 1890, the population increased from 2,060 to 6,812 after immigrants came from around the world to work in the granite industry. At one point in time, Barre had 3,500 granite cutters. (Courtesy of Maps of New England.)

On the Cover: Skin brown from the sun and covered in sweat from the hot summer air, these unidentified Barre quarry workers hauled granite 10 hours a day. Early settlers used granite for building foundations, fence posts, doorsteps, and window caps. A tavern built in 1802 by Silas Willard is a good example of the use of granite in its foundation. Early quarrymen used granite to manufacture millstones used to grind grain on Millstone Hill. The granite on a nearby hill, known as Cobble Hill, was used to manufacture paving stones called cobble. (Courtesy of the Vermont Granite Museum.)

IMAGES
of America

BARRE

Doreen Chambers and Brooke Lorentzen

ARCADIA PUBLISHING

ISBN 978-1-4671-2091-3

Published by Arcadia Publishing
Charleston, South Carolina

Printed in the United States of America

Library of Congress Control Number: 2013943962

For all general information, please contact Arcadia Publishing:
Telephone 843-853-2070
Fax 843-853-0044
E-mail sales@arcadiapublishing.com
For customer service and orders:
Toll-Free 1-888-313-2665

Visit us on the Internet at www.arcadiapublishing.com

Contents

ACKNOWLEDGMENTS

Barre is an expression of our fondness for the colorful history of Barre, Vermont. We would like to sincerely thank Patricia Meriam of the Vermont Granite Museum, Ed Larson of the Barre Granite Association, Valerie Beaudet of the Firehouse Inn and Ladder 1 Grill and Pub, and the Barre Historical Society for lending us a majority of these photographs from their collection. For kindly donating photographs, we would like to express our special thanks to Dave Allen; Old Maps; West Chesterfield, New Hampshire; Ashley Fleck Morris; Greg Fleck and Carol Fleck; Bob Somaini of the Barre Antique Mall; and Todd Paton, Rock of Ages. The unmarked postcards and images are from the authors' personal collection.

We would also like to express our thanks to Barre director of cemeteries and parks Dwight Coffrin for taking the time to drive to Hope Cemetery and mark a particular memorial so we could locate it to take a picture.

Finally, we wish to express our heartfelt appreciation to Arcadia Publishing acquisitions editor Caitrin Cunningham for her help and ongoing encouragement.

INTRODUCTION

Artistic is the best word to describe Barre because it is an open art gallery of sculpted figures and carved designs created out of beautiful granite. Barre, called the "Granite Center of the World," is centrally located in Washington County in what is considered by geologists as a very old mountain range of mostly solid granite that is about 150 to 500 million years old.

The story of when and how the 19,900 acres of wilderness became what is now known as the town of Barre, Vermont, began on November 6, 1780, when 65 proprietors named the land Wildersburg. Historians claim that all the proprietors came from Wildersburg, Massachusetts. Proprietors never settled here, but instead they sold the land for a profit to others living in Massachusetts and Rhode Island. The people who settled in Barre were adventurous men and women of great physical and mental strength.

Records show that in 1788 the first settlers—Capt. Samuel Rogers and John Goldsbury and their families—followed the Coös indian trail through the dark virgin forest to get to their land. Other early settlers were as follows: Col. Benjamin Walker (justice of the peace); Dea. Jonas Nichols, Joseph Sherman, Joseph Dwight, Maj. Nathan Harrington (selectmen); Job Adams (constable); Isaac S. Thompson, Apollos Hale, and Elias Cheney (listers).

At first, settlers were quite isolated and had little opportunity to communicate with anyone. The settlers' wives and family members were full partners in the task of daily living. They quickly adapted to their new environment, and each family made their own clothing from what was grown in the garden, or woven from a woolly sheep in the barn. Trees were used to build log cabins, furniture, and tools. Horses and oxen were great helpers to settlers because they carried heavy loads and pulled wagons and sleds.

By 1790, the wilderness was transformed into a small number of settled communities with a population of about 76 people. As the settlements grew in population, they eventually merged into one settlement along the valley. It did not take too long for the settlers to start complaining about the town's name, and they decided to rename it. In 1793, the new name was decided by the highest bid at a town meeting and ended with a playful fistfight between Joseph Thompson and Jonathan Sherman. The drama ended with a big smirk on Sherman's face and a shout of triumph: "Barre is the name by God." Thus began the colorful history of Barre, Vermont.

Granite was discovered in 1812 by Robert Parker and Thomas Courser on what was known as Cobble Hill. Shortly after, granite was also discovered in the areas of Graniteville and Websterville (in South Barre near Williamstown) known as Millstone Hill.

The principal streams in Barre are the Stevens Branch and Jail Branch. The Jail Branch stream was named after a log jail that had been built on its bank, and the Stevens Branch stream was used to power a number of mills in the village. In 1818, Joshua Thwing built the first machine shop and grain mill in Barre. In Hamilton Child's book *Gazetteer of Towns*, he writes, "Smith, Whitcomb, and Cook were the proprietors of the Barre iron works, a merchant and custom grist-mill, and a saw-mill."

Industry and machine manufacturing replaced Barre's manual-labor-based economy. It began with the mechanization of the woolen mills and manufacturers. William Moorcroft started the first woolen mill to manufacture white flannel, and it used 5,000 pounds of wool each year. New granite-cutting tools were also developed.

The Central Vermont Railroad reached Barre in 1875. Railways helped move goods, foods, and people faster than horse-drawn wagons, and life moved along reasonably well. Trade expansion was made possible by improved roads, vehicles, and a street railway connected by an electric line from Main Street in Barre to Montpelier, Vermont.

The Long Depression (1873–1879) triggered mass emigration from Europe. During that time, immigrants were recruited from around the world to work in quarries, sheds, and manufacturing. The Scots came first, followed by the Italians and then many other immigrant groups, which tripled Barre's population between 1880 and 1990. Immigrants were welcomed and became a valuable part of the Barre community. They assimilated into the culture—many starting their own businesses in the area. The granite industry flourished, as exemplified by the number of quarries expanding from 8 to 56 and used 3,500 granite cutters. Many immigrants carried their skill of stone carving with them as seen in chapter four.

In 1922, Canadian labor wars triggered mass emigration from Canada. The timing was good for the Barre granite quarry owners, as they needed more work completed because their own granite workers were on strike. The decision to fill the positions with Canadians resulted in hostility between the strikers, owners, and the immigrant French Canadian workers. A new immigration law came into effect in 1930, and Barre's population started to stabilize. In 1930, one third of all Barre granite firms merged to form the Rock of Ages Corporation.

In 1937, the Vermont Planning Board in *Vermont: A Guide to the Green Mountain State* wrote, "Notoriously a free-spending and pleasure-seeking people, the stoneworkers are largely responsible for the vigor of Barre life. The swift circulation of money, the swarming streets and stores, the whole fast and lusty tempo that sets Barre apart from the rest of the Vermont, is created by the hard-working, hard playing stonecutters. It is characteristic of many busier towns in the State to relapse into quiet with nightfall, but not so Barre."

With the rapid population growth, the town government was unable to keep up with the town's demands, and it was decided to split Barre into two governing bodies. Photographs in the third chapter begin in March 1985, when the village was incorporated as Barre City and the town of Barre. Although incorporated separately, both are in the town of Barre.

Later images tell a story of a variety of social and political movements including anarchists and socialists, temperance, women's suffrage, and protecting the rights of workers and children. The Italians also brought with them strong political opinions favoring revolutionary change in government. These political opinions added to the social and political drama that impacted on the lives and times of Barre residents. Radical at the time, Italians helped organize labor-union strikes to prevent exploitation of the granite workers. They also were strong advocates for the poor. While many opposed violence, others supported it. Luigi Galleani (1861–1931) was the editor of an anarchist newspaper in Barre for 15 years. Luigi fought hard to make a better world for neglected groups of people. He was deported to Italy in June 1919, after a series of violent incidents by his followers.

The final chapters show the evolution of Barre through visual images of clothing fashions, fun, and fancy fire trucks.

The Aldrich Public Library website states, "Today, Barre is one of only a handful of Vermont communities with a culturally diverse population, boasting some fifteen distinct ethnic groups, including Danish, English, Finnish, French, German, Greek, Irish, Italian, Lebanese, Norwegian, Polish, Scottish, Spanish, Swedish and Yugoslavian, as well as Yankee peoples." Barre also has a population of French Canadians.

One

First Settlement

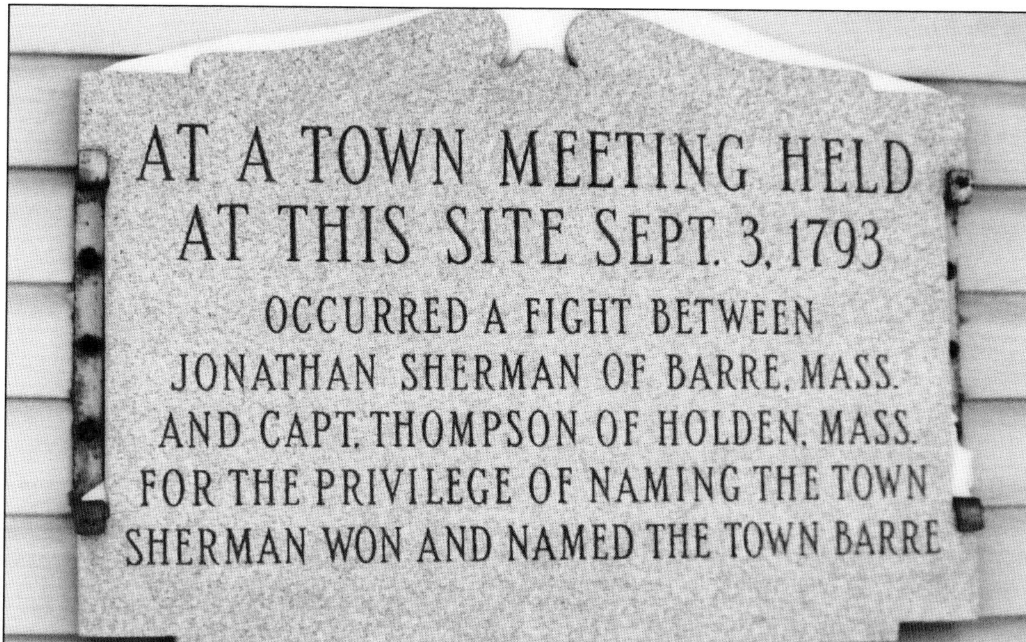

Unhappy with the name of Wildersburg that was chosen by the proprietors, settlers decided to rename the town. Pictured is a granite plaque mounted on the outside (originally the inside) of Calvin Smith Farm's barn wall that memorializes how settlers decided to rename where they lived.

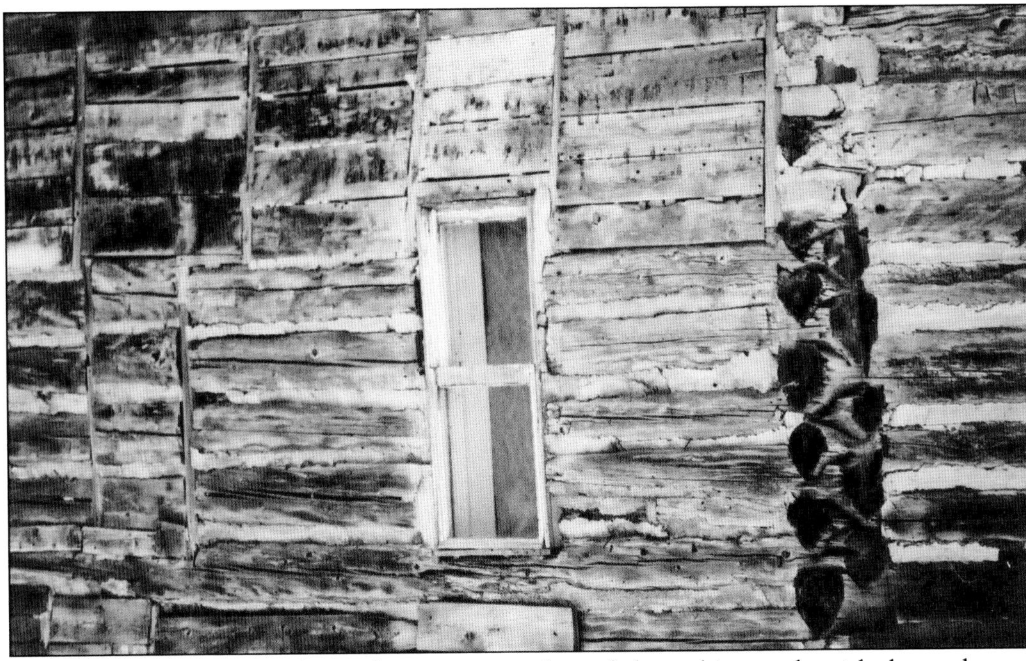

Wood was plentiful, and the settlers constructed rough log cabins made with downed trees. Historically, moss or mud was used as insulation and bark as roofing material. If they had windows, they were filled with oiled paper or covered with animal skins. Settlers did not have glass, nails, or hardware to use in their homes. They lived in these cabins until they could build framed houses.

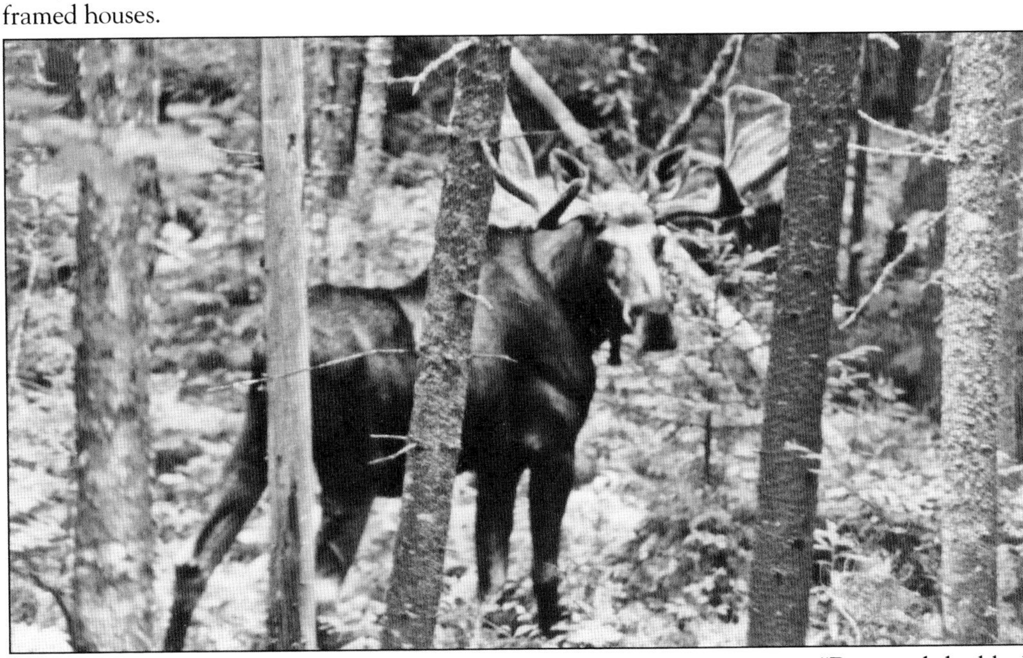

The History of Washington County in the Vermont Historical Gazetteer states, "Deer and the black bear were found very plenty in the first of the settlement, and occasionally the American monsal [*sic*], or moose. The bear still contests the rights of civilization, rather too successfully for our sheep pastures at times."

Located in Elmwood Cemetery is the slate gravestone of the first family of settlers to move into Barre, Rebeckah (1759–1834) and John Goldsbury (1735–1825). The settlement in this area of Barre was called Gospel Village.

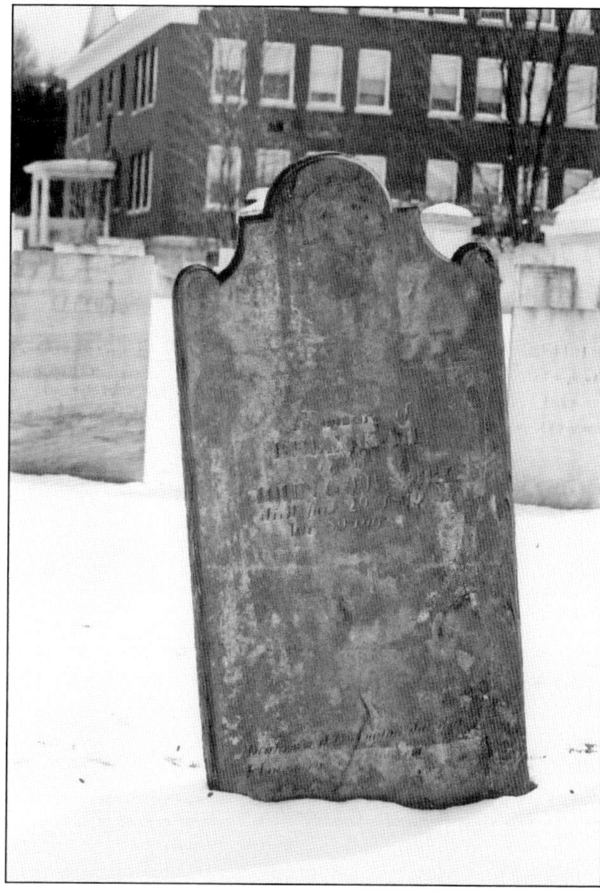

Cultivating the land was the means of producing the family's food. Most farms had chickens, pigs, horses, oxen, and a few cows. Beans, squash, pumpkins, and corn could be stored in root cellars during the winter, and they supplemented the garden produced vegetables with butternuts, blackberries, strawberries, and grapes.

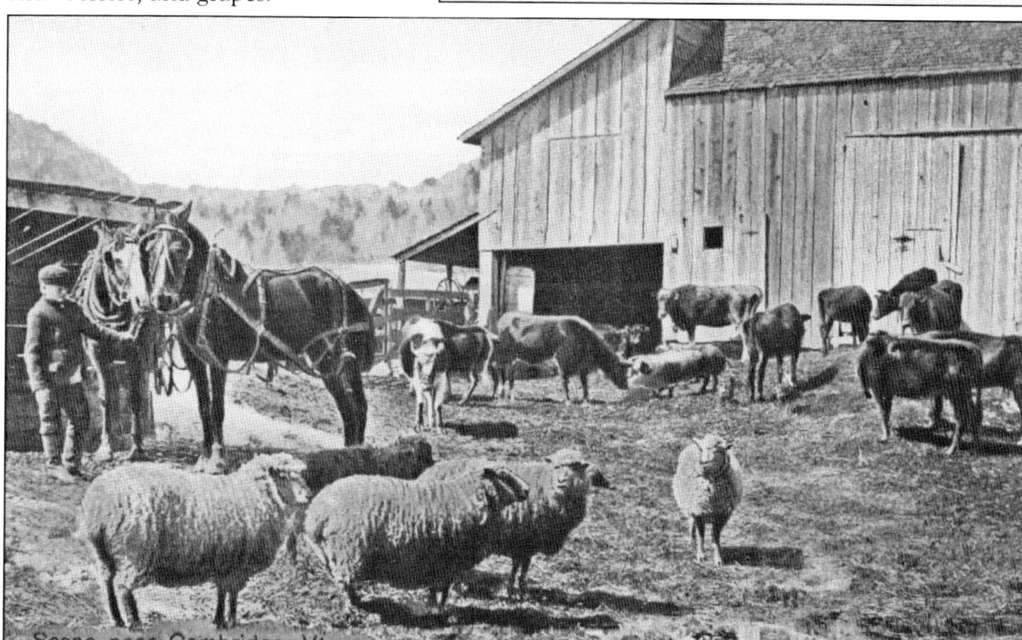

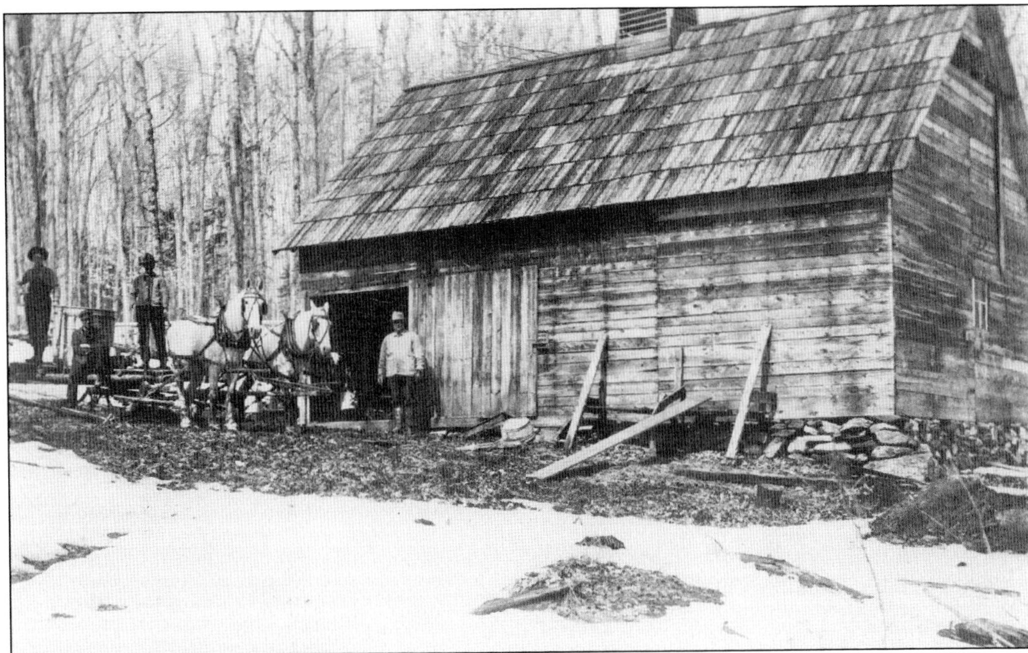

Maple syrup was the primary source of sugar for early settlers. This image shows a team of horses next to the sugar house. The chemistry of the soil combined with chilly nights and warm days of early spring produces the sugar inside of the maple tree. Early settlers may have killed many maple trees by using an ax to cut big notches in the trees to get to the sap. (Courtesy of Ainsworth Public Library, Barre, Vermont.)

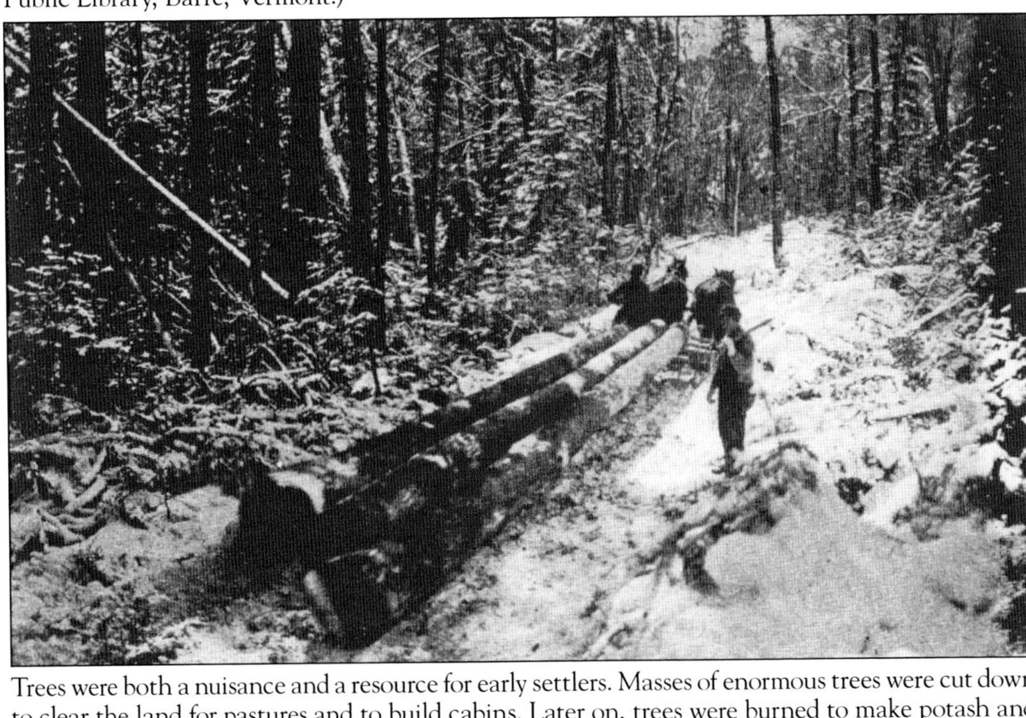

Trees were both a nuisance and a resource for early settlers. Masses of enormous trees were cut down to clear the land for pastures and to build cabins. Later on, trees were burned to make potash and used for commercial lumbering, which led to the white pine tree becoming scarce in the 1860s.

Pastures were cleared of rocks, and stone walls were built up around pastured areas with the discarded stone often by the effort of many generations as can be seen in this image. Stones were also used for outbuildings and foundations. Later, stone walls may have been dismantled to support town roads.

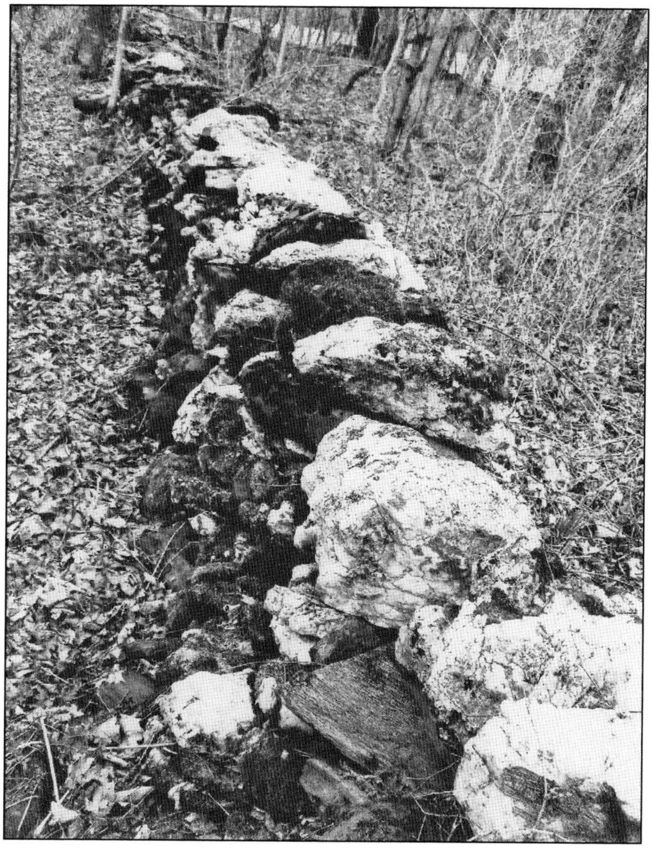

This is the Morrison farm in rural Barre. Hamilton Child reported the following in *The History of Washington County in the Vermont Historical Gazetteer*: "In 1816 the winter snow remained on the ground until the middle of June. Settlers were unable to plant their crops and their apple trees and berries never produced fruit resulting in much hardship."

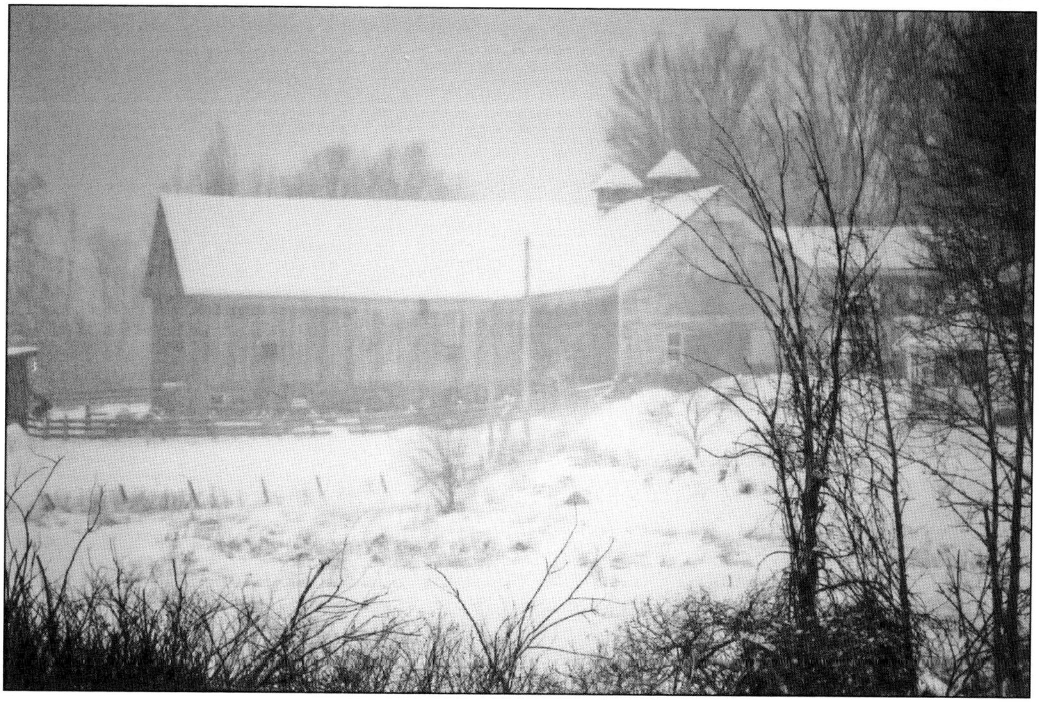

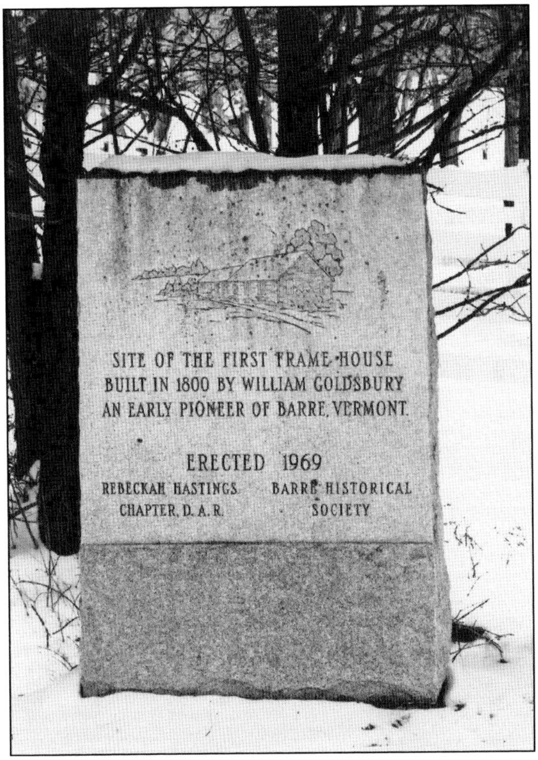

An exciting period in history was memorialized by a marker on West Hill erected in 1969 by the Barre Historical Society to indicate the site of the first framed house built in 1800 by William Goldsbury. The building burned to the ground in 1960.

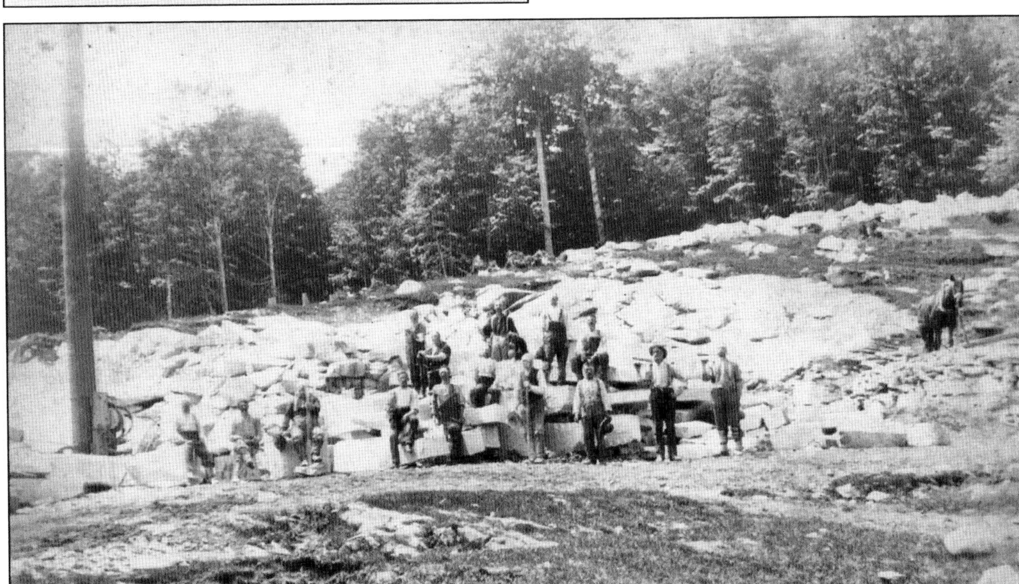

In 1815, Robert Parker and Thomas Courser began cutting surface granite used for millstones (used to grind grain) on their property, and the area was later named Millstone Hill. Granite was later discovered in South Barre in the areas of Graniteville and Websterville. Pictured is the early way of pulling treasure from the ground and hauling granite from the quarries to the sheds about three miles downhill. (Courtesy of Paul Bagalio and William Roy and the Vermont Granite Museum.)

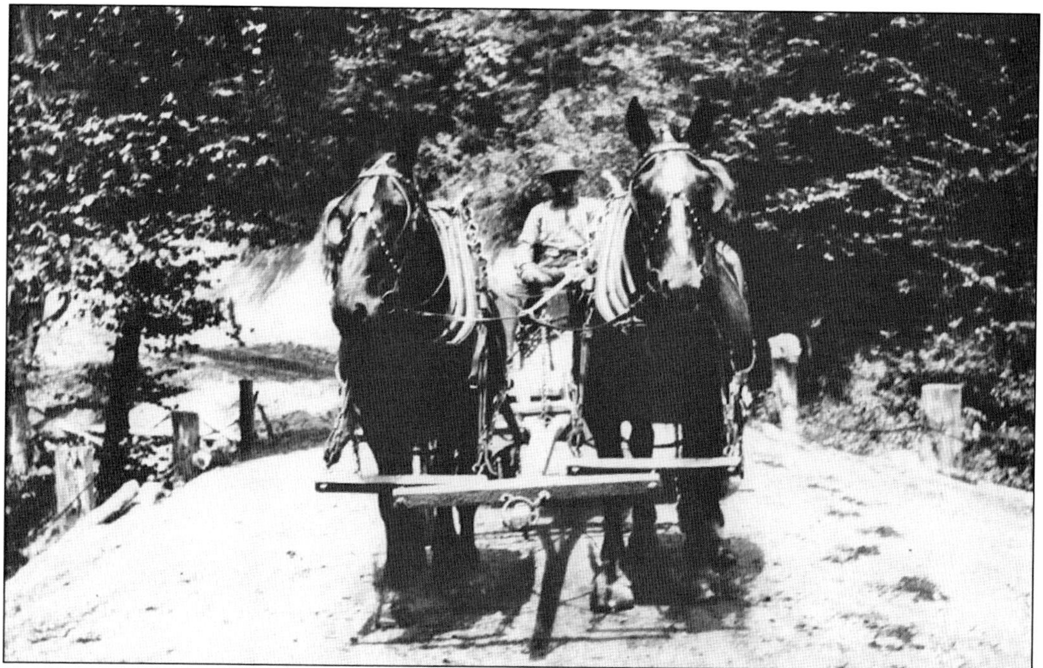

An unidentified man is in a horse-drawn wagon, which was the primary means of travel in settled communities. Earlier settlers did not have the luxury of the wagon when they arrived, but by necessity settlers built what they needed: rudimentary carts, tools, sleds, and furniture.

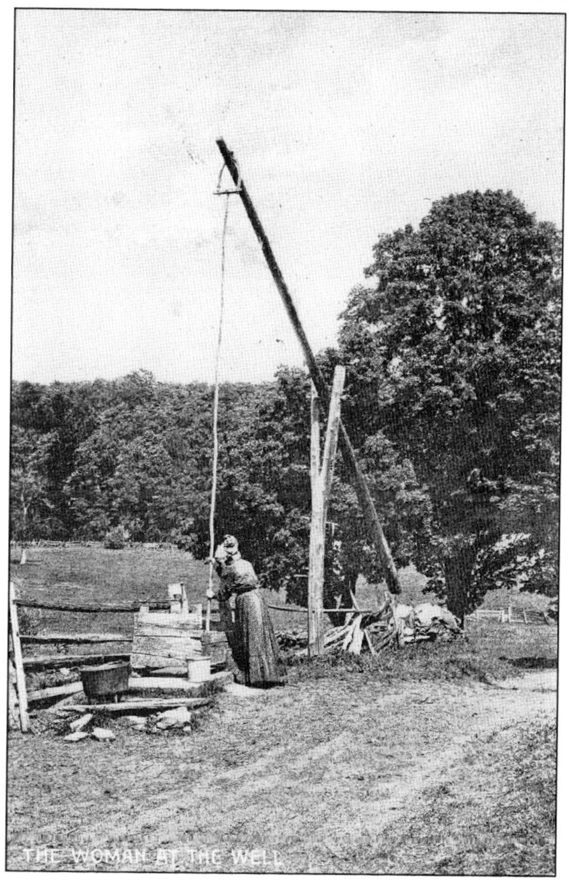

Life was lived simply. This image of a Barre woman getting water from the family well features a useful wooden device created to help lift the bucket out of the well.

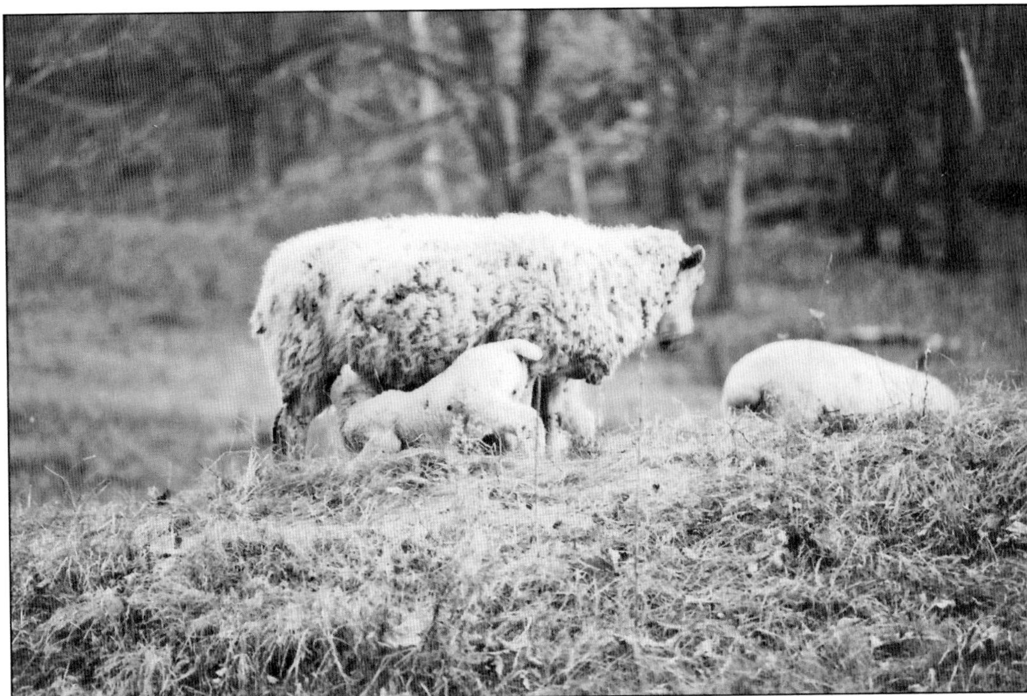

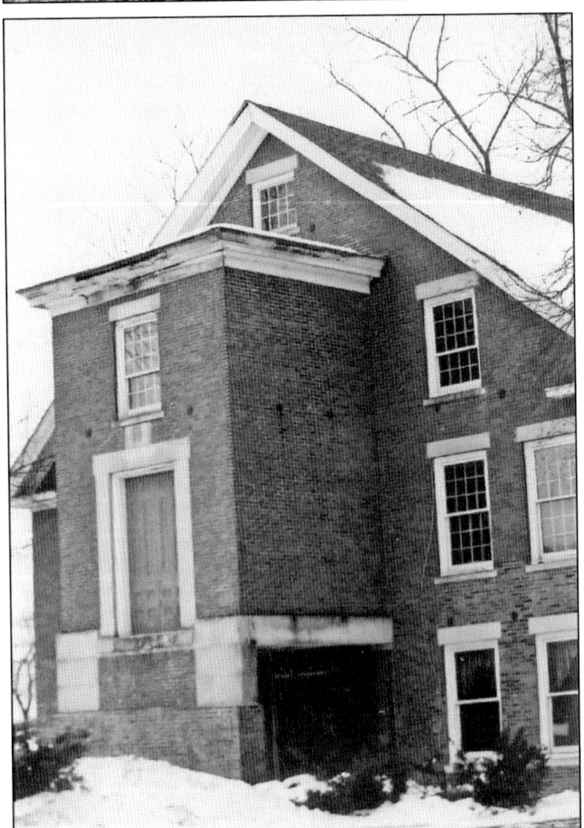

Early on in Barre's history, the principal industries were dairy production, lumbering, and farming. Prior to 1850, settlers raised sheep for the businesses of carding wool and making clothing. John Baker and Ira Day started the first wool carding businesses in Barre.

The Thwing Mill Building was named after Joshua Thwing, who was known for building the first machine shop and grain mill. Prior to the mill being built, settlers had to travel to other towns with their meal for grinding. In Hamilton Child's *Gazetteer of Towns*, he reported, "In 1818, Joshua established the first iron foundry in the state."

Two

Early Barre

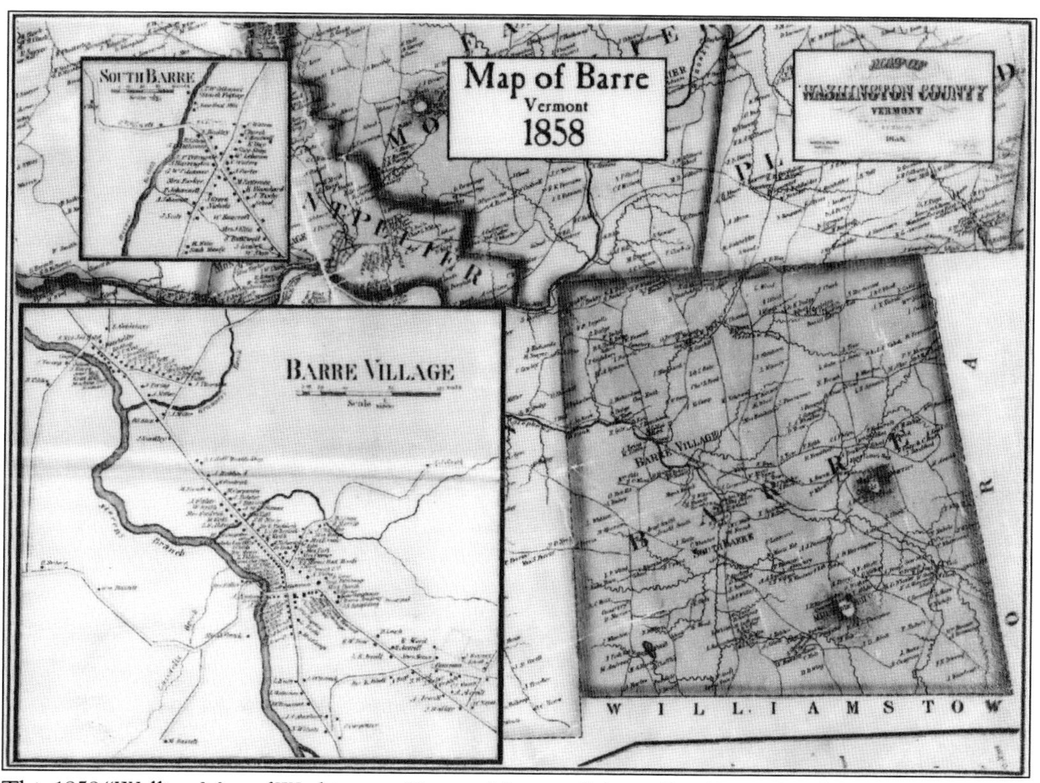

This 1858 "Walling Map of Washington County, Vermont" shows East Barre, South Barre, Graniteville, and Barre Village. This map captures the businesses and residential homes as the settlement grew into a lively town with a population of over 1,845. (Courtesy of Maps of New England.)

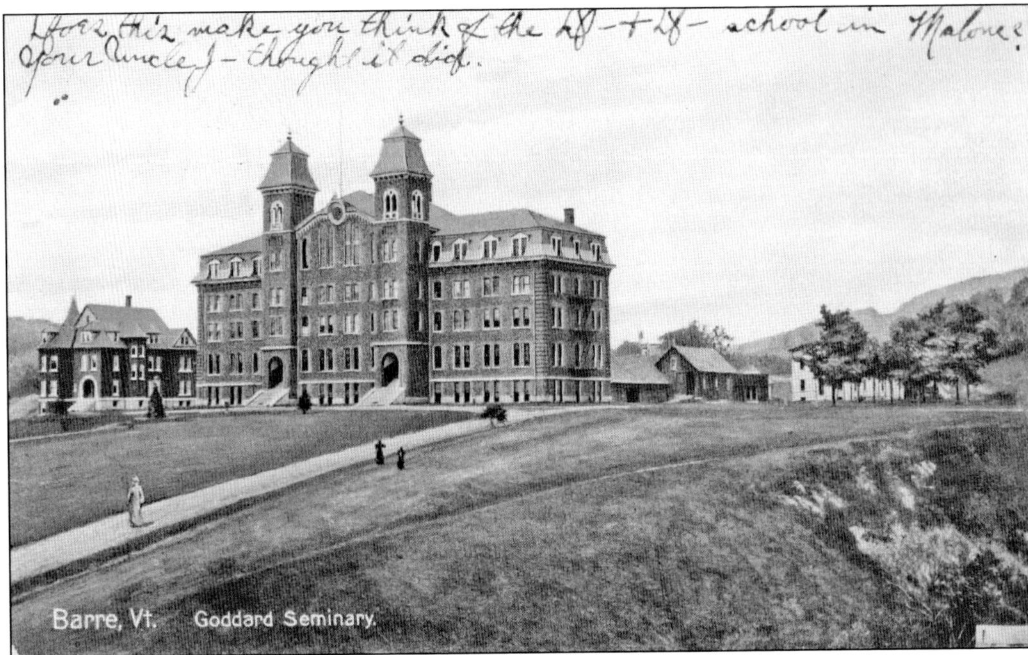

This 1870 postcard published by the Hugh C. Leighton Company shows Goddard Seminary (currently the municipal auditorium) founded in 1863. In 1938, the old Goddard Seminary moved from Barre to Plainfield, Vermont.

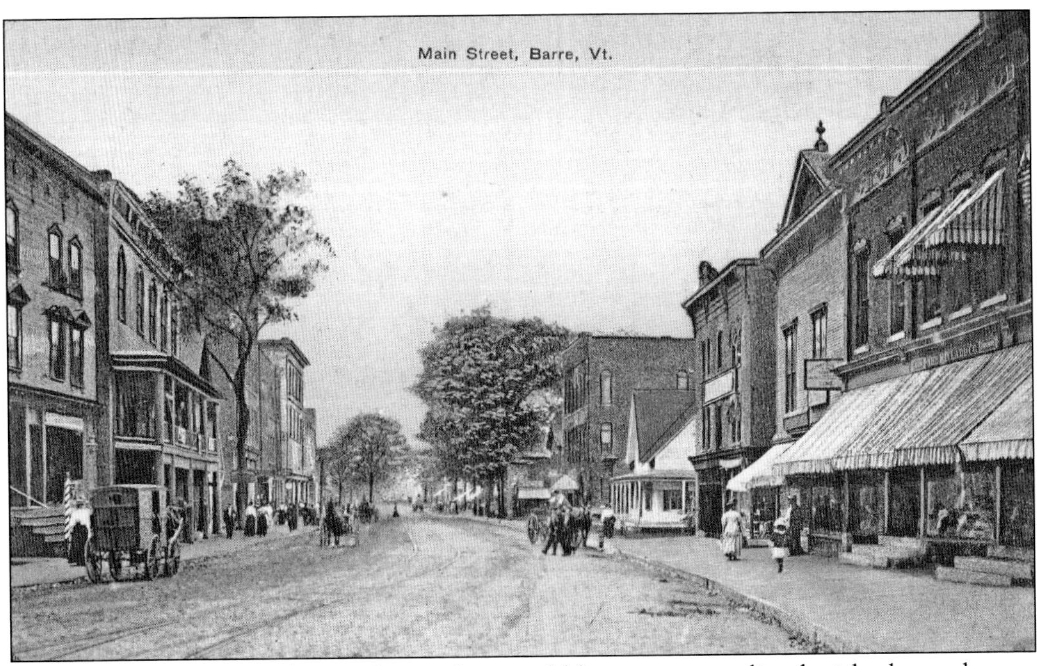

This early photograph of Main Street shows cobblestone streets lined with elm and sugar maple trees.

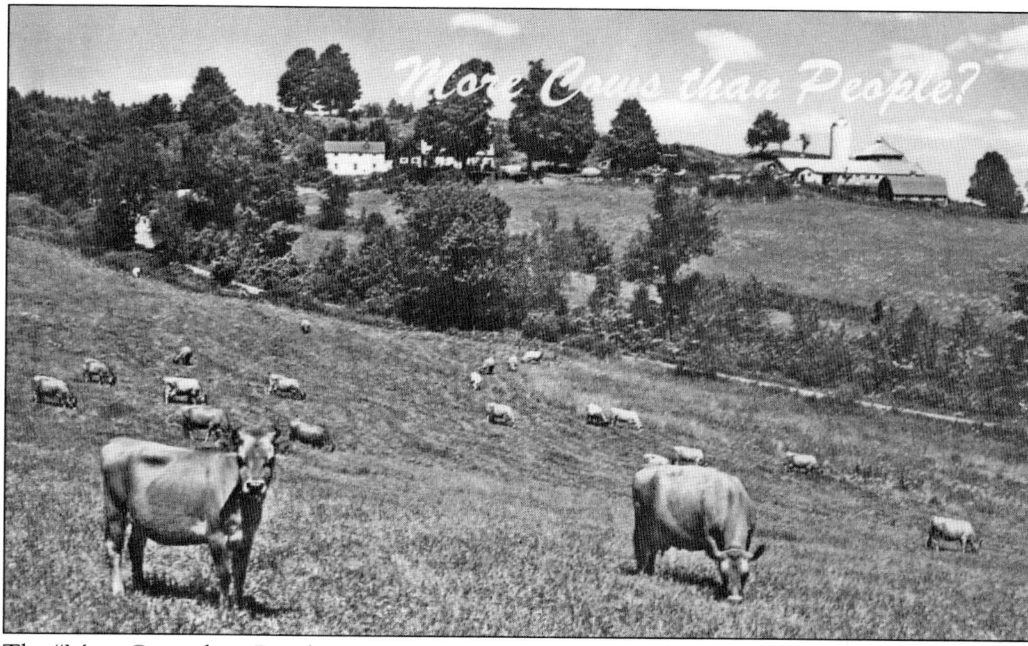

The "More Cows than People" postcard above shows the Booth Brothers Farm in 1850. This is a typical dairy scene representing the principal farm industry of the Green Mountain State. It was published for Vermont Products Supply Company in Barre. The beautiful Booth Brothers Farm is still in use today.

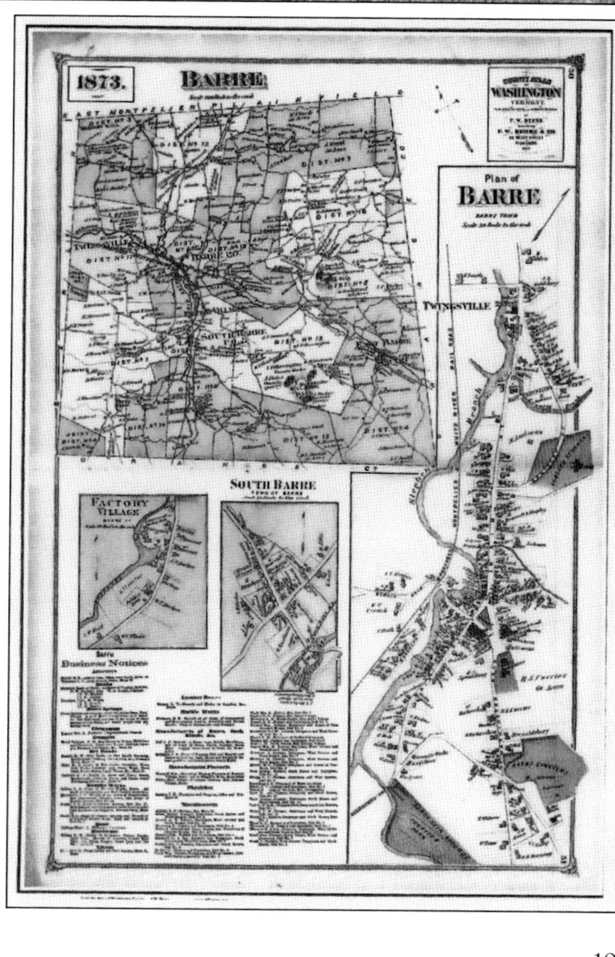

This 1873 Beers Atlas Map shows the population when it had grown to over 2,000. Thwingsville (also spelled Twingsville) is shown on the insert at the lower right-hand corner. (Courtesy of Maps of New England.)

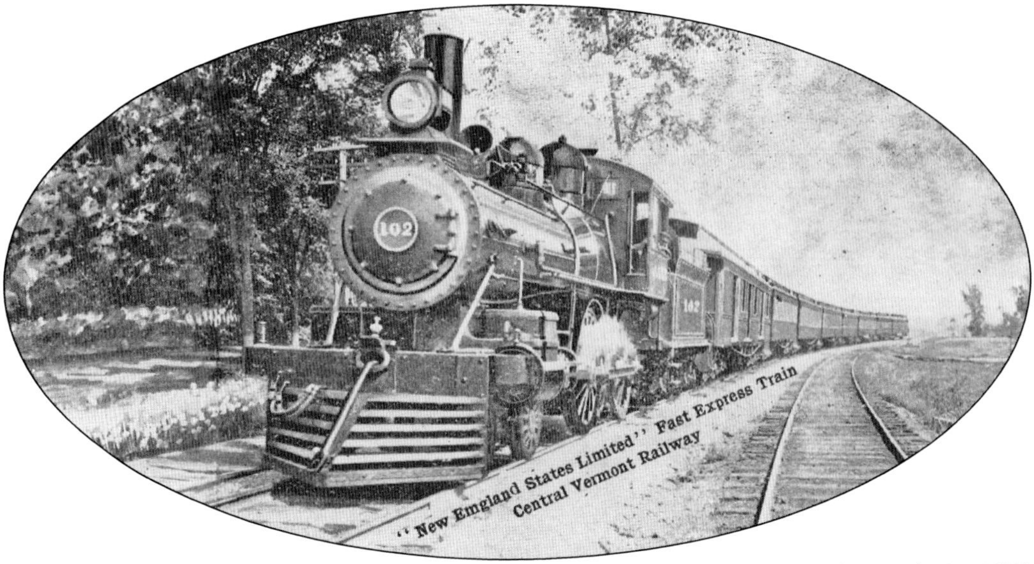

The fast express train of the Central Vermont Railroad is chugging down the track. In 1875, the first Central Vermont Railroad train came into Barre. Thomas W. Bailey was the passenger conductor since the road was opened; Dexter Moody was the baggagemaster; and James Bowers, Robert Gregg, David Daniels, and Albert Caswell were engineers.

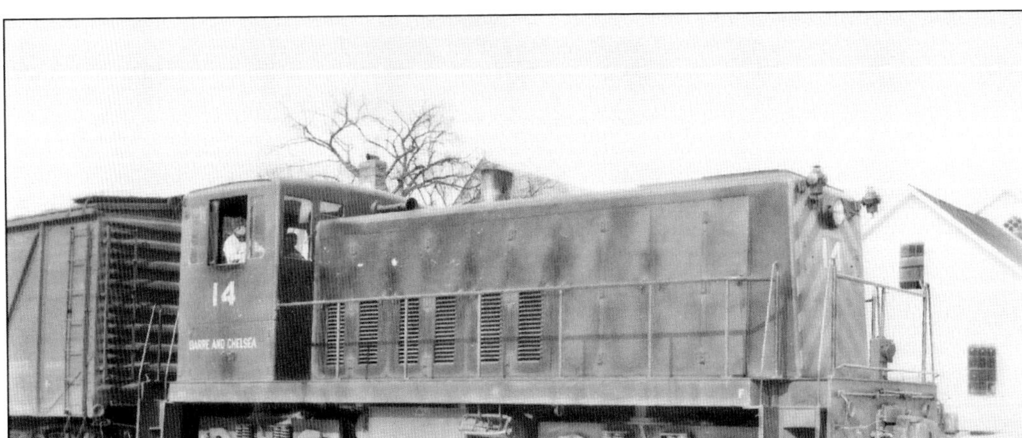

Edmund Fuller's *Vermont: History of the Green Mountain State* says, "Getting the stone from Millstone Hill which climbs 1740 feet in three miles to the working sheds was not solved by the Central Vermont Rail Road. In 1889, the so-called 'Sky Route,' actually the No. 14 Barre and Chelsea Railroad, was built by the city connected every quarry with the shed."

The Long Depression (1873–1879) triggered mass emigration from Europe. During that time, immigrants were recruited from around the world to work in the quarries, granite sheds, and manufacturing plants.

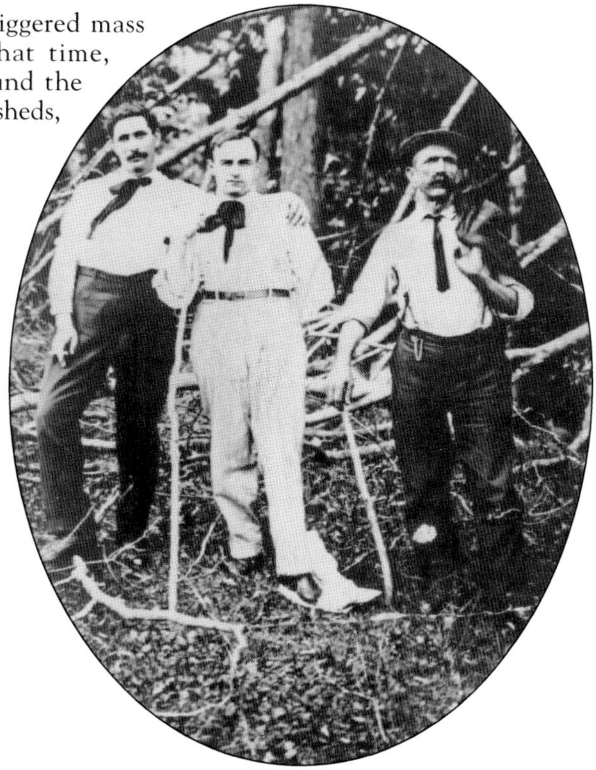

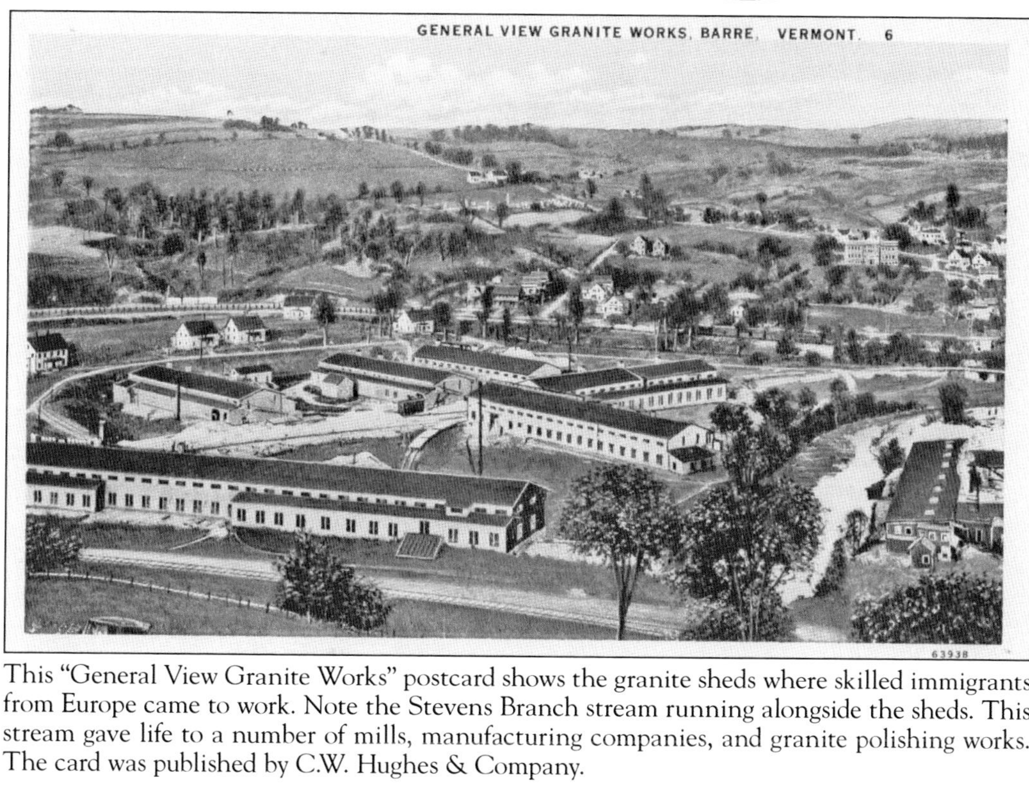

This "General View Granite Works" postcard shows the granite sheds where skilled immigrants from Europe came to work. Note the Stevens Branch stream running alongside the sheds. This stream gave life to a number of mills, manufacturing companies, and granite polishing works. The card was published by C.W. Hughes & Company.

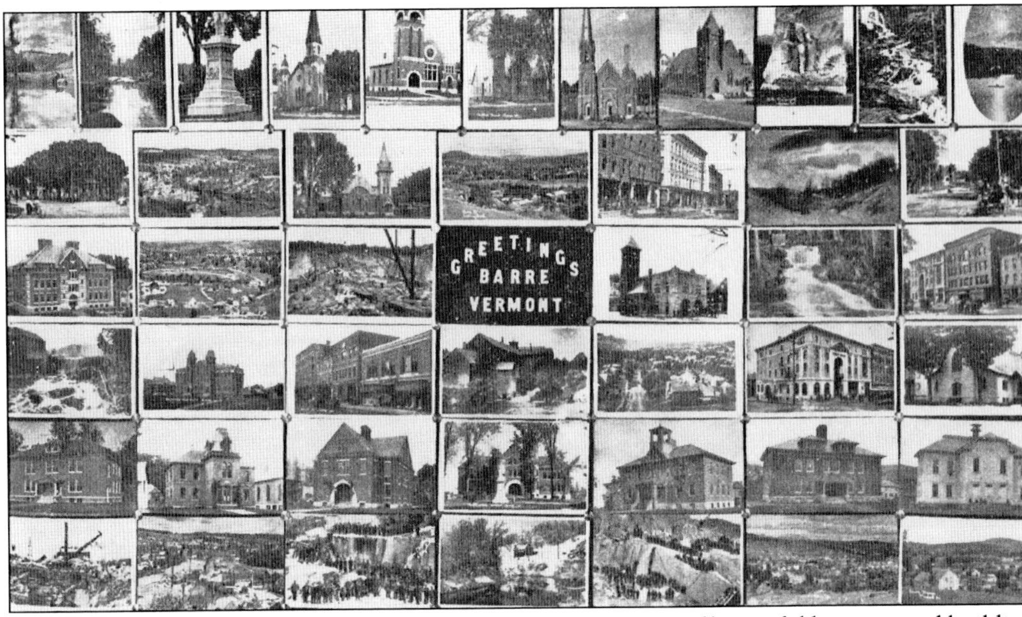

Skilled immigrants brought from their home countries a variety of beautiful housing and building styles uniquely shaped by a variety of cultures, political ideas, and traditions—as shown in this image published by the Post Card Company in Burlington, Vermont.

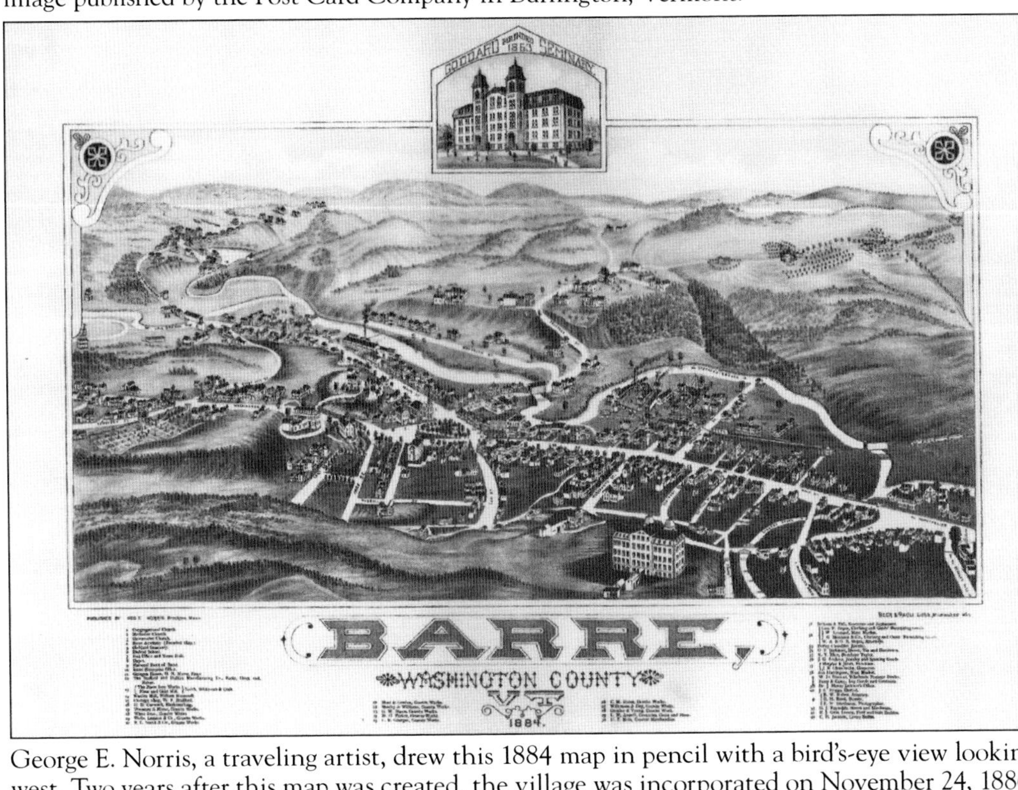

George E. Norris, a traveling artist, drew this 1884 map in pencil with a bird's-eye view looking west. Two years after this map was created, the village was incorporated on November 24, 1886. To show its importance to the town, George enlarged the drawing of Goddard Seminary on a rise overlooking the city. (Courtesy of Old Maps of New England.)

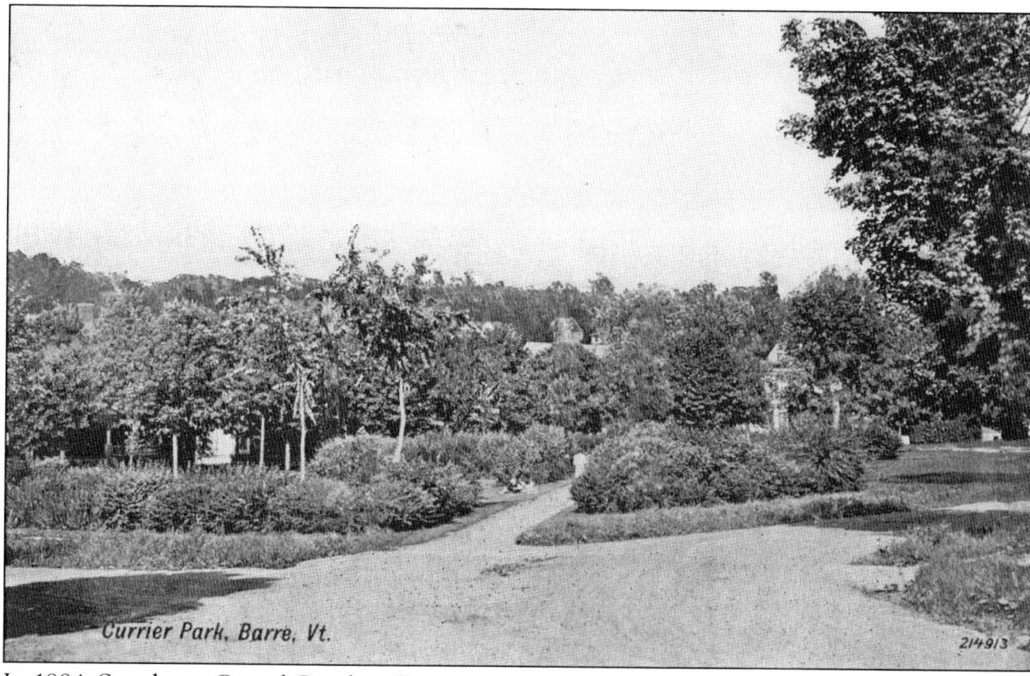

In 1884, Steadman C. and Caroline F. (Currier) Chubb presented two acres of land to the town with the stipulation that it be used for a public park (shown) to be named Currier, also known as Chubb Park. The park and surrounding houses have been designated as the Currier Park Historic District. The houses were built in the Italianate, Queen Anne, and Colonial Revival architectural styles.

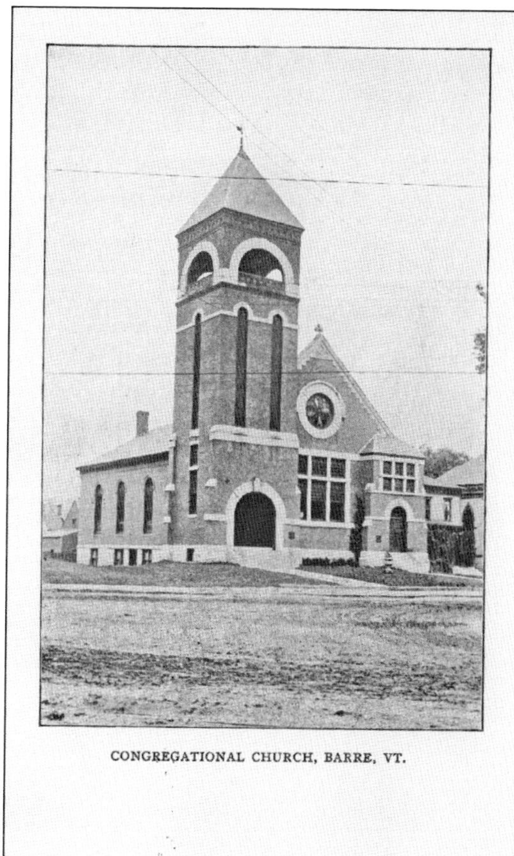

In Hamilton Child's *Gazetteer of Washington County, Vt., 1783–1889*, he reports, "The Congregational church was organized in November 14, 1799. Until they constructed a church and located a pastor, its 12 members held services in houses, schools, or barns. The first church was built in Gospel Village. In 1840, the brick church was built on the present site in the village."

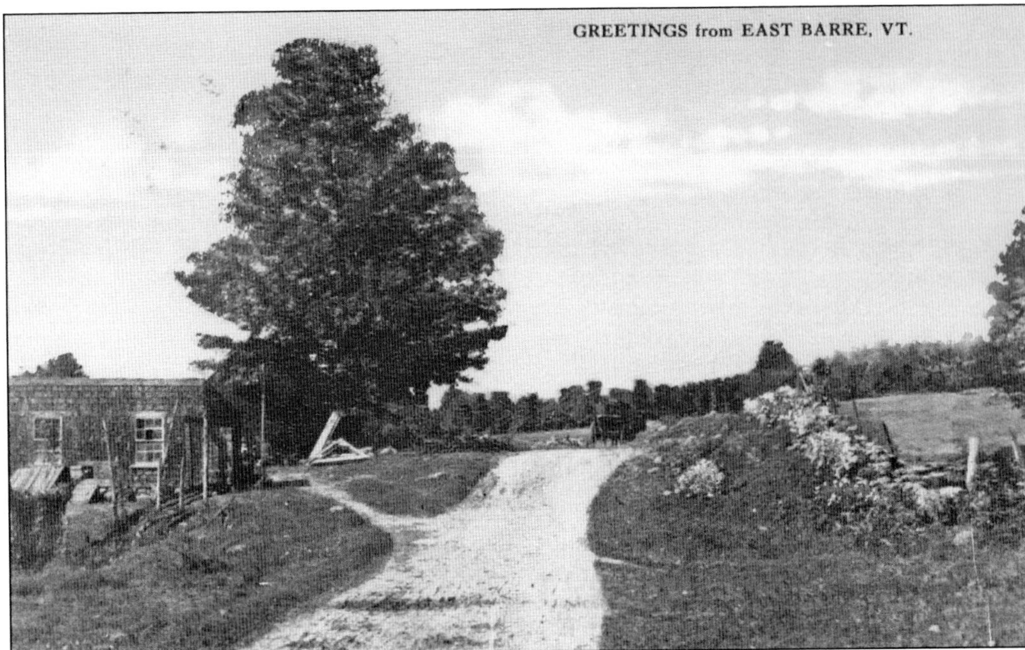

This "Greetings from East Barre, VT" (1921) postcard shows a small home in East Barre, which lies in the southeastern part of the township. The Jail Branch River passes through this village and furnishes the town with its waterpower. The early settlement cluster in East Barre had a post office, a granite shop, a blacksmith shop, one store, and about 20 dwellings. The postcard was mailed to Mrs. W. Cole of 65 Merchants Street from Lettie.

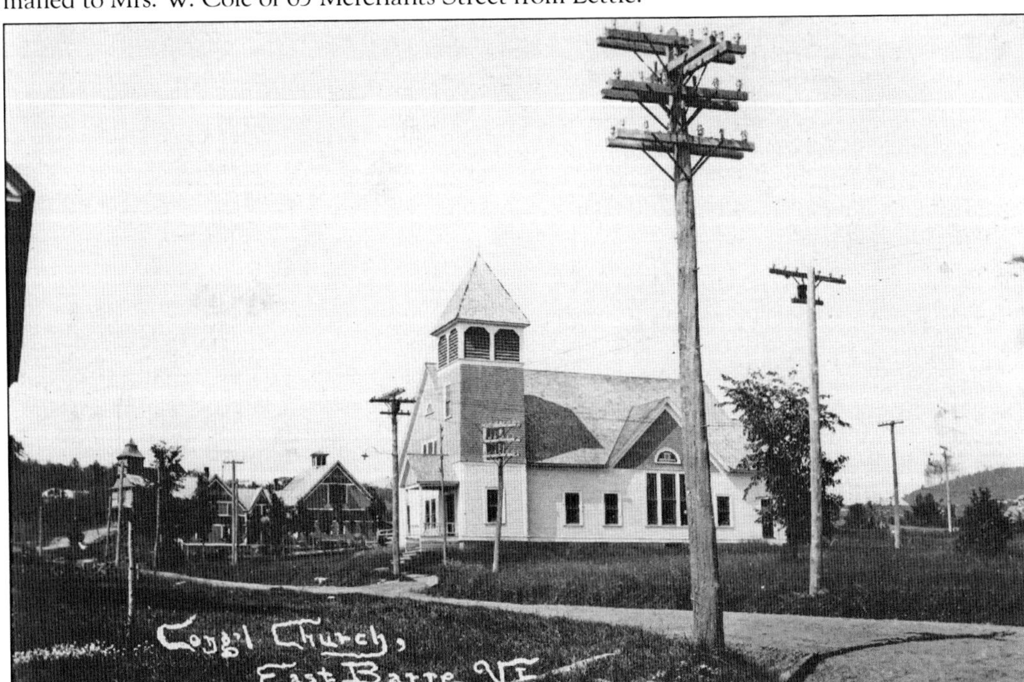

The East Barre Congregational Church was organized in 1894.

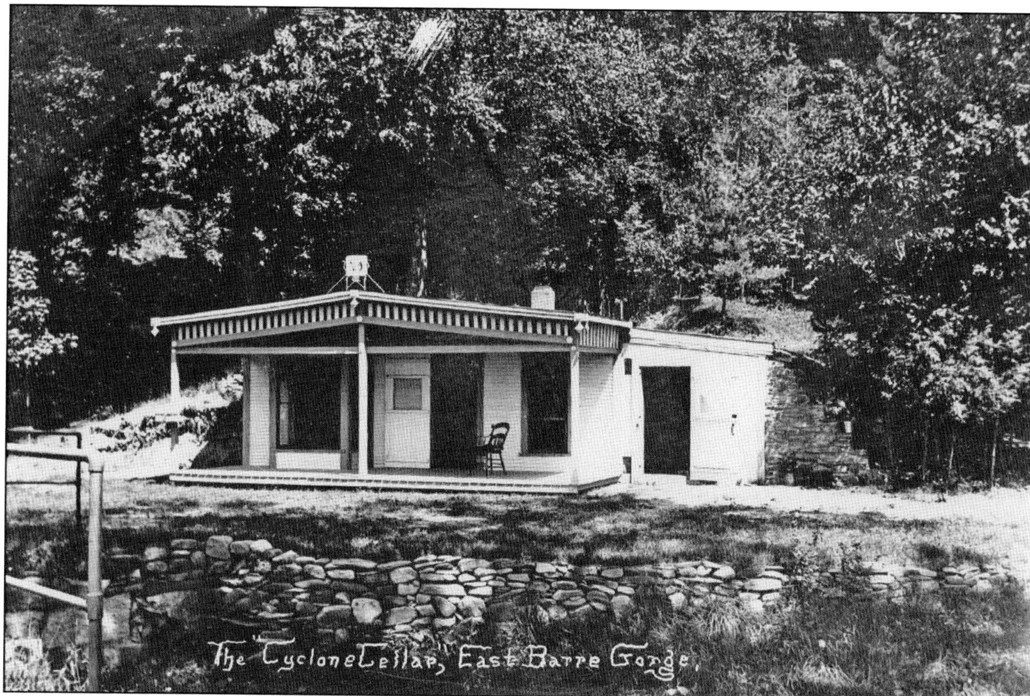

The "Cyclone Cellar in East Barre Gorge" postcard shows what is known locally as the old Dugout Restaurant. The only tropical cyclone to make a direct hit on Vermont in its early recorded history was in 1938.

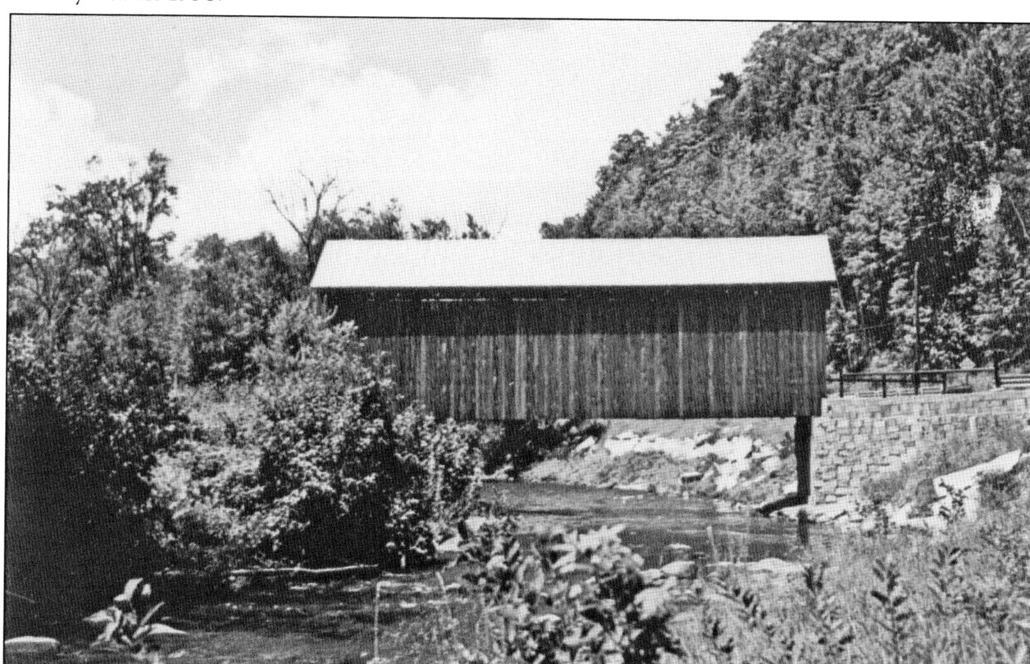

Robert River Robbins built the Robin's Nest Bridge in the early 1960s to replace an exact duplicate lost in the flood of 1927. The other side of the postcard says, "Short, but 'Sweet' in historic sentiment is this old covered bridge in East Barre, Vermont." (Courtesy of John H. Knox)

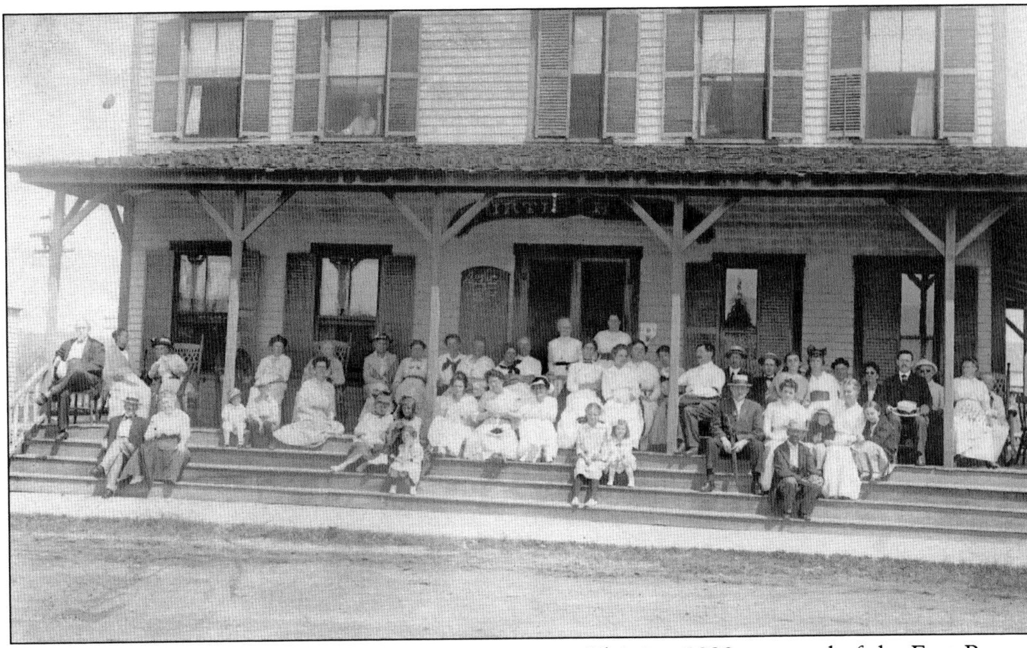

This is a 1920 postcard of the East Barre Hotel. It was located in the East Barre settlement, known as Carnes Mill. This settlement supported its own railroad depot, grocery stores, a business block, dance hall, opera house, fire department, livery stables, lumberyard, photography store, jeweler, and many other businesses.

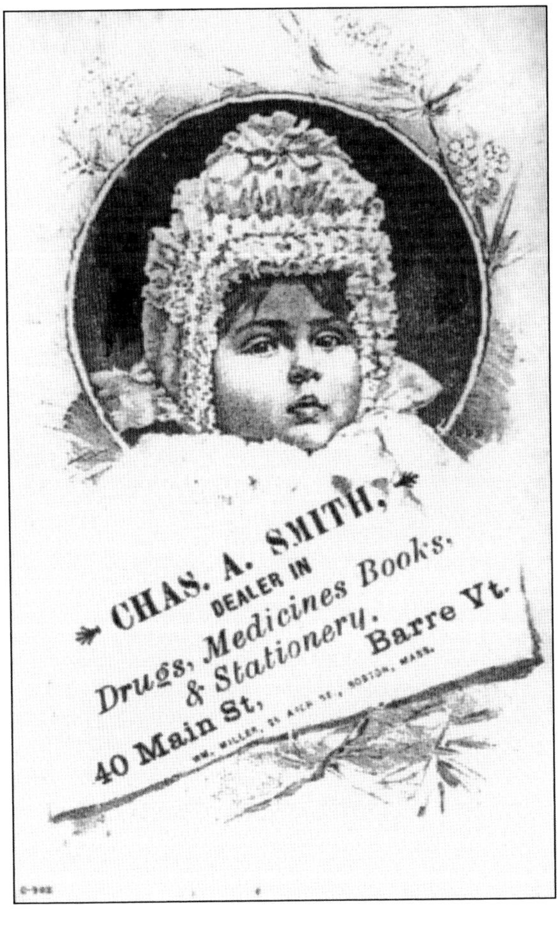

By 1884, Barre had several flourishing manufactories, 40 granite businesses, many merchants, lawyers, doctors, and businesses. (Courtesy of H.H. Hay.)

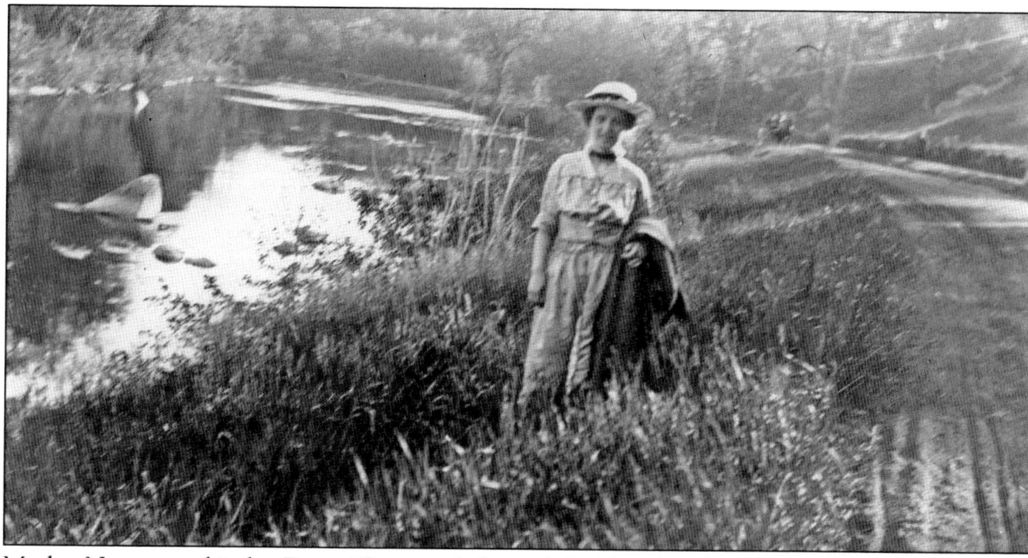

Mother Nature was kind to Barre. She provided it with fertile soil and an abundance of water, making it suitable for agriculture. Shown is an unidentified woman taking a stroll along the Stevens Branch stream. The swift water that flowed down the slopes of the Green Mountains into the Stevens Branch stream made it strong enough to turn mill wheels, which was very important for industrial growth.

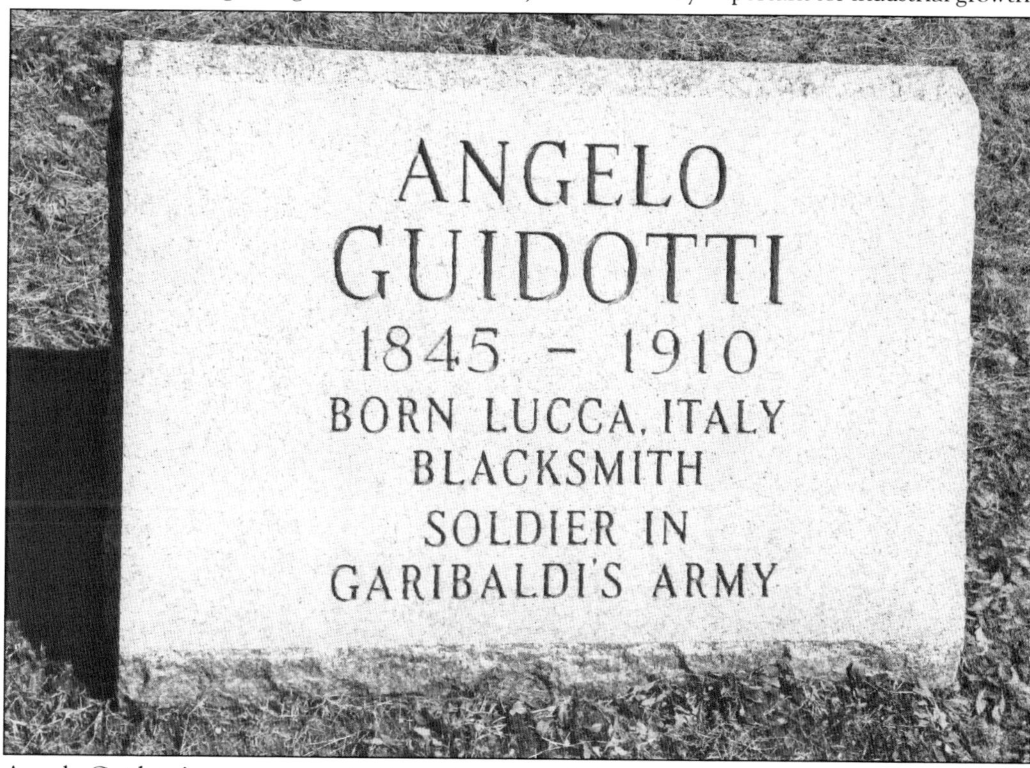

Angelo Guidotti's gravestone is in Hope Cemetery. Guidotti worked as a blacksmith on Second Street in Barre City and could shape iron into tools, horseshoes, and wagon wheel rims. He also made the nails that fastened the horseshoes to the horses' feet. The sound of his hammer striking the anvil was a familiar sound in Barre. East and South Barre also had their own blacksmiths.

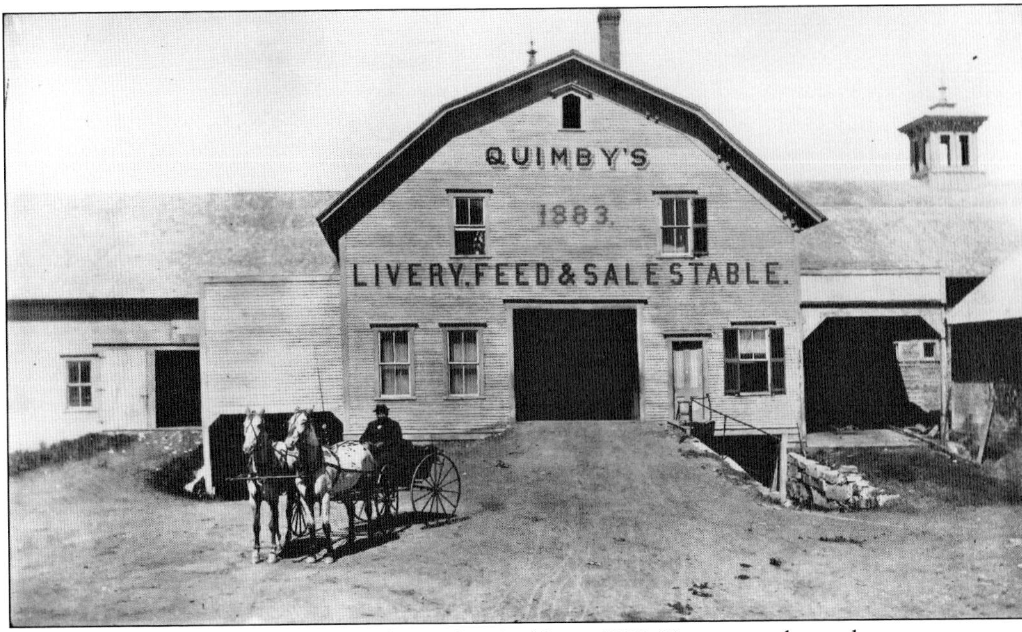

This is Henry Quimby's Livery, Feed & Sales, Stable in 1889. Horse travel was the most common method of transportation in the 1800s. (Photograph by O.J. Dodge, courtesy of Aldrich Public Library, Barre, Vermont.)

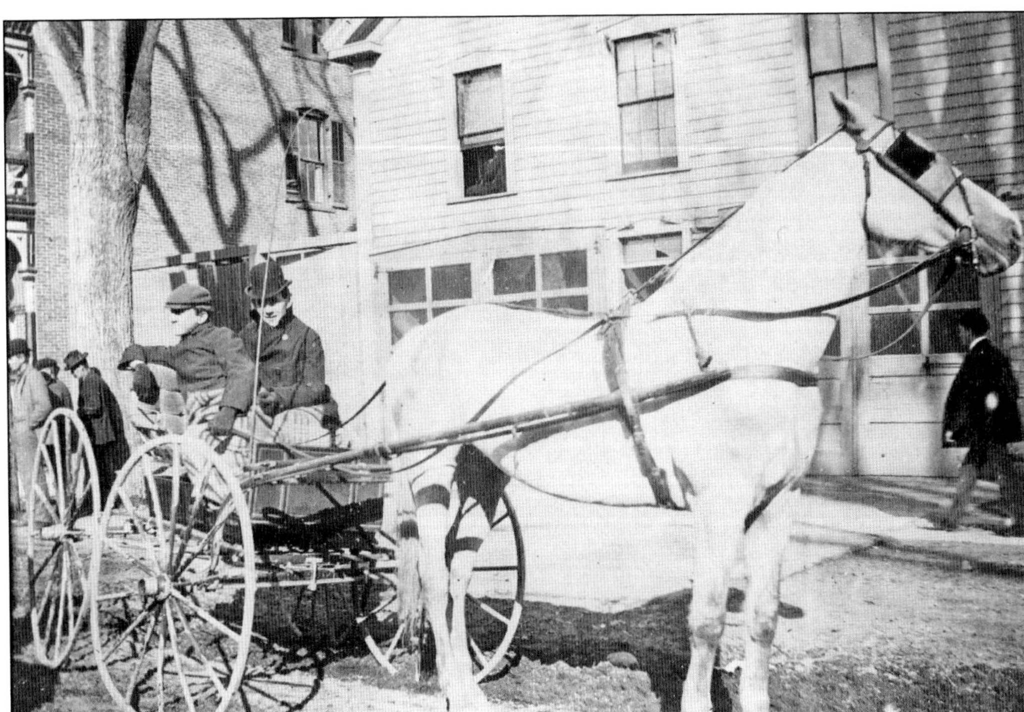

The postcard shows a white horse pulling a four-wheeled wagon. Horse-drawn carriages were used for transporting goods and people from the 18th century until the early 1900s.

Three

Barre City

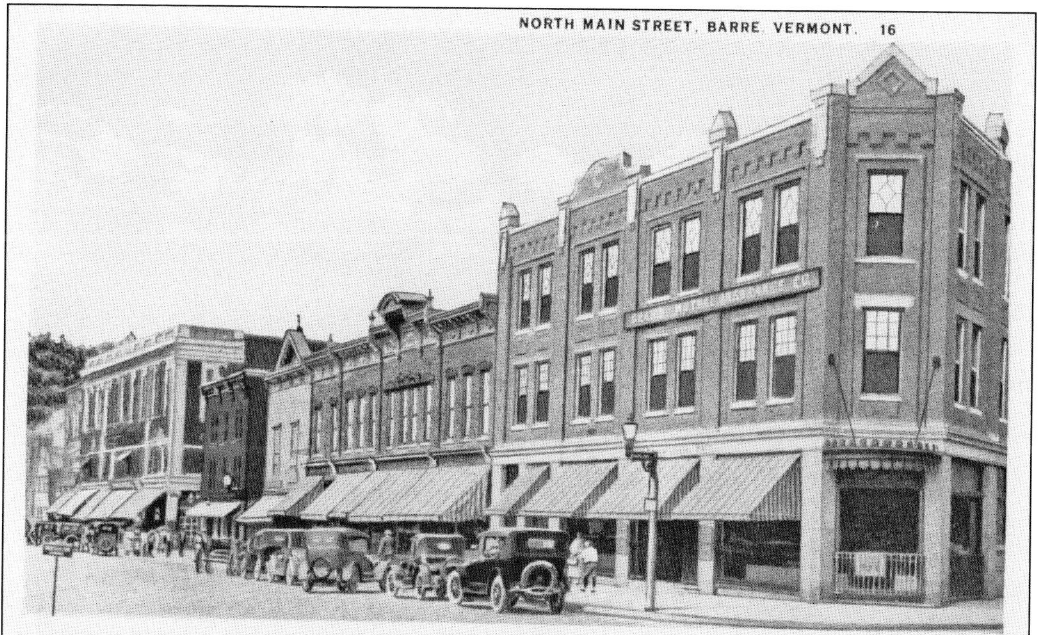

As Barre's population grew, the need for infrastructure grew along with it resulting in an increased cost burden for residents. The last straw came when town officials proposed spreading the costs among all its residents to pay for village streetlights. It may have helped in the decision to split Barre village off from Barre Town, which led to Barre village being incorporated as a city on March 5, 1895. This image shows North Main Street's Aldrich Block. The advertisement postcard was created for Palmer's five-and-ten stores. Hugh C. Leighton Company published it.

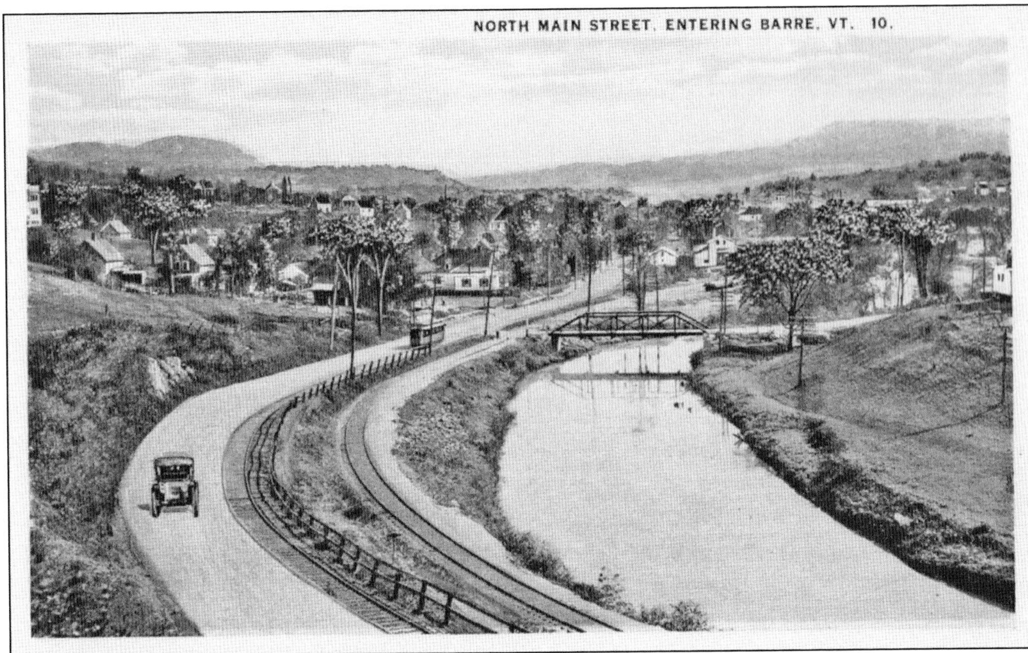

This 1875 postcard published by Charles W. Hughes shows the road entering Barre from North Main Street. There are train tracks that run along the river and a trolley car. Railways helped move goods, foods, and people faster than horse-drawn wagons.

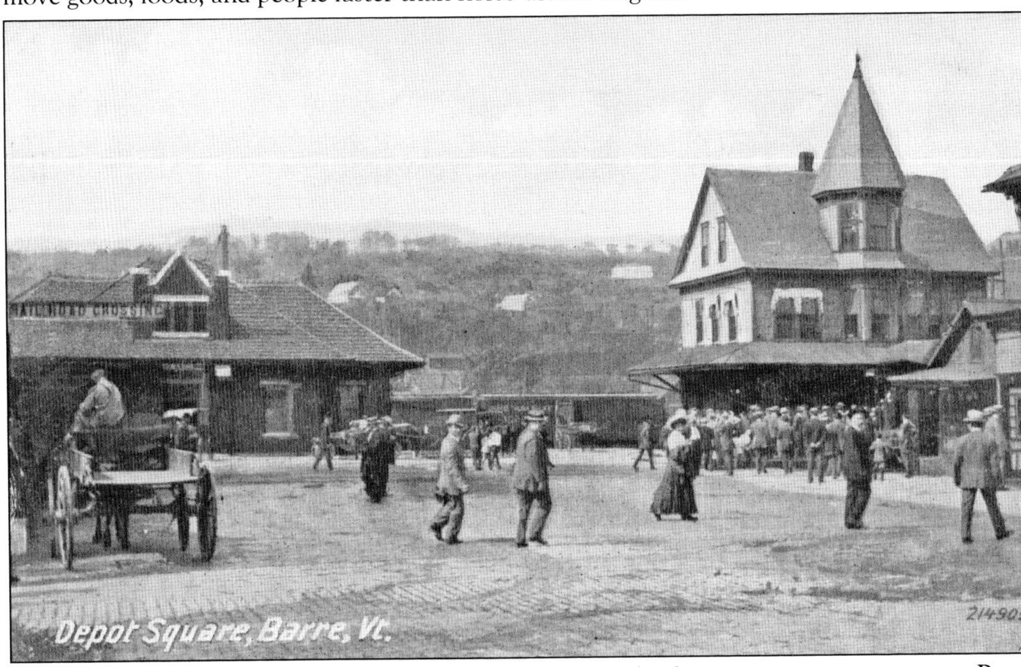

This 1912 postcard shows Depot Square in Barre village. The first passenger train came to Barre in 1870, and trains left Barre daily except Sunday. In 1875, the first telegraph office opened in Depot Square and the first telegram was sent on October 1, 1875. The *Vermont Heritage Network* indicated that "Telegraph stations were often located in railroad depots since the telegraph lines typically followed the rail lines."

Fred W. Sherburne, a photographer, took the image of this young woman wearing a style of spectacles named pince-nez. These spectacles were supported without earpieces, by pinching the bridge of the nose. Sherburne established his photography business in 1865, was a member of the Masonic lodge, and a Knight Templar.

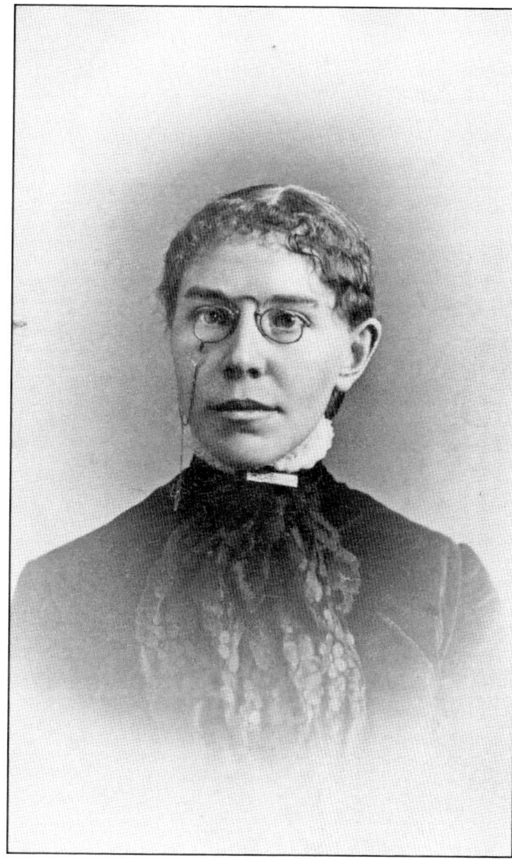

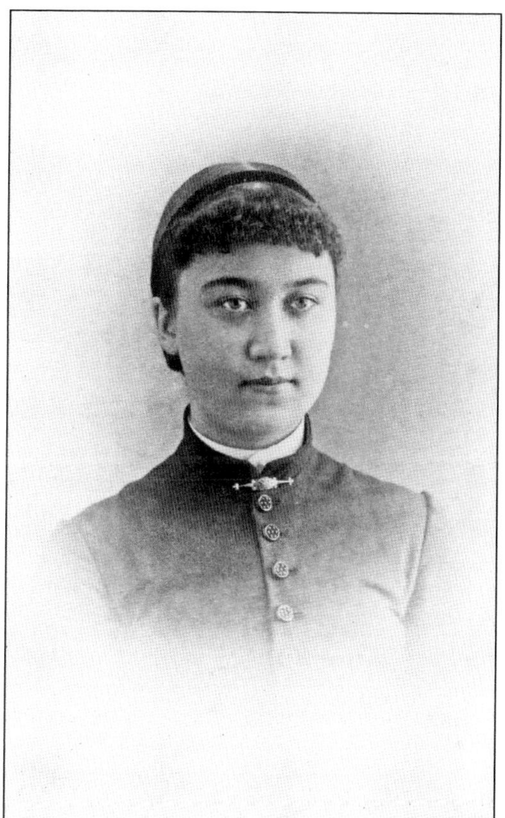

Sherburne took this "carte de visite" image. These small photographs became very popular during the American Civil War and were traded among friends and family members.

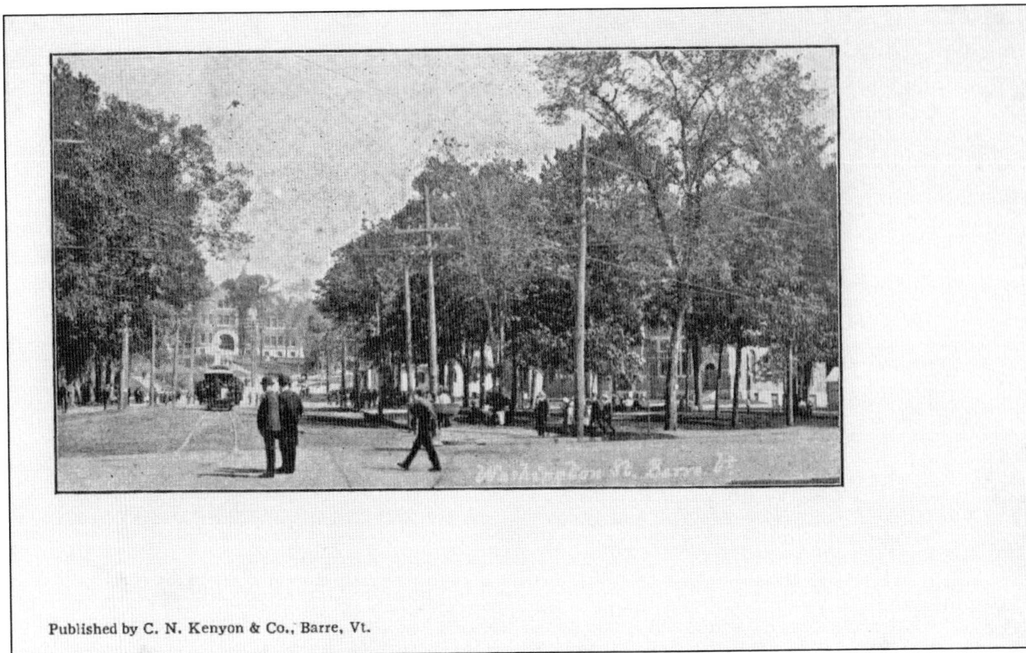

The view is looking up Washington Street to the Spaulding School. The men crossing the street are wearing bowler hats, which remained popular through the first half of the 1900s. The photograph was originally published by C.N. Kenyon & Company.

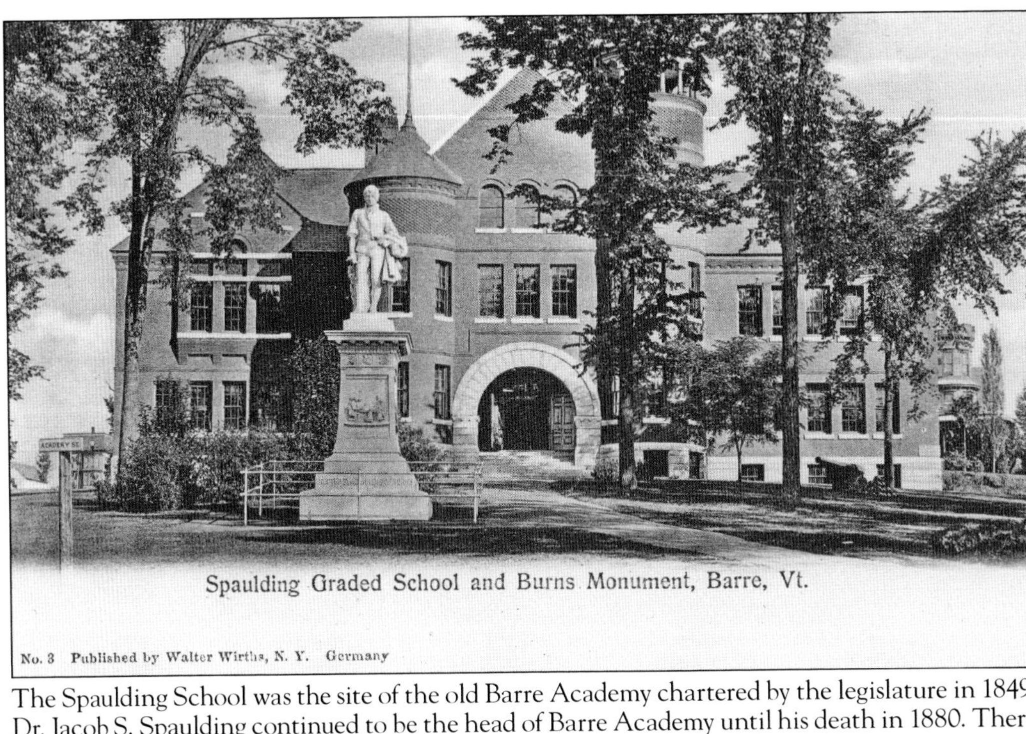

The Spaulding School was the site of the old Barre Academy chartered by the legislature in 1849. Dr. Jacob S. Spaulding continued to be the head of Barre Academy until his death in 1880. There is a cannon on the right side of the lawn.

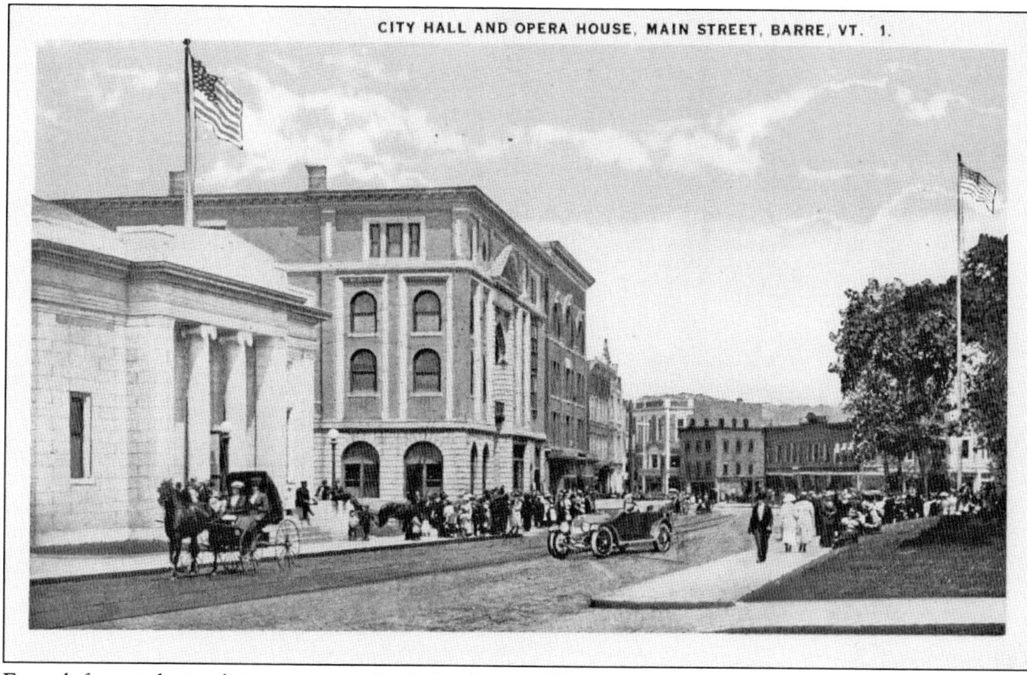

From left to right in this image are the federal post office, Barre City Hall, the opera house (located on the top two floors), and Beckett Block. With the introduction of the technological marvels of the 19th century, the automobile was replacing horse-drawn carriages.

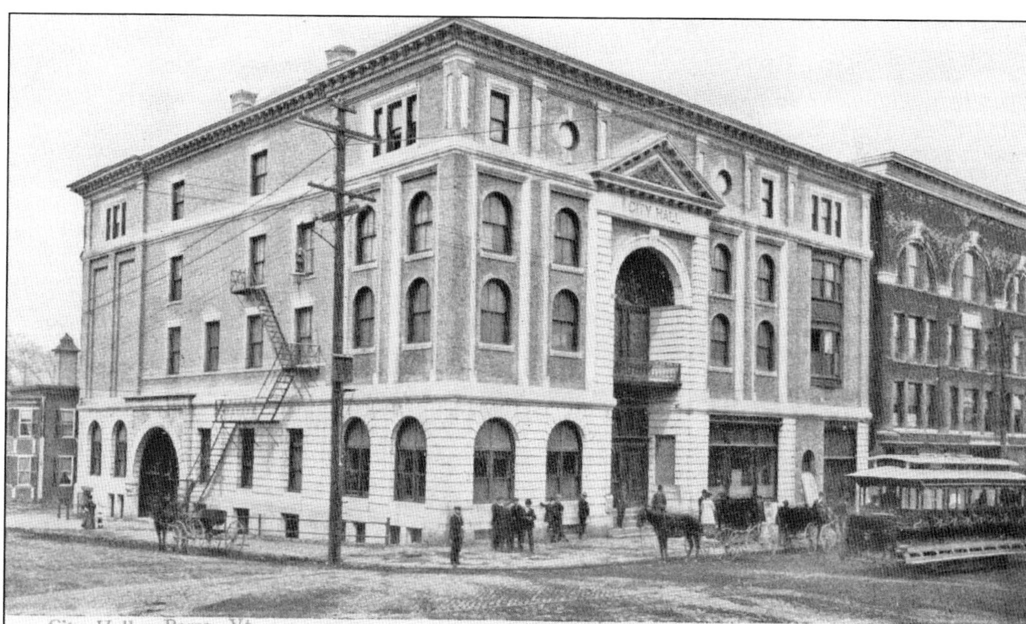

Established in 1898, a trolley line ran down Main Street in Barre to sister city Montpelier. The trolley was abolished in 1927.

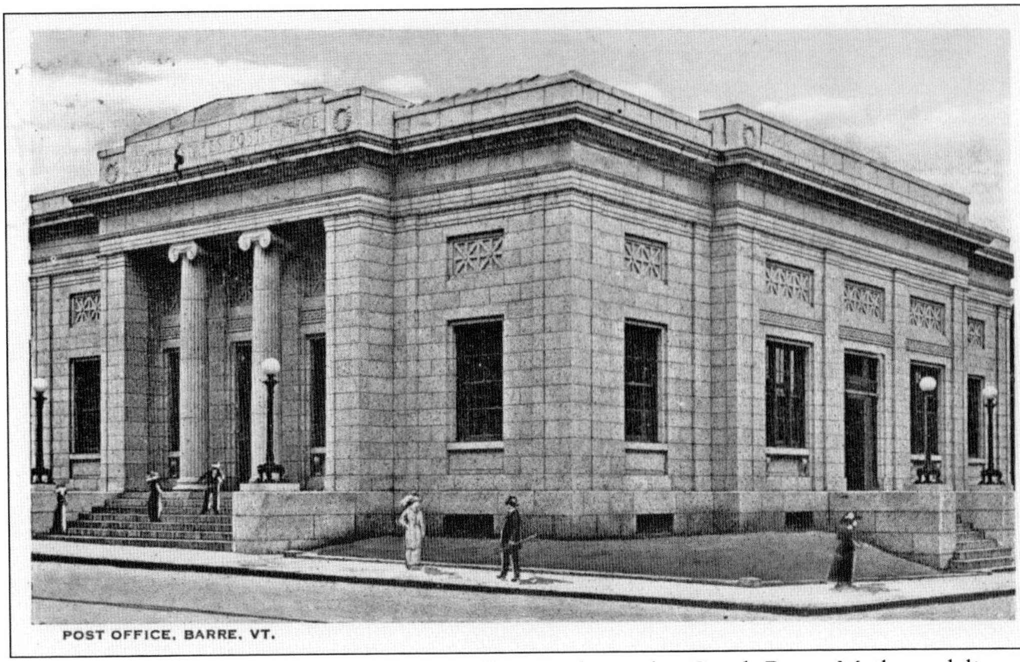

In the early history of Barre the town post office was located in South Barre. Mail was delivered from a postman on horseback and later by the old stagecoach drawn by six horses. Finally, mail was sent from the federal post office in Barre City and rerouted to adjacent towns. The postcard is dated 1922, and the photograph is by Lincoln Lillie.

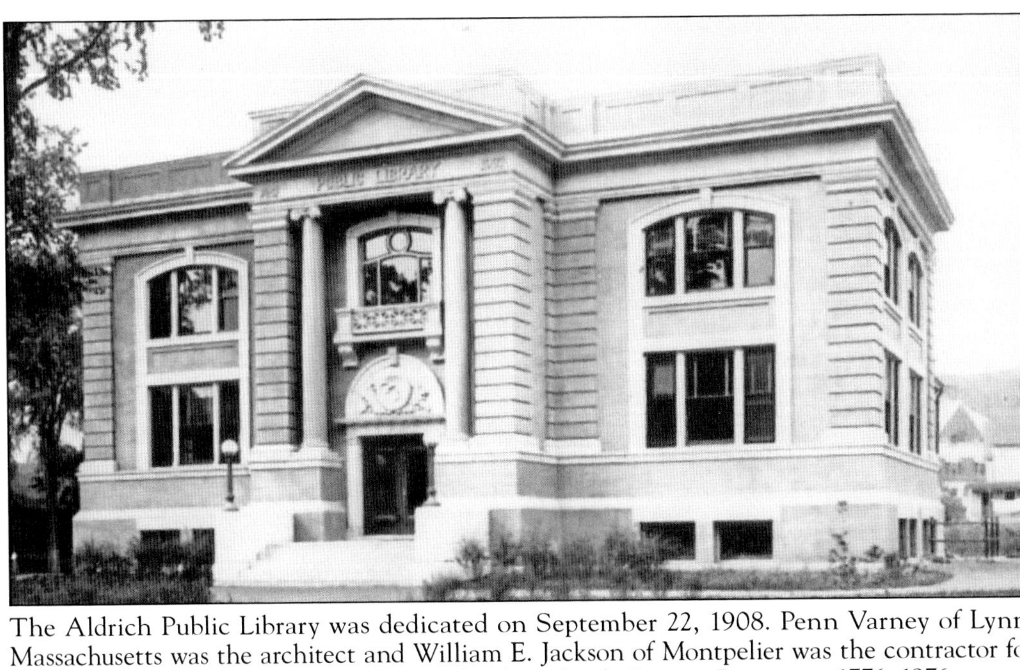

The Aldrich Public Library was dedicated on September 22, 1908. Penn Varney of Lynn, Massachusetts was the architect and William E. Jackson of Montpelier was the contractor for the $39,000 Classical Revival building made of gray brick. *Barre in Retrospect, 1776–1976* reports, "The delicately-carved frieze shows the Passing of the Torch of Learning."

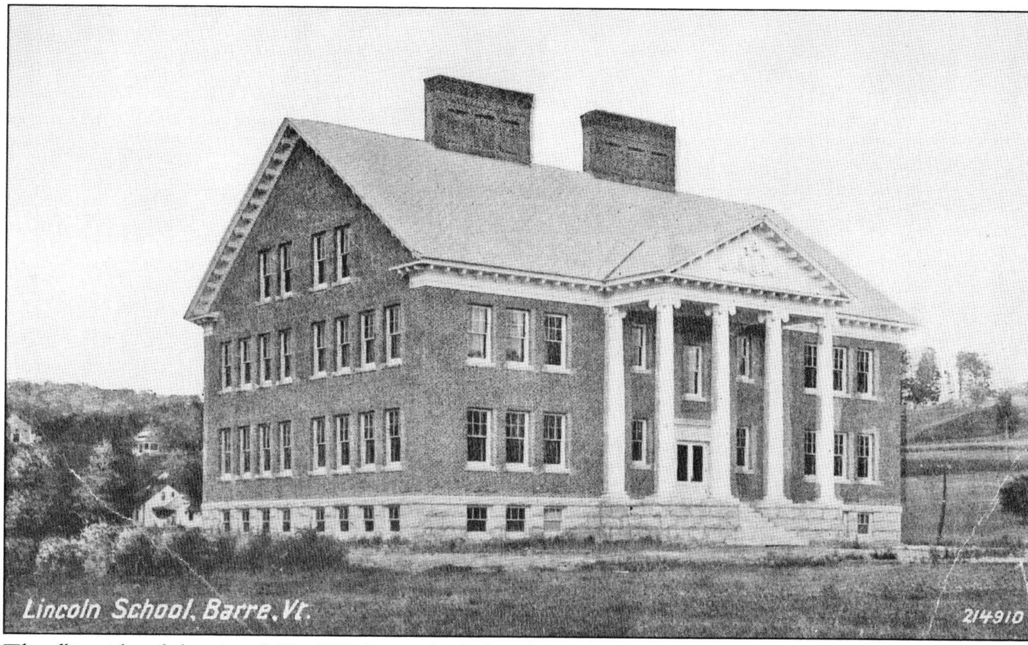

The flip side of the April 29, 1912 Lincoln School postcard says, "Dear Mirian Thomas, This is a picture of one of the several large brick school houses here. They have splendid schools and many beautiful buildings in Barre." The Leighton and Valentine Company published this card.

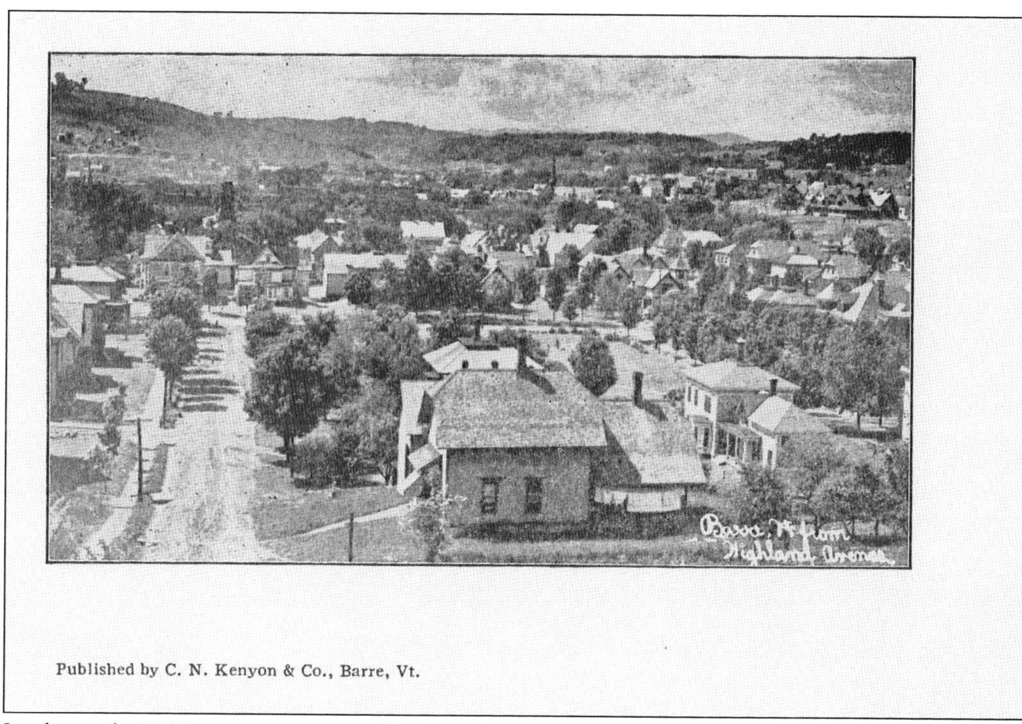

In the early 1900s, private citizens began to take black-and-white photographs and have them printed on paper with post card backs. This picture shows Barre as seen from Highland Avenue with the main road down the hill unpaved.

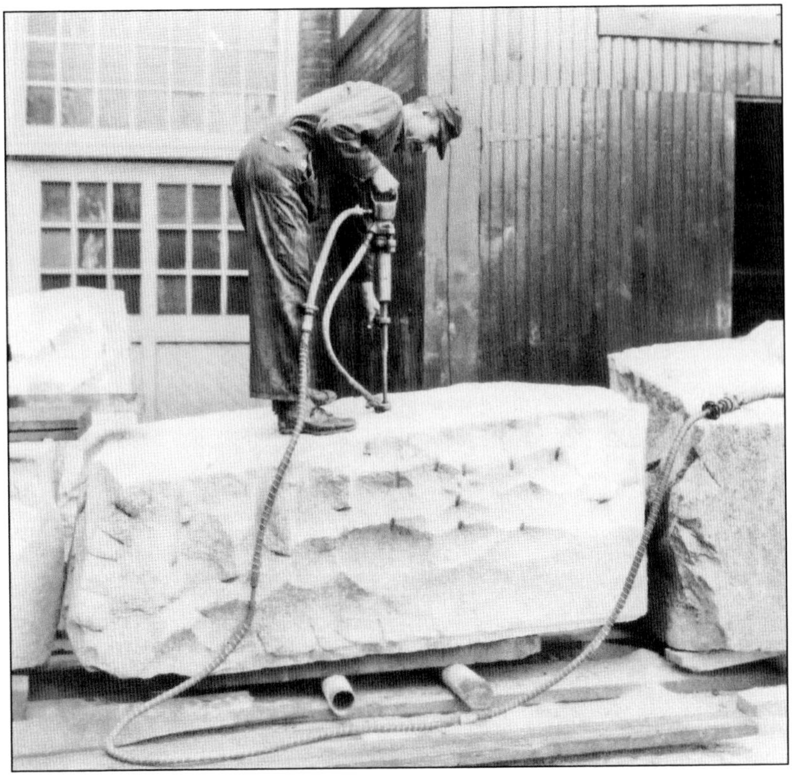

During the Industrial Revolution, new manufacturing processes were developed that helped change almost every aspect of daily life. Technological developments included manufacture of machine tools, farm machinery, typewriters, sewing machines, telegraphs, telephones, cameras, electricity, pneumatic drills, power cutting tools to cut granite, and new modes of transportation.

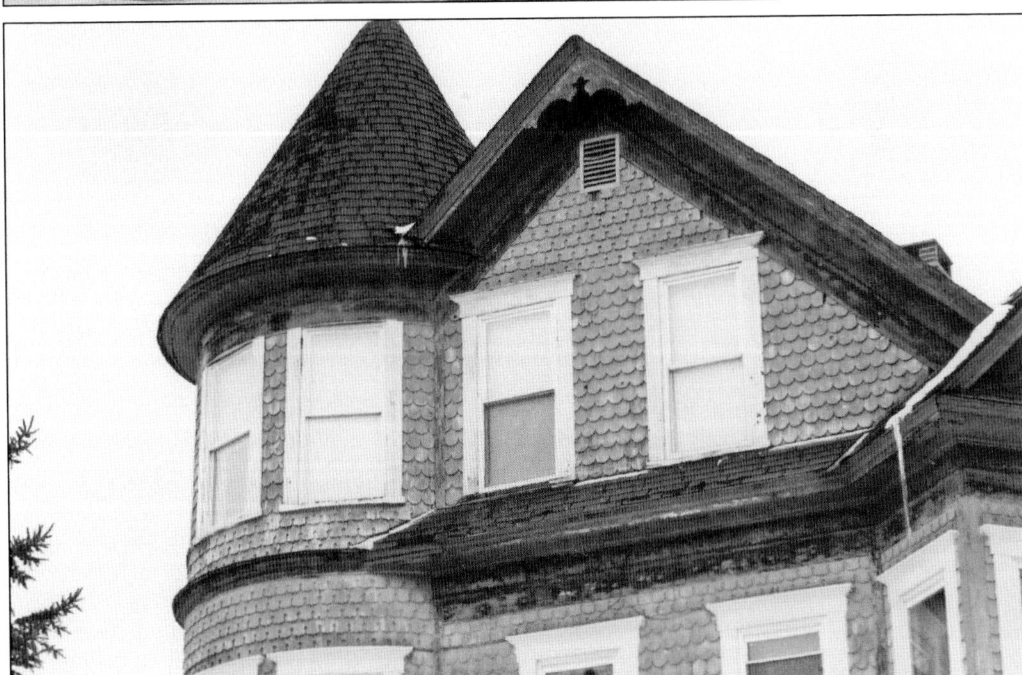

The Thursday, May 1, 1902, *Barre Evening Telegram* reported that the new Barre Emergency Hospital, pictured, was opened on Hooker Hill in the old Hooker residence. Dr. W.F. Gilman directed the hospital.

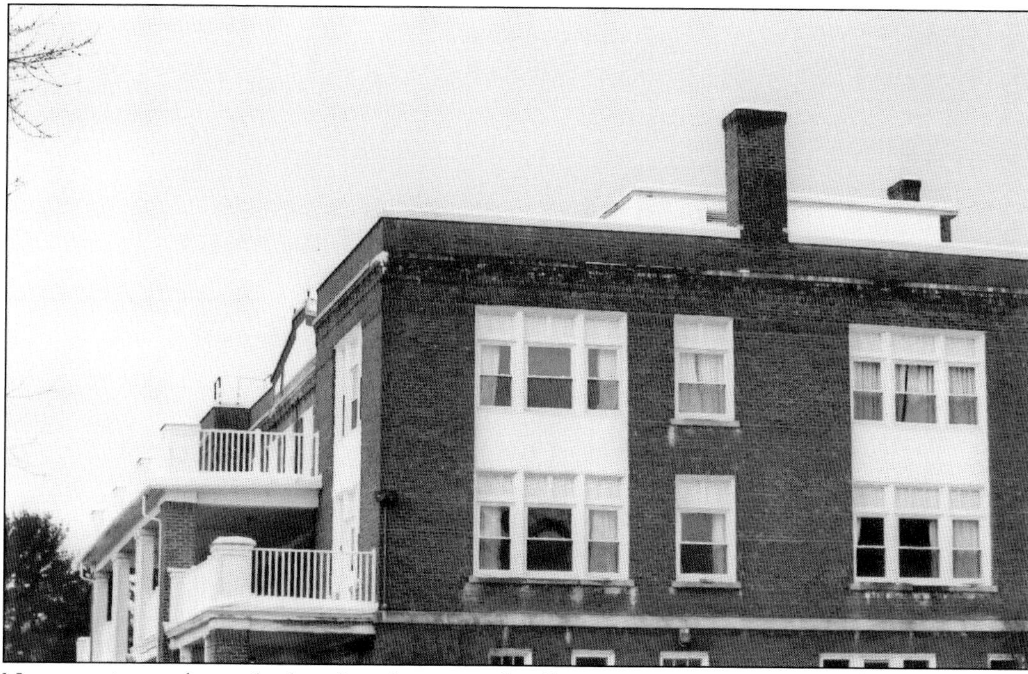

New granite tools resulted in fine dust particles floating in the air during the manufacturing process, which were inhaled by the granite workers and caused serious health problems. Early on, it was called grinder's asthma by the shed workers and tuberculosis by the doctors, but later on it was known as silicosis. The Carmelite Monastery building on Beckley Hill was built to treat patients with silicosis. The Carmelite Monastery was used until 1968.

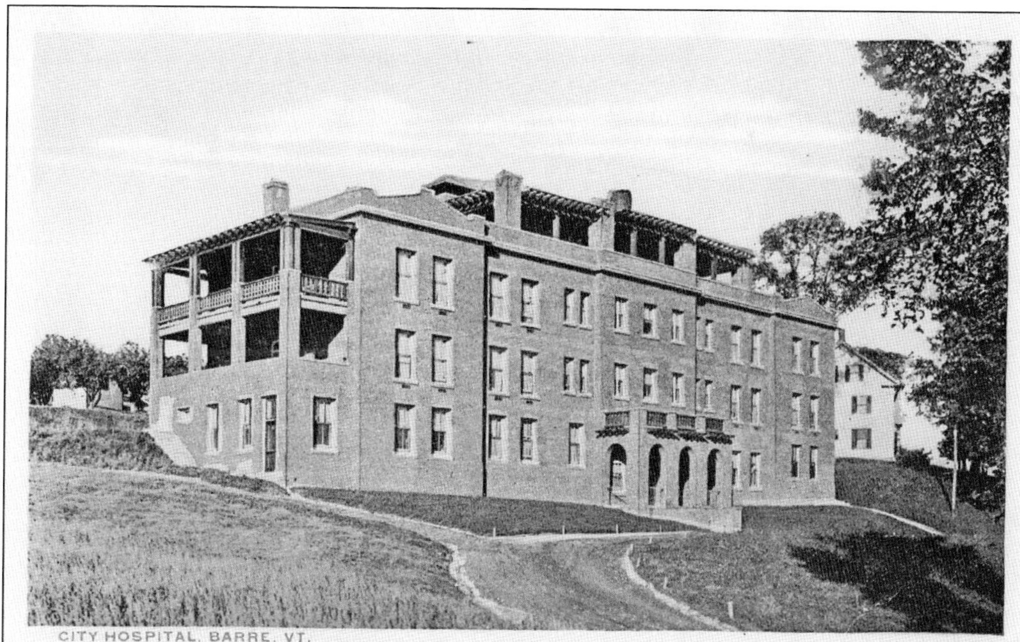

In 1914, the Barre City Hospital was built on Washington Street as pictured. The postcard is dated 1930, and C.W. Martin took the photograph.

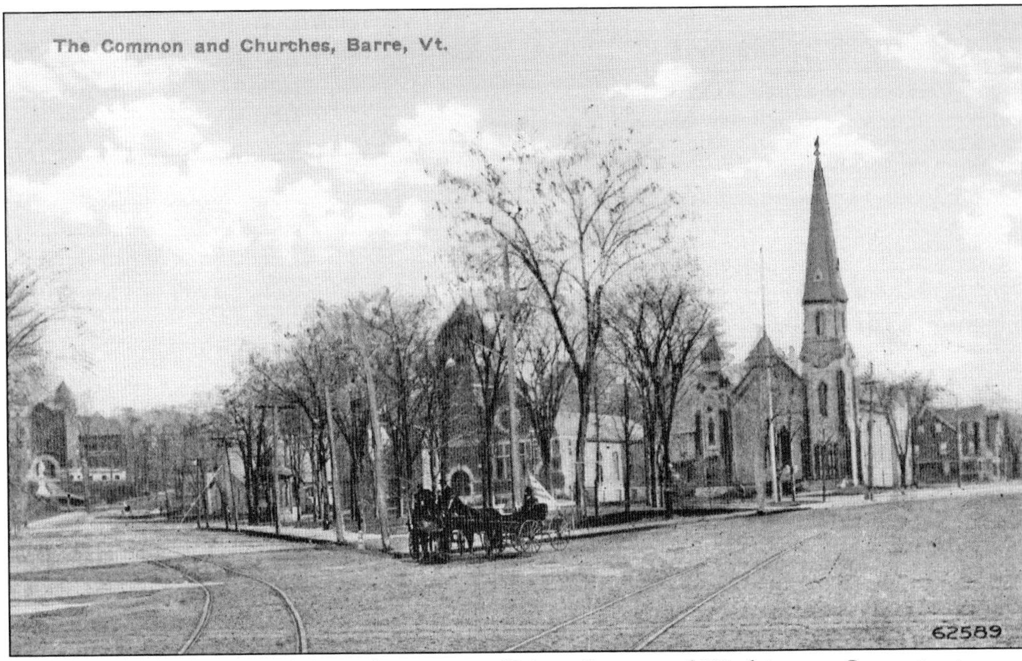

The village park as viewed from the corner of Main Street and Washington Street is pictured. This and the next three pictures show changing Barre from 1899 to 1950 as it developed into a thriving city.

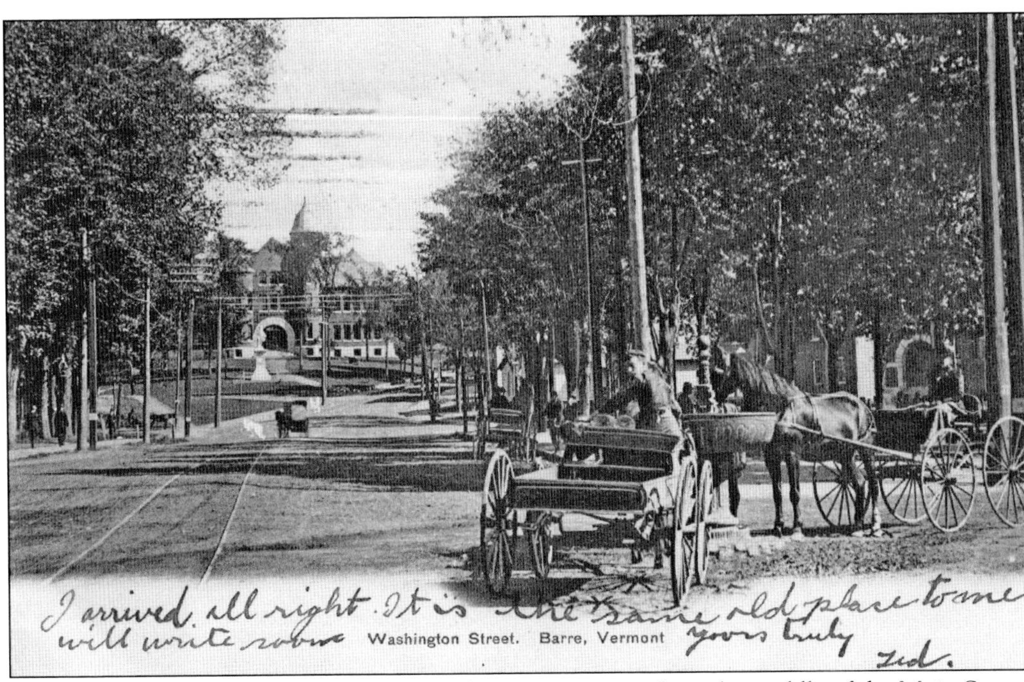

This is a 1907 postcard of a horse drinking from a water trough in the middle of the Main Street. Note the electric poles in this postcard. The view is looking up Washington Street to the Spaulding High School. The postcard was published by the Springfield News Company.

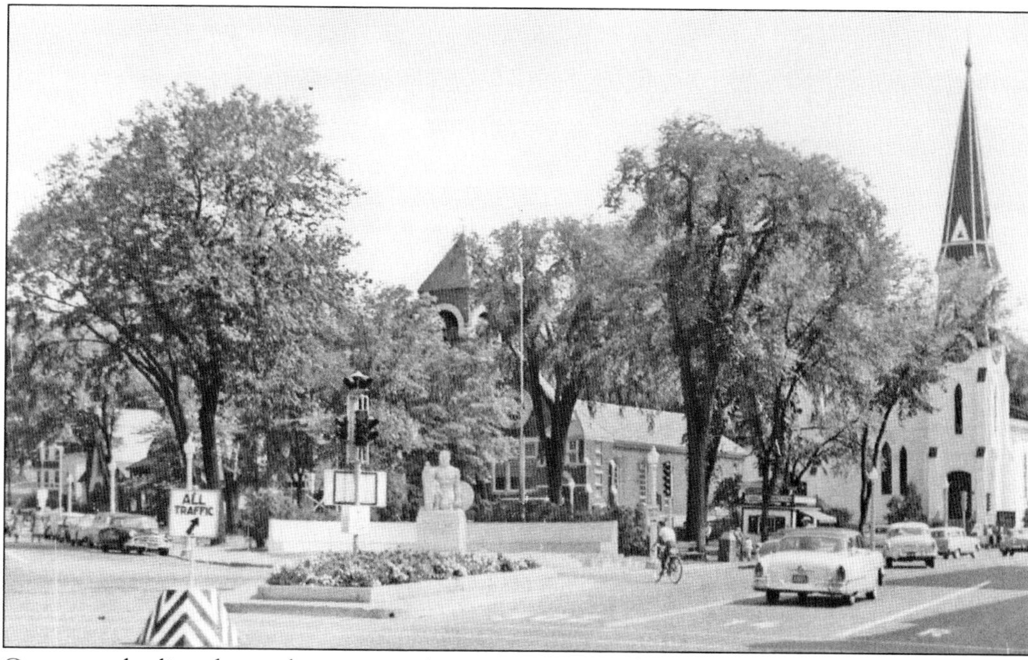

Cars started ruling the roads as seen in this image. Increased signage was used because of a greater need to control the flow of traffic. Mike Roberts's image is dated 1950.

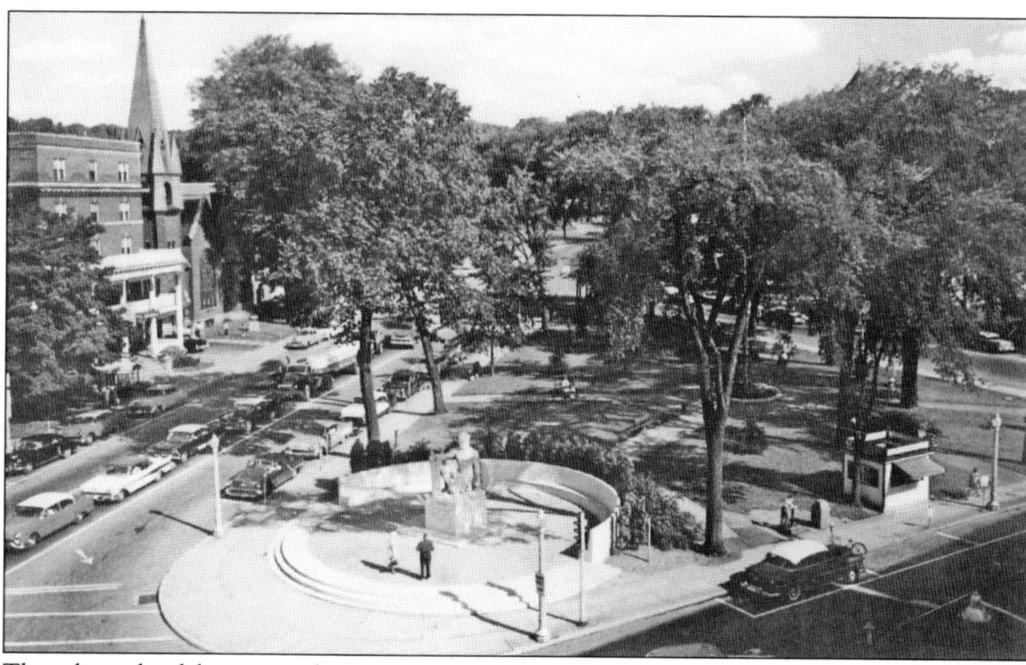

The other side of the postcard says, "Barre Municipal Park, Vermont. Showing Soldiers Memorial Monument erected in 1919. It was the work of Barre Craftsmen, sculptured from the local quarries." Stephen Warner took the photograph.

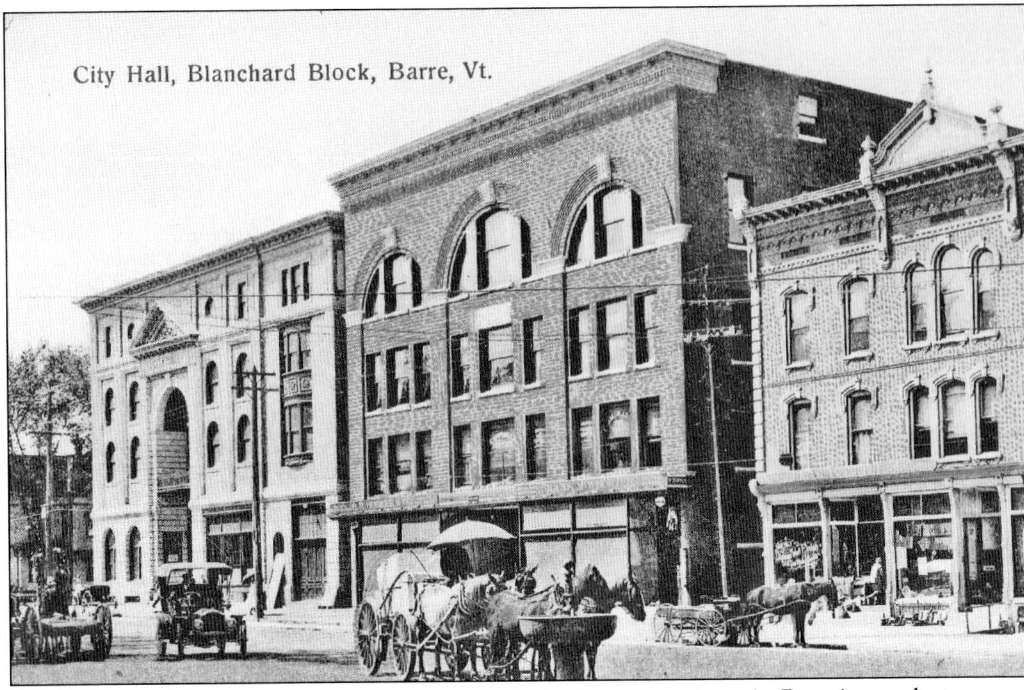

Seen here is city hall, on the left, and Blanchard Block in Barre City. As Barre's population grew, Main Street became passable for stagecoaches and horse-drawn wagons.

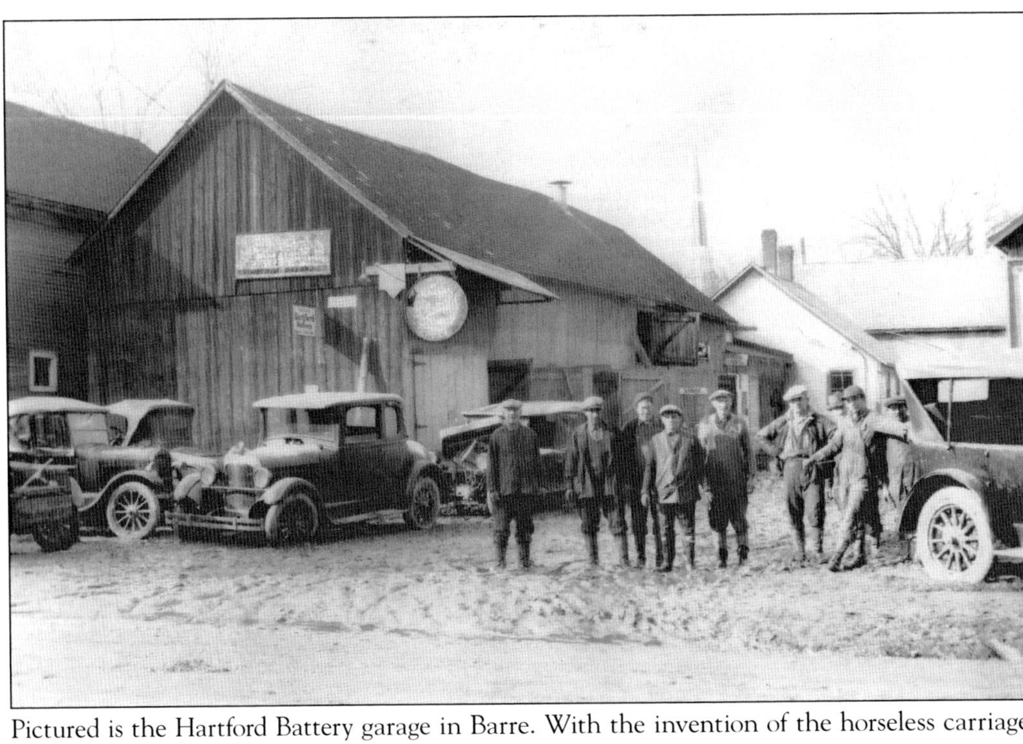

Pictured is the Hartford Battery garage in Barre. With the invention of the horseless carriage, garages soon replaced livery stables.

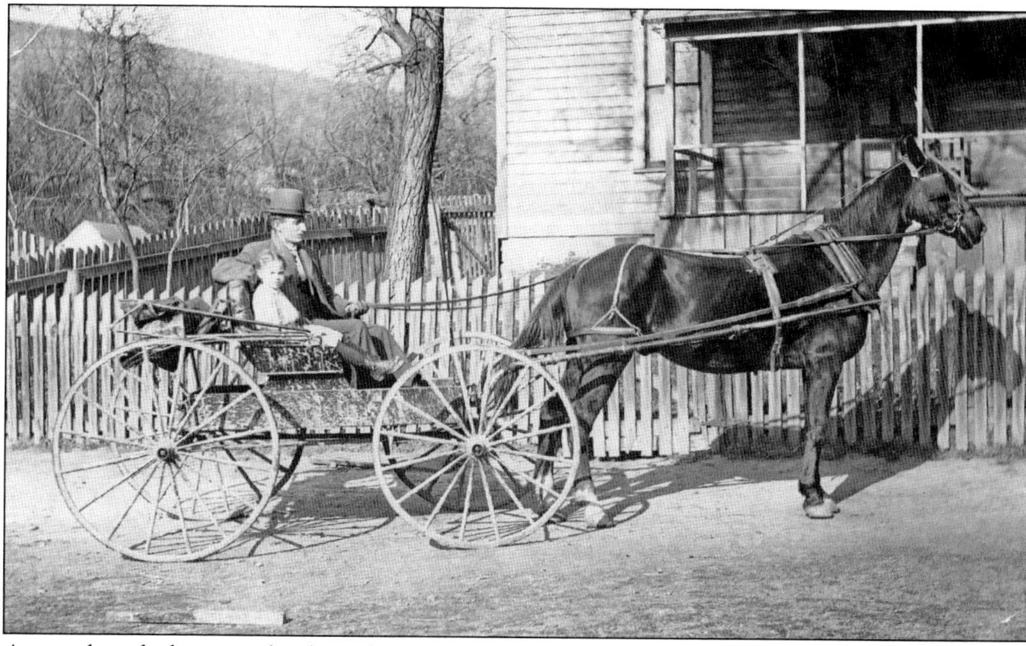

An unidentified man and girl are shown sitting in a horse-drawn two-seated buggy. These smaller buggies were used in town and for short trips into the country.

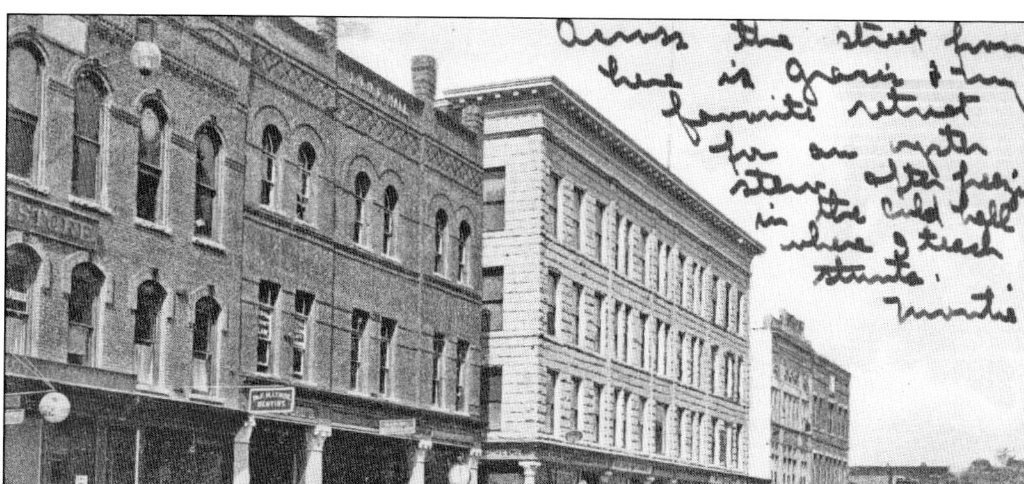

Parking was not a problem in downtown Barre, but it did require hitching posts for the horse-drawn buggies. There are advertising signs for services and products hung along Main Street. (Courtesy of Hugh C. Leighton Co.)

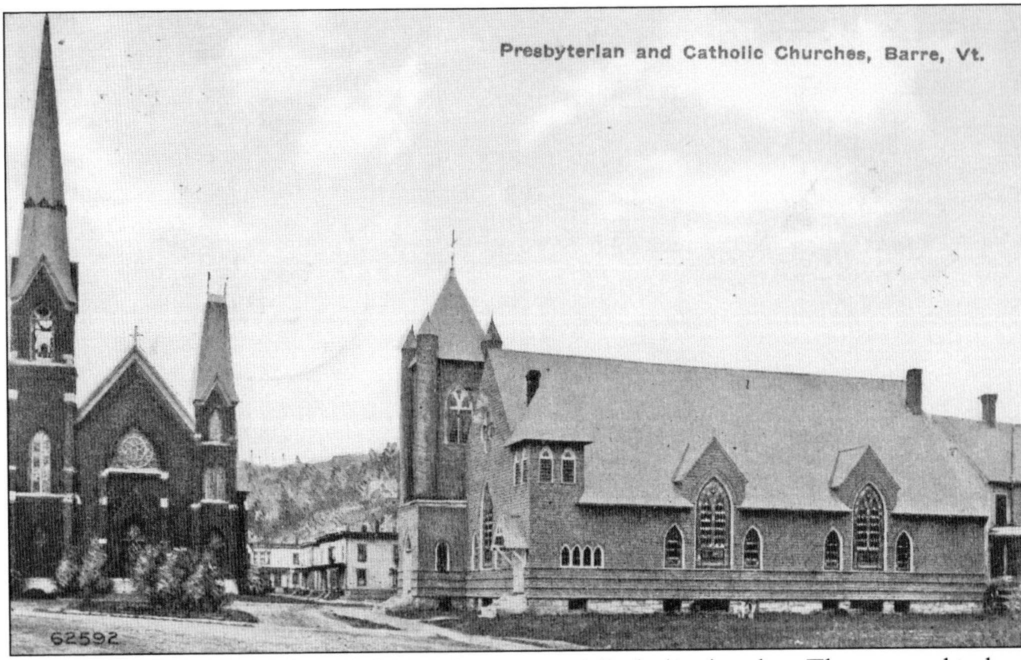

The Italians and Scots organized the Presbyterian and Catholic churches. The postcard is dated November 4, 1910.

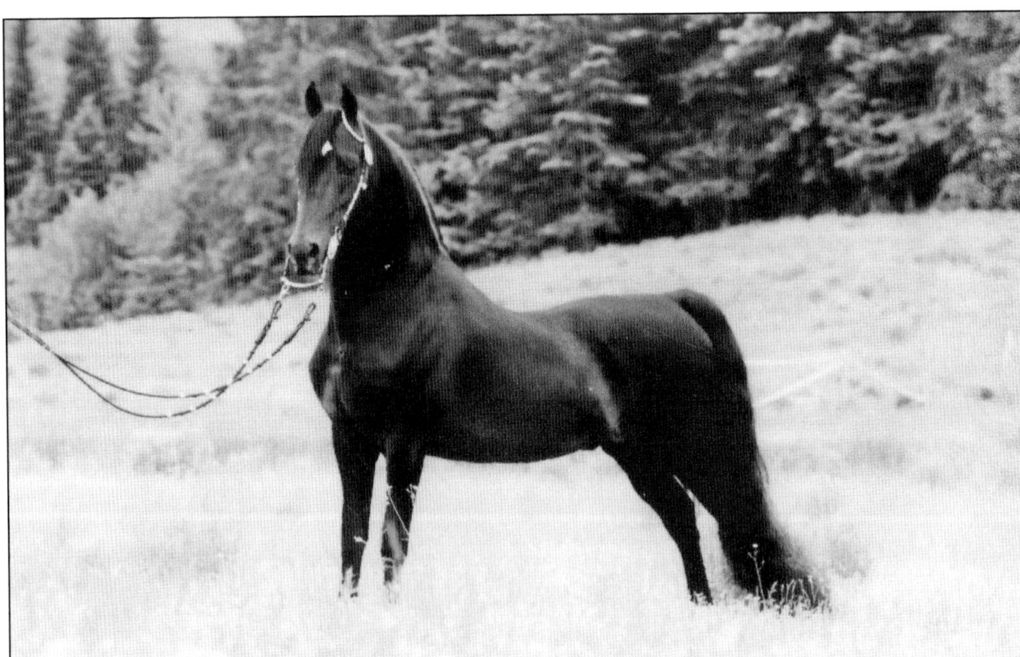
Jockey Hollow was the site of a fairground, Granite City Trotting Park, stables, and other sporting events. Barre ranked among the best in raising Morgan horses of distinction. Treble's Tanqueray, a descendent of the famous Justin Morgan horse, is pictured here. (Courtesy of Ashley Fleck Morris, Greg Fleck, and Carol Fleck.)

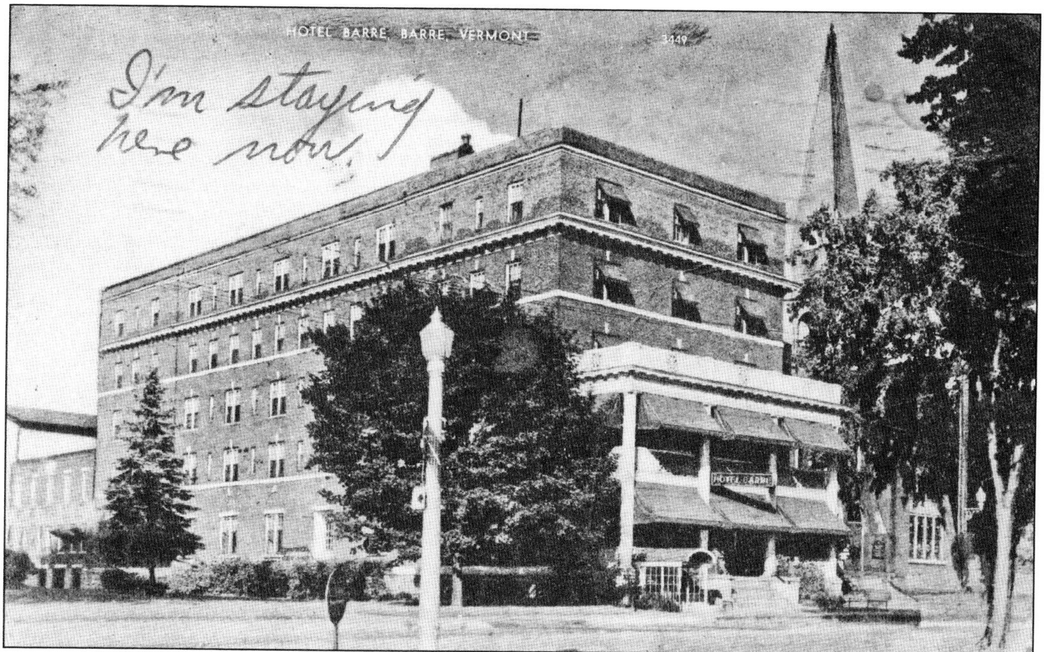

Hotel Barre—with its 70 rooms—filled a great need. Scrawled in red pen on the flip side of the May 28, 1950, postcard it says, "Dear Molly, Isn't this a cultured looking postcard? I am working in Barre for a couple of days and will move to Burlington tomorrow. I love the writing in red ink, Love Barb."

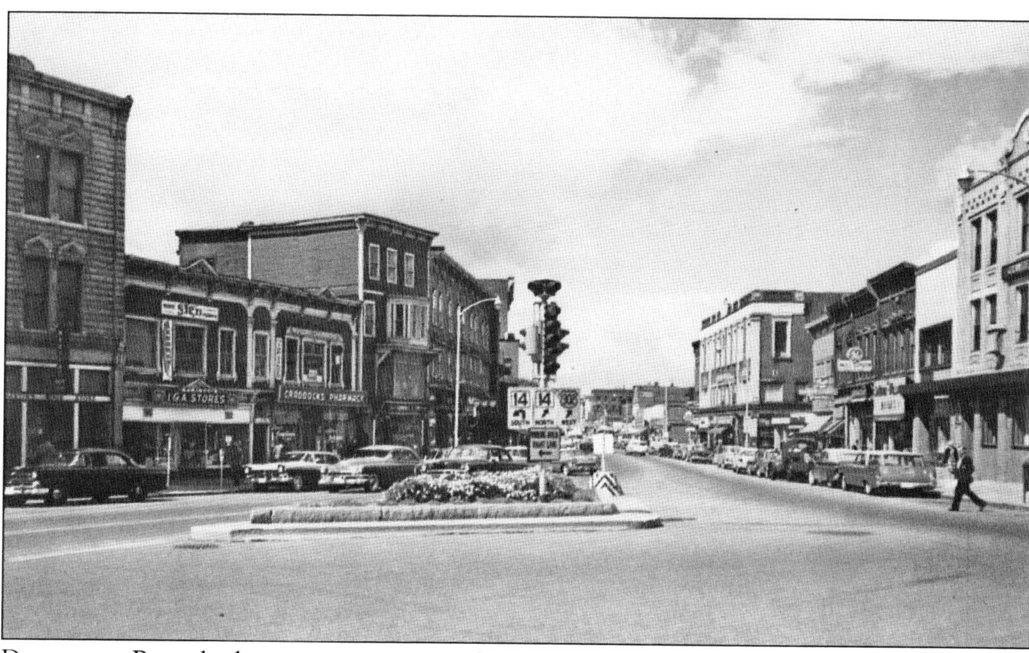

Downtown Barre had swarming streets and stores, showing a fast paced mid-1900s. With the problems caused by the increasing use of automobiles, electric traffic lights were installed on Main Street.

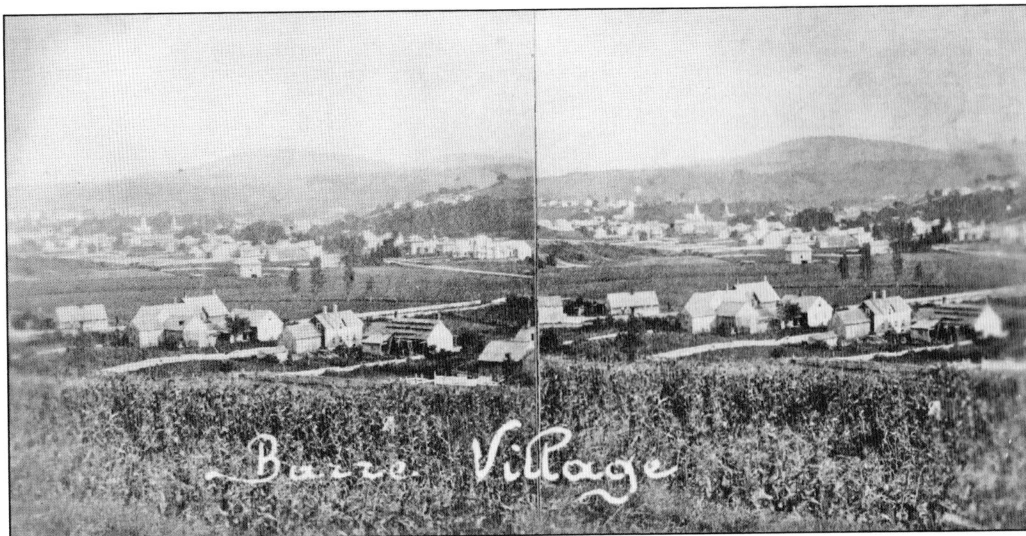

This 1870 image shows a few big white Federal-style houses, a valley, the top of a church steeple, and rolling green mountains in the background. With a population of 1,882, the village was the heart and soul of Barre. It was the place to go to get a taste of culture, friendship, education, and start a business.

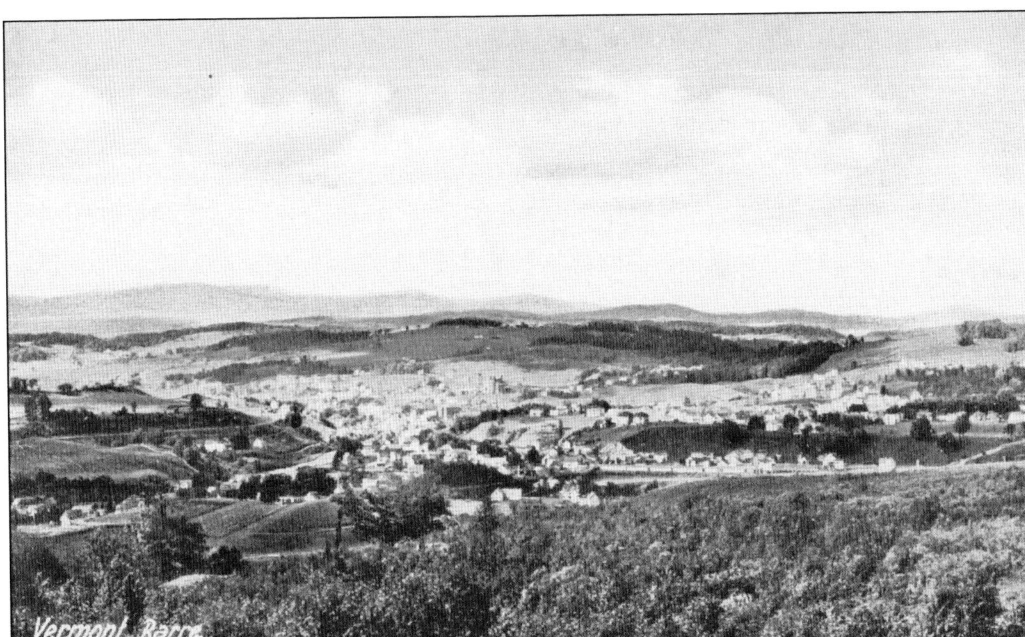

In the 1900s, communication improved because there were newspapers, a post office, telephones, books, a telegraph, and radios. By 1920 the Barre population had grown to 10,008.

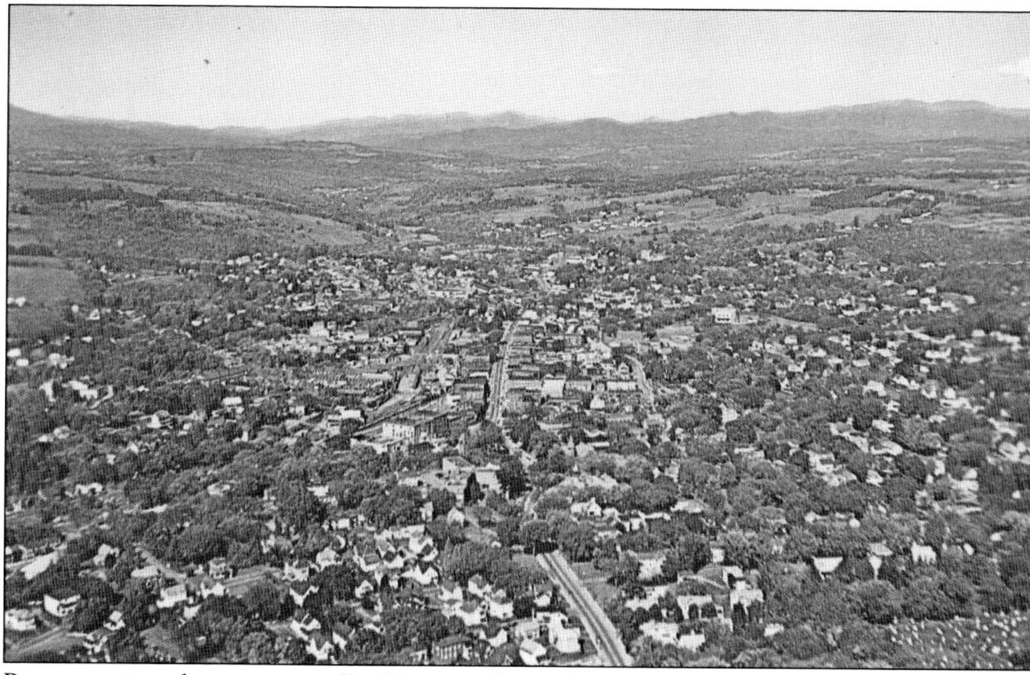
Barre continued to grow rapidly. The population hit its peak in 1915 when the population was 10,922.

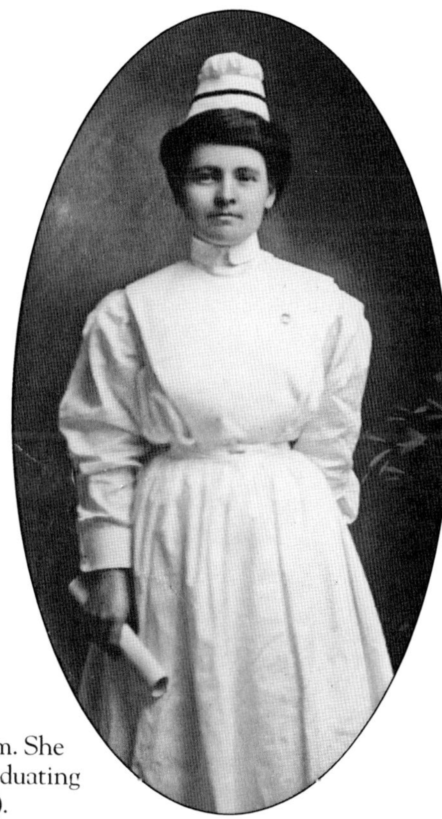
A proud woman poses in a white cotton starched uniform. She holds her rolled-up nursing diploma in her hand after graduating from Montpelier's Vermont College for Women (1953).

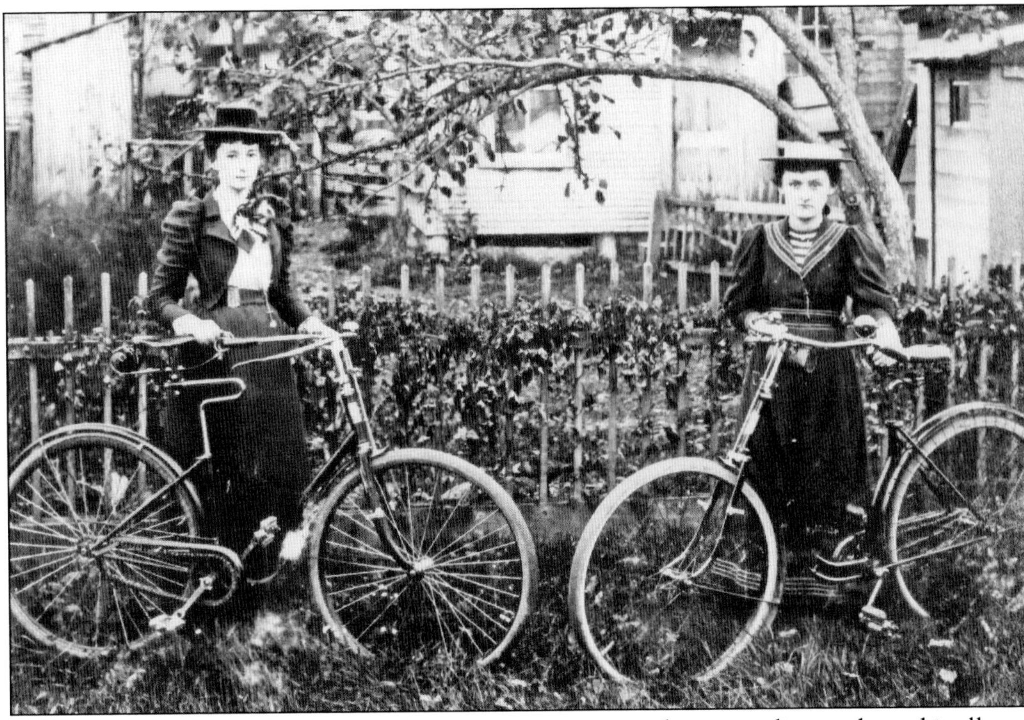

In the late 1800s, the bicycle inspired an interest in creating better quality roads, and it allowed residents to visit surrounding towns like Montpelier. The back of this photograph says, "Fred Ladd's wife?" (Courtesy of Aldrich Public Library, Barre, Vermont.)

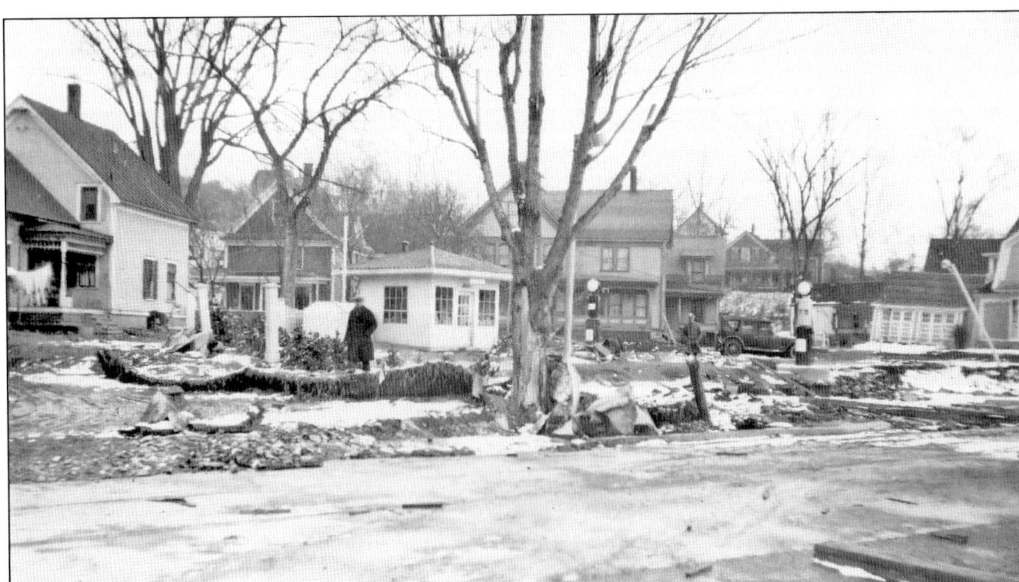

Two unidentified men scan the devastation from a spring flood. Note the gas tanks on the right side of this image.

Four

The Granite Center of the World

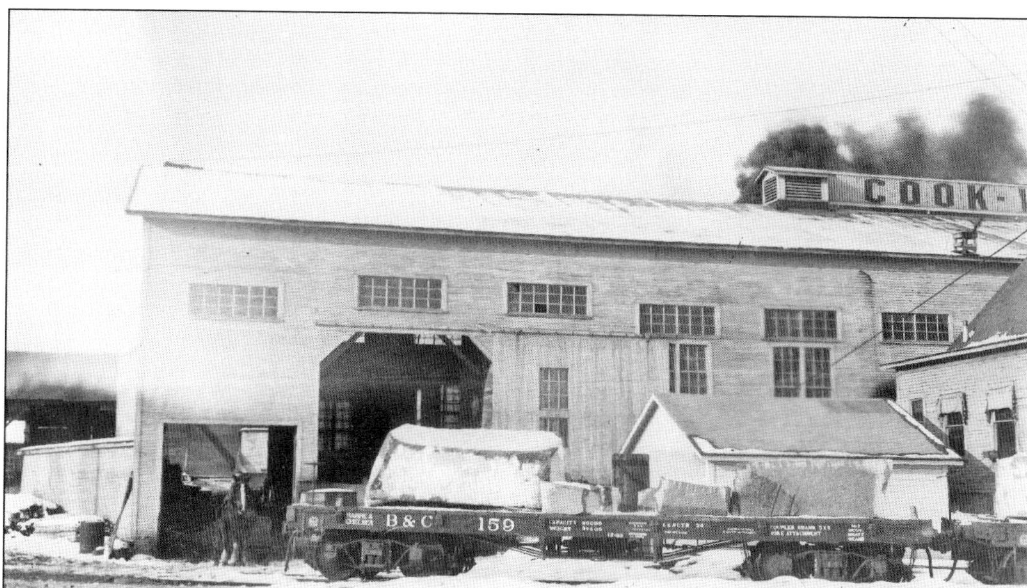

The Barre and Chelsea Rail Road Engine (Granite City) No. 4 transported huge blocks of granite from the quarries to the sheds; they were freighted down steep winding tracks by way of switchbacks. Early on, this building pictured was used as a gristmill, sawmill, and the Thwing Foundry. Later, it was used by Smith, Whitcomb & Cook as a granite shed. (Courtesy of the Vermont Granite Museum.)

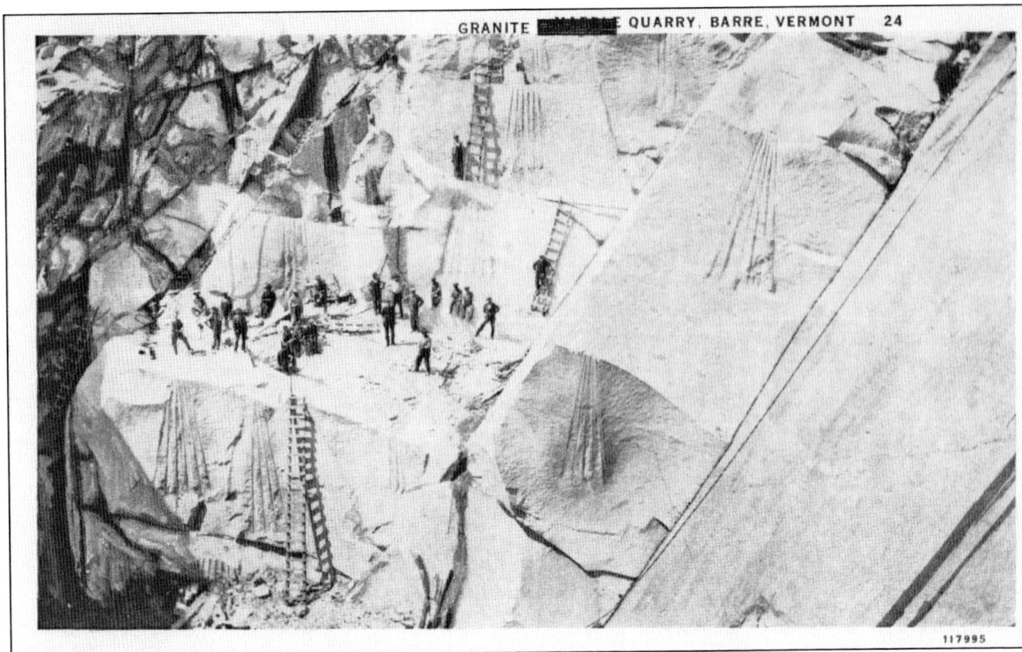

Men are working in a granite quarry in 1932. The opposite side of the postcard says, "Dear father, we came up to see the quarries. Wish you could see them. Take care of yourself. We'll be there soon if all goes well. With love —Helen." C.H. Hughes & Company took the photograph.

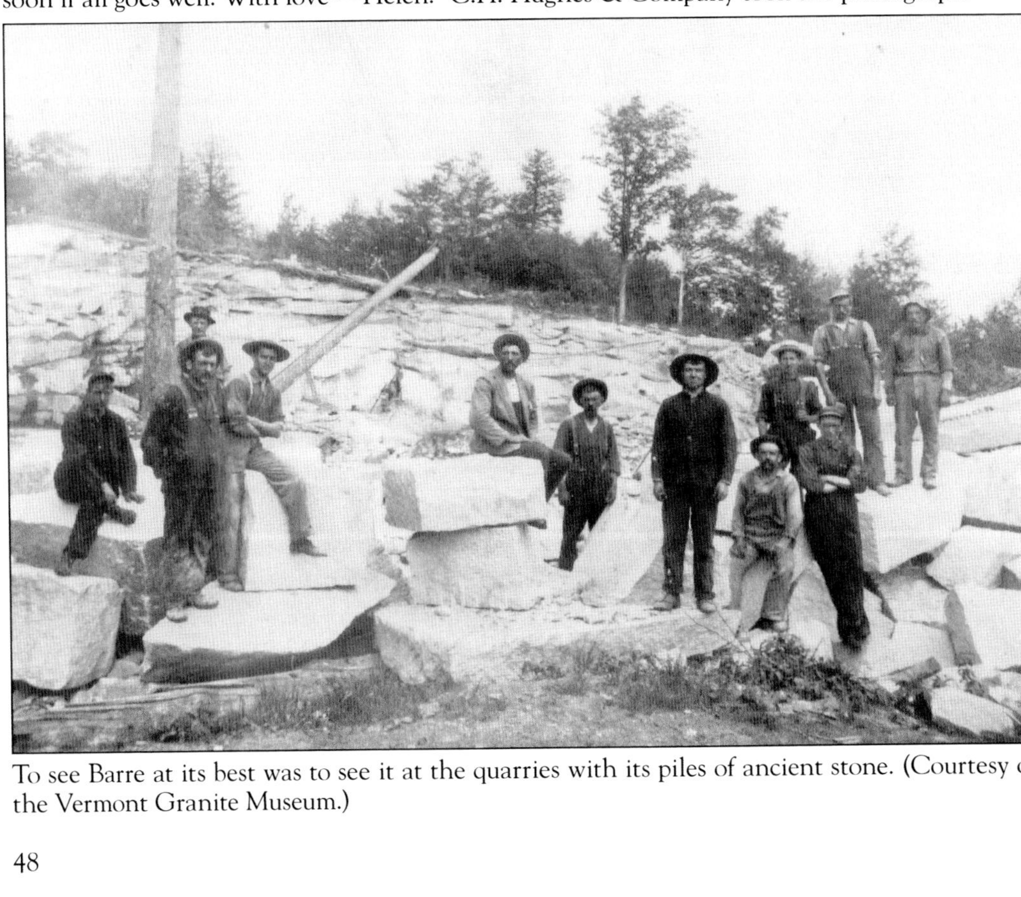

To see Barre at its best was to see it at the quarries with its piles of ancient stone. (Courtesy of the Vermont Granite Museum.)

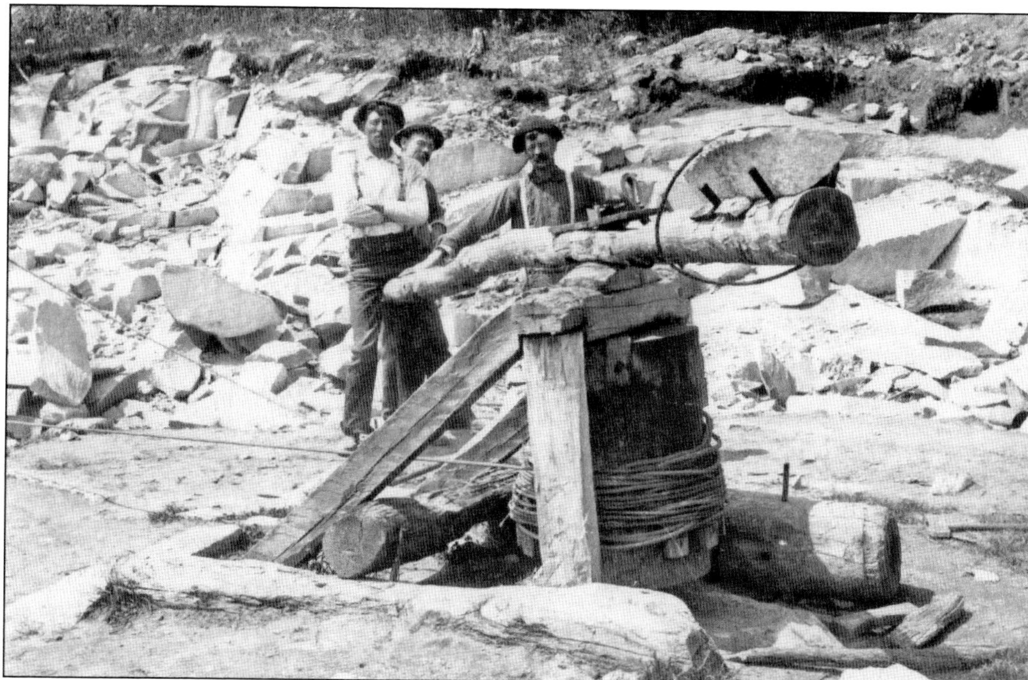

With no electricity, useful wooden devices were used to move large heavy blocks of granite around in the stone yard. (Courtesy of the Vermont Granite Museum.)

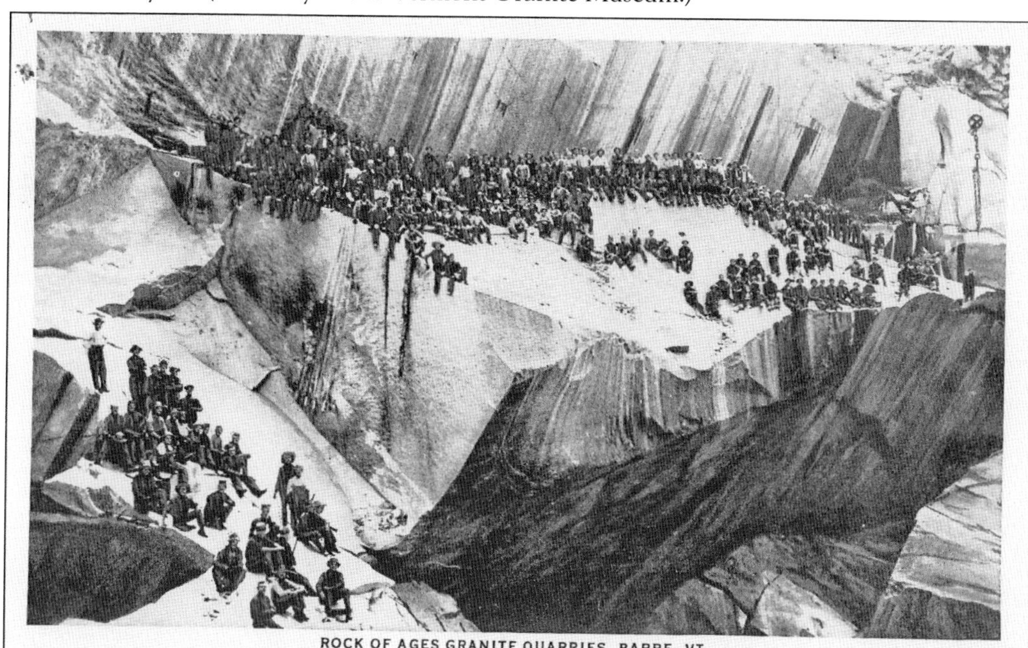

The back of the undated postcard says, "Largest block of granite ever quarried. Vermont ranks first in the production of granite and in Barre, the Granite Center, are located the Rock of Ages quarries which are the most extensive yet developed anywhere. Here are shown 300 workmen stationed on a block 200 feet long, 80 and 24 feet thick. It weighed 69,000,000 Lbs. and 1,700 flat cars were required to transport it." (Courtesy of the Curt Teich & Company, Inc.)

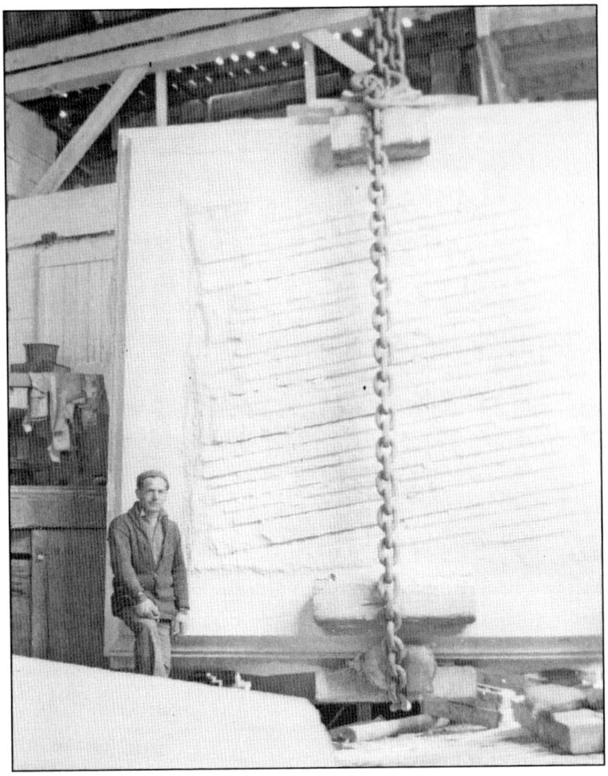

Granite weighs about 180 pounds per cubic foot. Thick, tough chains were used to lift the granite out of the quarries onto freight cars and then haul them to the finishing plants. (Courtesy of the Vermont Granite Museum.)

In this photograph by A.M. Troup is a group of workers from the Wells-Lamson Quarry Company. The end of the granite is marked as 103 tons. With the ability to import and export goods, the granite industry soared. (Courtesy of Aldrich Public Library, Barre, Vermont.)

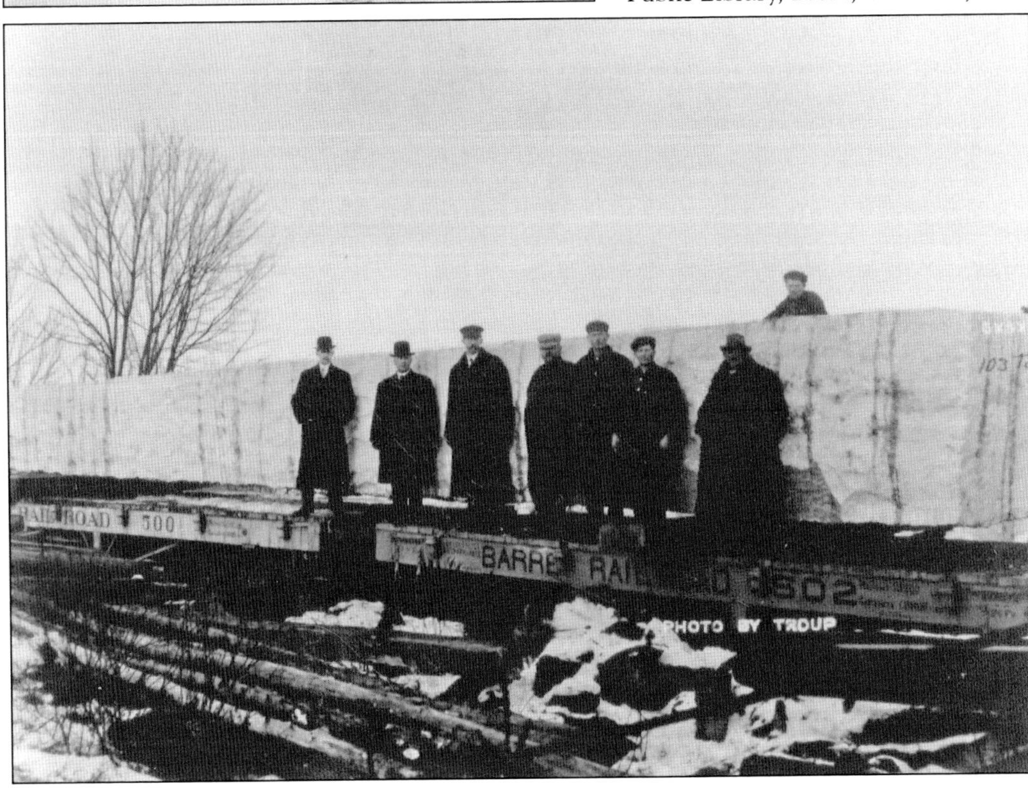

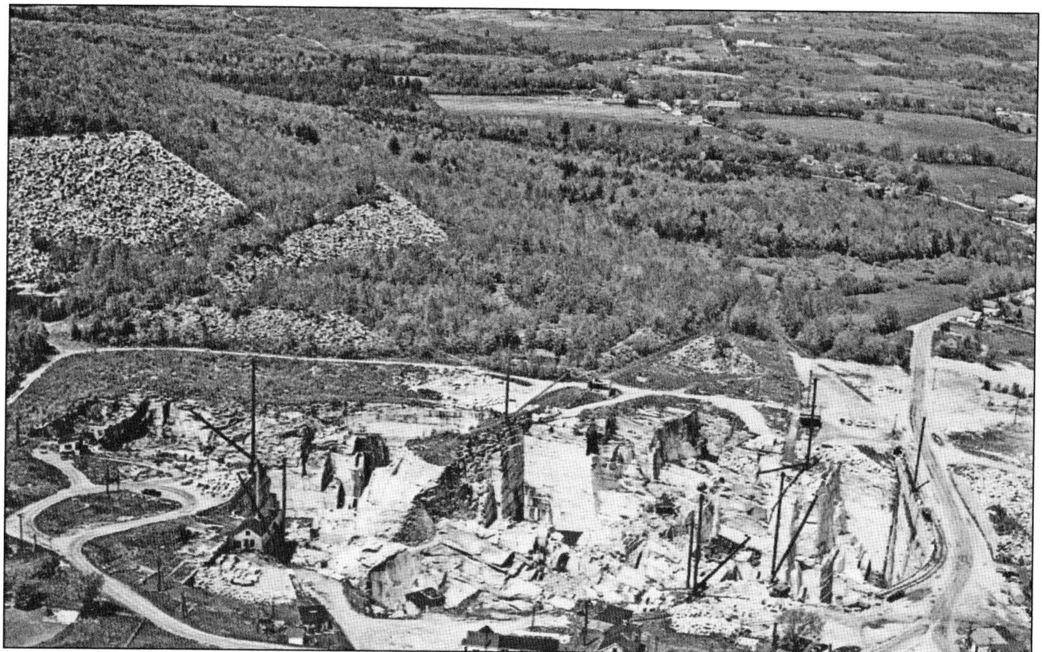

The Wells-Lamson Granite Quarry as seen from above in this photograph by Frank L. Forward. The 115-foot derricks brought huge granite blocks to the surface. The switchbacks were used to safely climb up the steep 1,025-foot incline toward the mountaintops. There were 35 miles of both sidings and switchbacks.

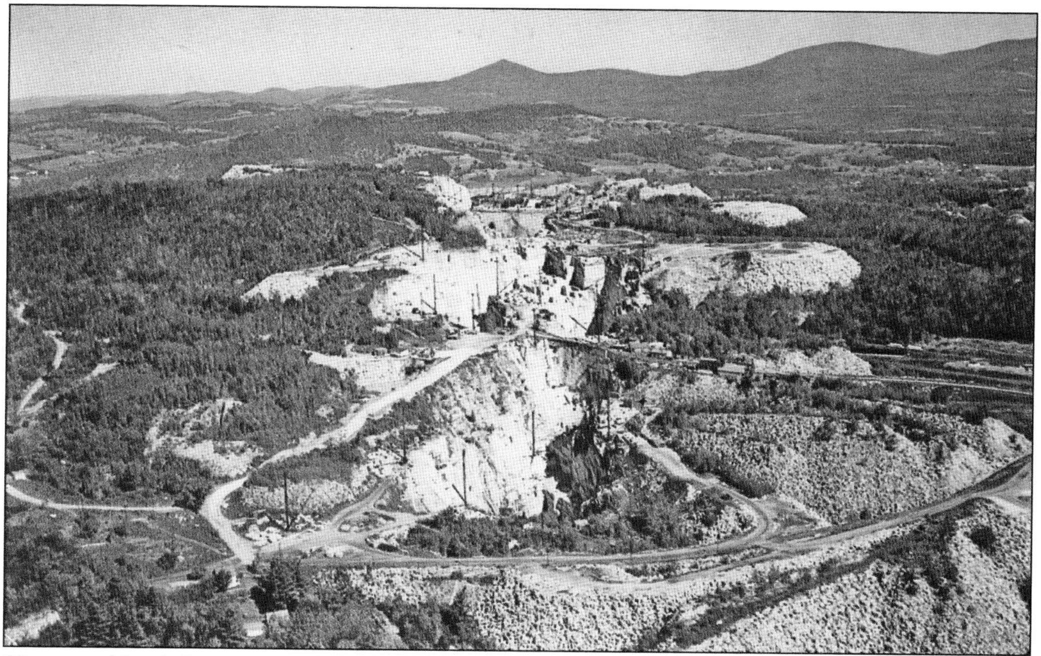

There could only be ten empty cars drawn by Barre & Chelsea Railroad locomotive, which weighed about 100,000 pounds, photographed here by John B. Hustler. Arthur Wellington Brayley's *The History of the Granite Industry of New England* (1913) reports, "The locomotive was built to 'hold on to the iron' by reason of its weight and sundry devices on its brakes."

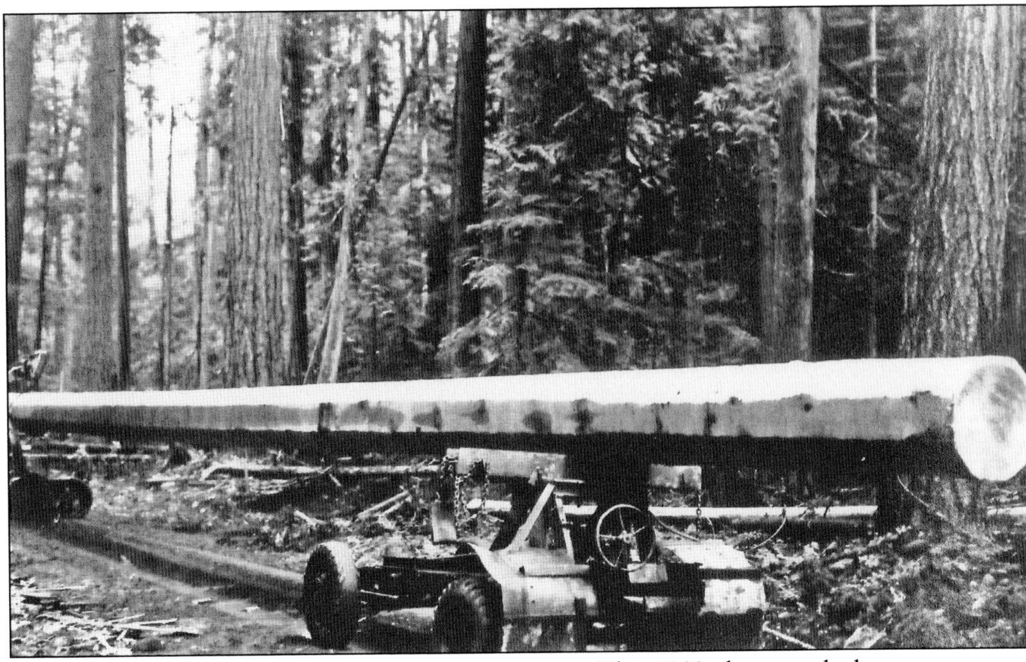

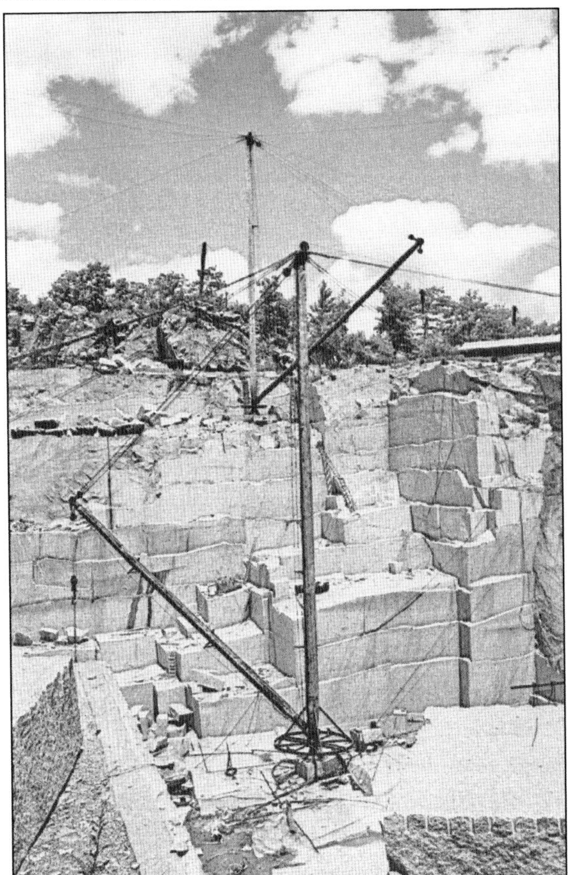

This 1902 photograph shows a mammoth 90-foot log cut in Oregon headed for a derrick to be used in one of the 68 granite quarries in Barre. In 1875, the Smith Quarry erected the first derrick on Cobble Hill. The log derrick had a 21–22 ton capacity, but later steel hoisting machines were used. (Courtesy of the Barre Granite Association.)

The derrick is pictured after it has been erected in the John Swenson Granite Quarries, which were owned by the same family since 1833. The Swenson family emigrated from Sweden. The opposite side of the postcard cites, "Buildings constructed from the Swenson granite are as follows: the Tomb of the Unknown Soldier, the approaches to the Pentagon, Tiffany's store in New York, Neiman Marcus Store in Dallas, and the Concord Public Library." Bromley & Company published the image.

This "Derrick Perched on Edge of Precipice" postcard shows the Rock of Ages granite quarry with a train perched on the top right corner. The bull wheel at the bottom of the derrick allowed the derrick operator to turn the mast and boom arm. The mast has a steel pin on the top, which is in the middle of what was called the "spider." (Courtesy of the Rock of Ages Corporation.)

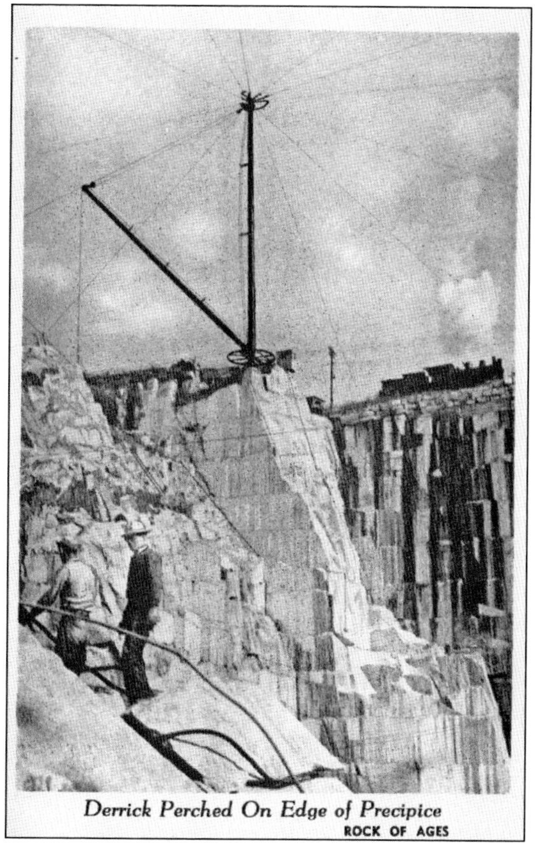

Immigrants came to Barre for work after escaping from crises in their own countries. (Courtesy of the Vermont Granite Museum.)

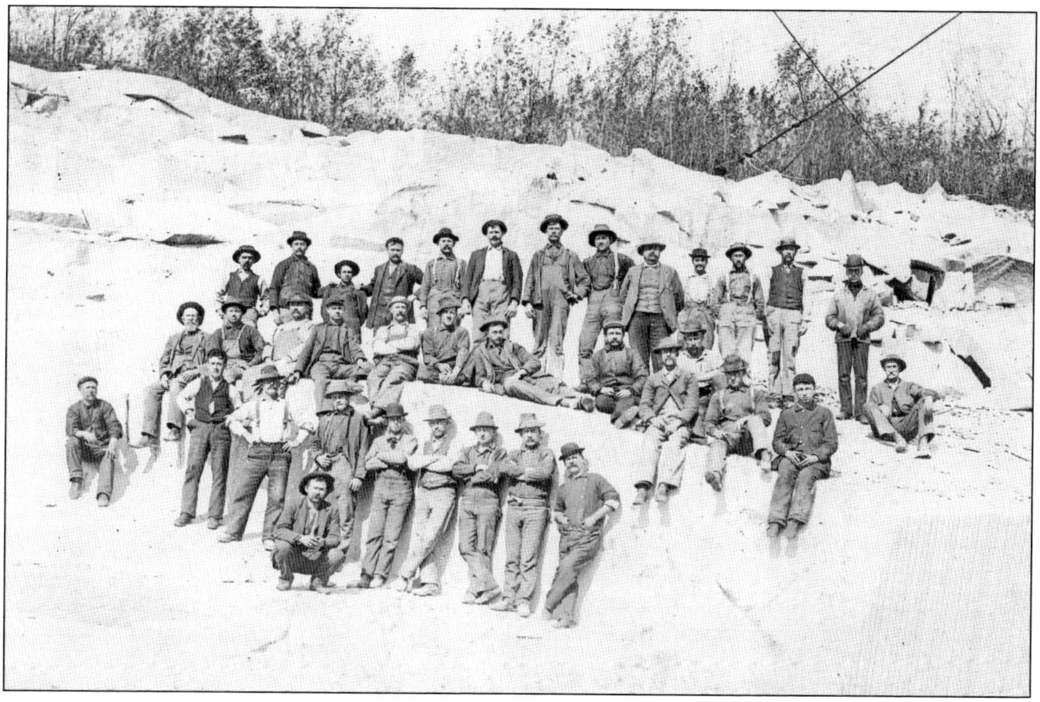

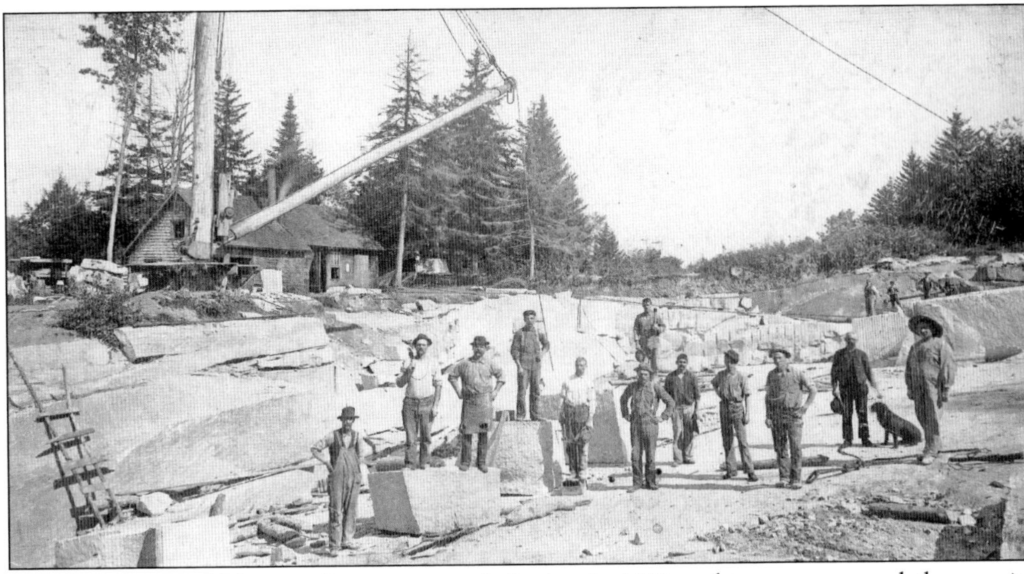

Robert Parker and Thomas Courser started digging in 1812 and it soon exposed the granite ledges on what is now known as Cobble Hill. This early image of quarry workers shows surface granite before it became a very deep pit. (Courtesy of Paul Bagalio, William Roy and the Vermont Granite Museum.)

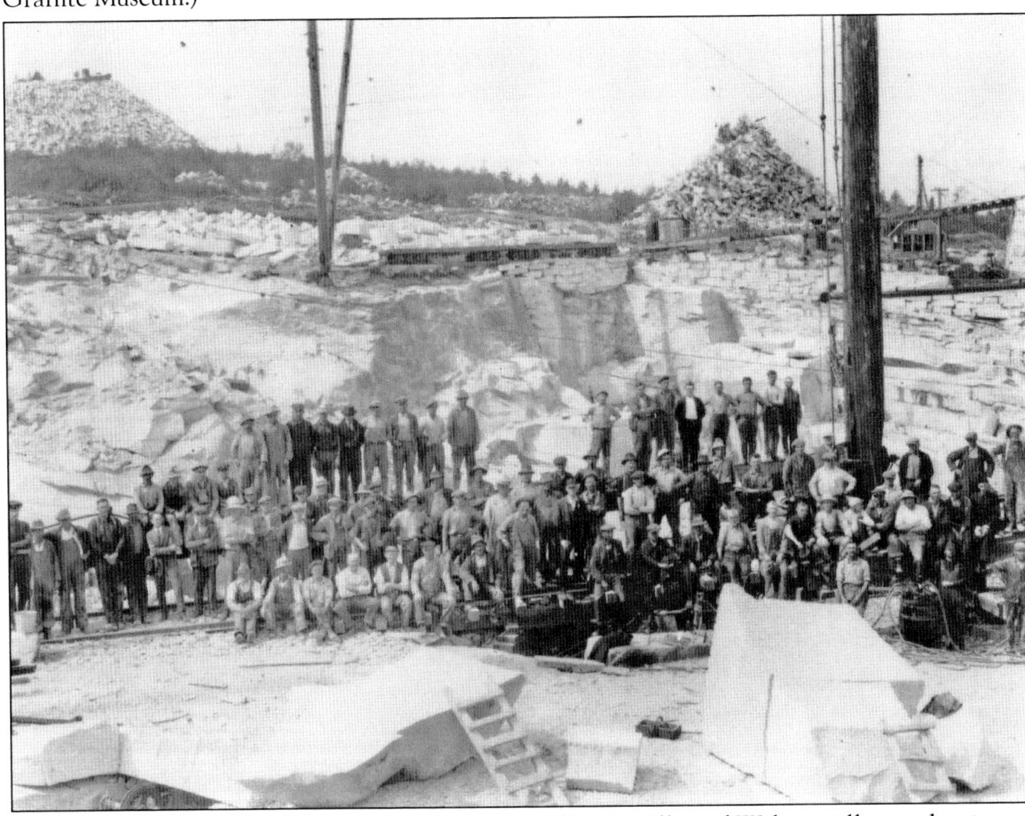

Shortly after, granite was discovered in the areas of Graniteville and Websterville on what is now known as Millstone Hill. (Courtesy of the Vermont Granite Museum.)

This postcard's perspective extends from a distance across the quarry to the tiny, circled man. The label encourages the viewer to "note size of men." The deep quarry pit is impressive in comparison to the earlier surface images. (Courtesy of the Rock of Ages Corporation.)

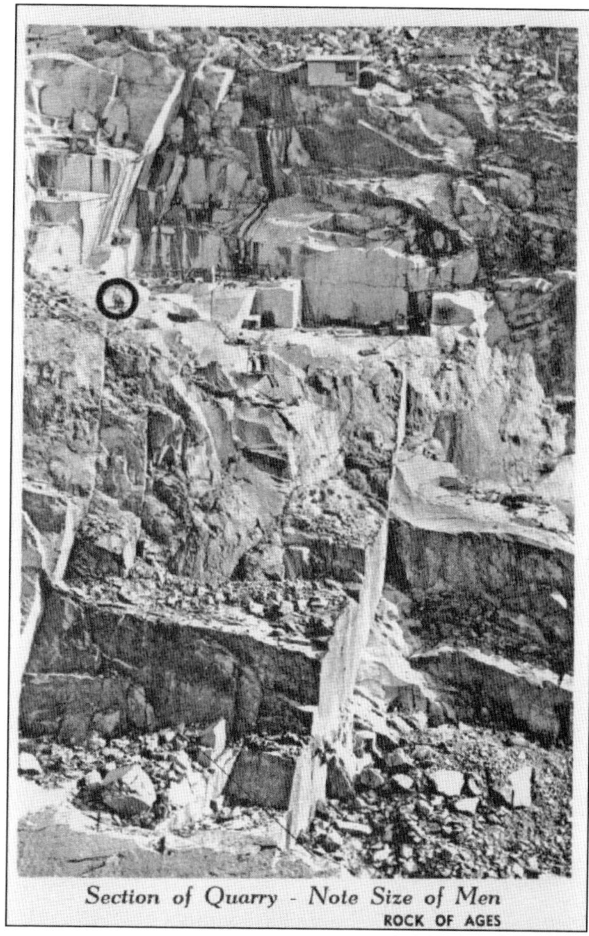

Smith & Wells established the Wells, Lamson & Company in 1880. (Courtesy of the Vermont Granite Museum.)

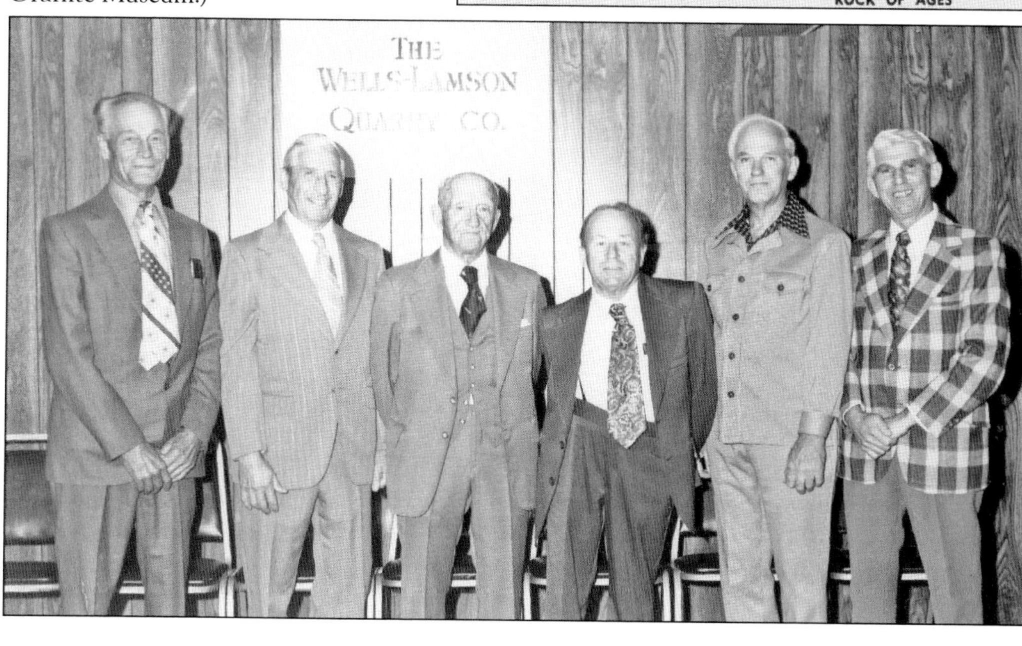

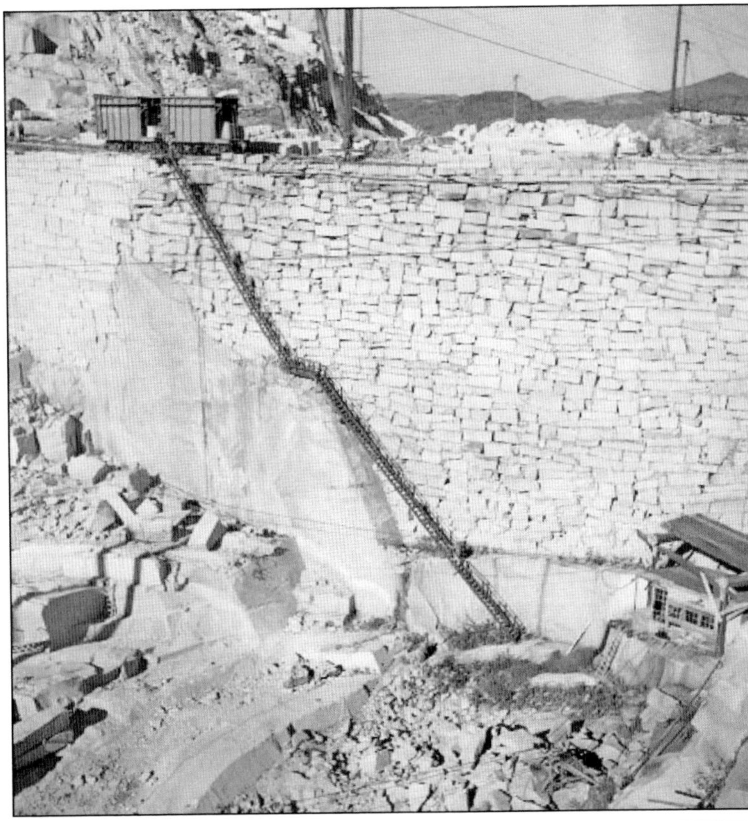

This 1941 aerial image of the Whitmore and Morse quarry in East Barre shows a ladder up the pit's wall to the train. (Courtesy of the Library of Congress, photograph by Jack Delano #LC-USF34-045982-E.)

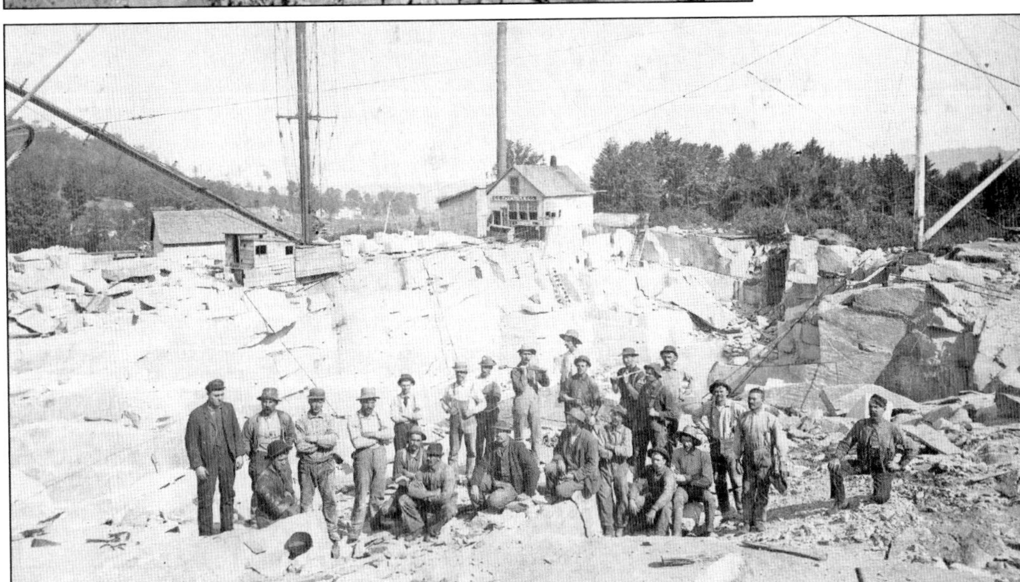

Other immigrant groups that lived and worked in Barre, Vermont, were Scandinavians, Italian, Spanish, English, Irish, Greeks, and French-Canadians. Almost all the immigrant workers were employed in the granite industry, and less than 30 percent of the granite industry workers were native-born. In this image from 1894 is a quarry owned by the C.E. Tayntor Company, and they employed 30 men. (Courtesy of the Vermont Granite Museum.)

In 1900, brothers Henry J., James M., William G., and Alexander D. Smith founded the Smith Brothers Granite Company. The brothers immigrated to the United States from Scotland. Dark granite was popular because it made a contrast between the polished and the hammered surfaces. (Courtesy of Paul Bigalio and William Roy collection, Vermont Granite Museum of Barre.)

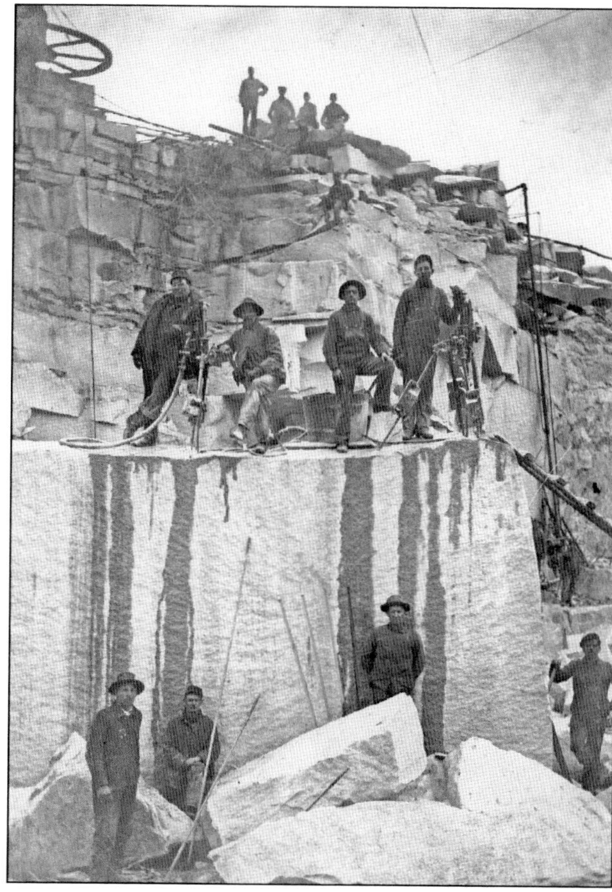

Arthur Wellington Brayley's *The History of the Granite Industry of New England* (1913) reports, "Mrs. Elizabeth (Murphy) Carroll, Barre, has the distinction of being the only woman in New England holding the position of sole proprietor and manager of a granite manufacturing business." This 1940 postcard shows a small wooden derrick shack where the operator engaged drum hoists and brakes.

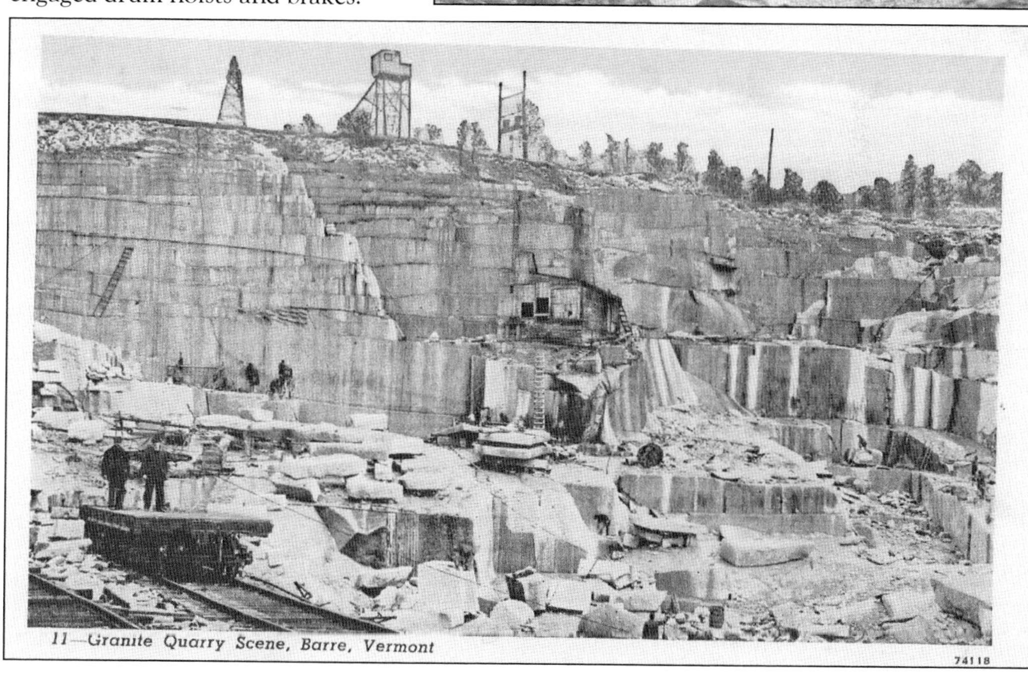

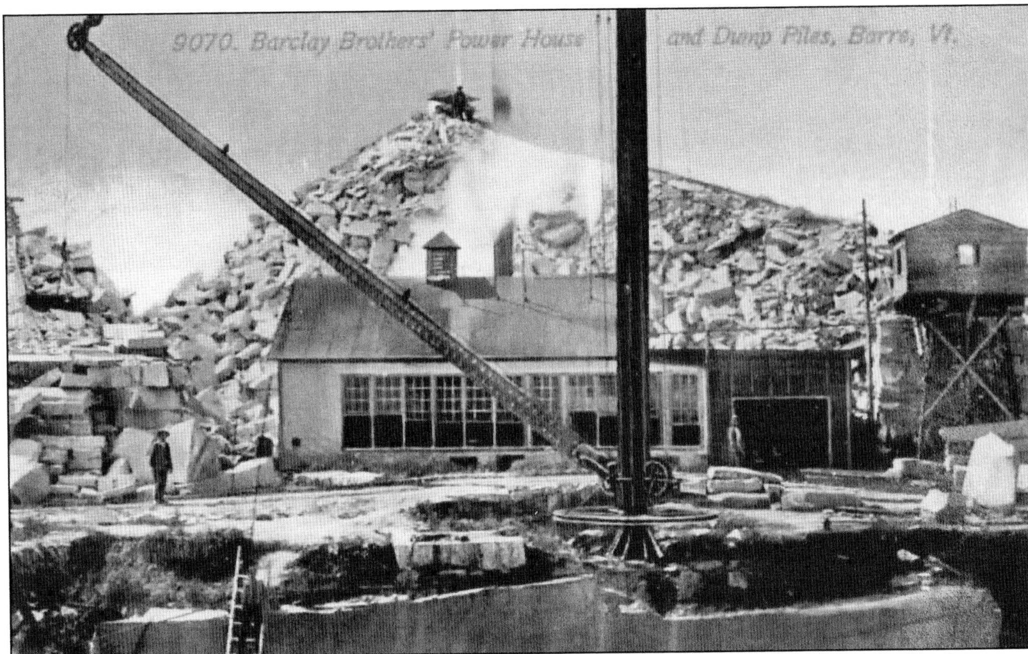

This 1912 image shows Barclay Brothers Power House with dump piles in the background. S.L. Littlejohn and William Barclay—granite cutters—had sheds on the bank of the river, north of the Jones Brothers' shed. They manufactured cemetery, monumental, and statuary work for wholesale and retail trade.

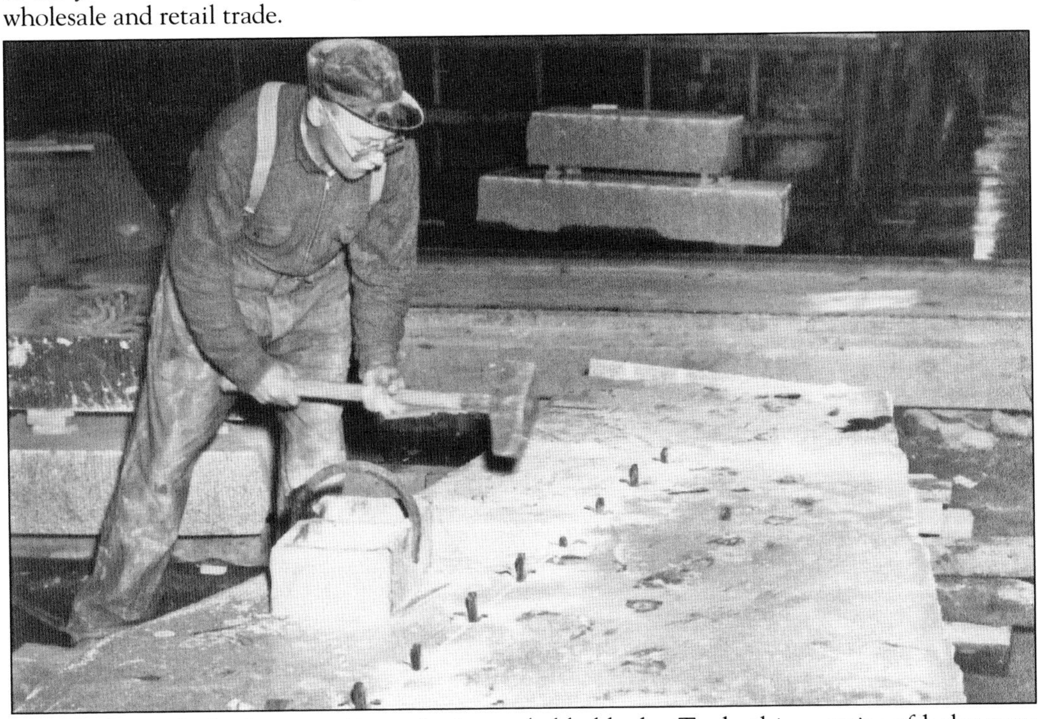

Granite has to be broken or split to obtain workable blocks. To do this, a series of holes were drilled along a line to be split by hitting an iron chisel with a sledgehammer, or by tapping with a hammer until it cracked along the rock's grain. (Courtesy of the Vermont Granite Museum.)

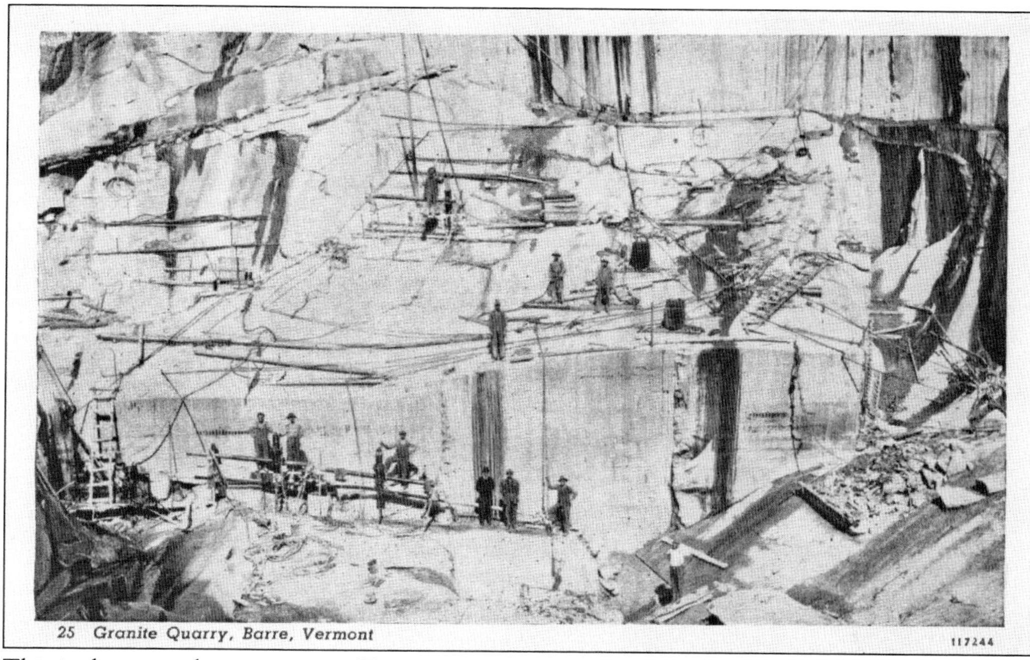

This is the second quarry opened by owners James Boutwell and Harvey Varnum, who formed Boutwell, Milne & Varnum Company (BM&V). They mined both medium gray and dark gray granite.

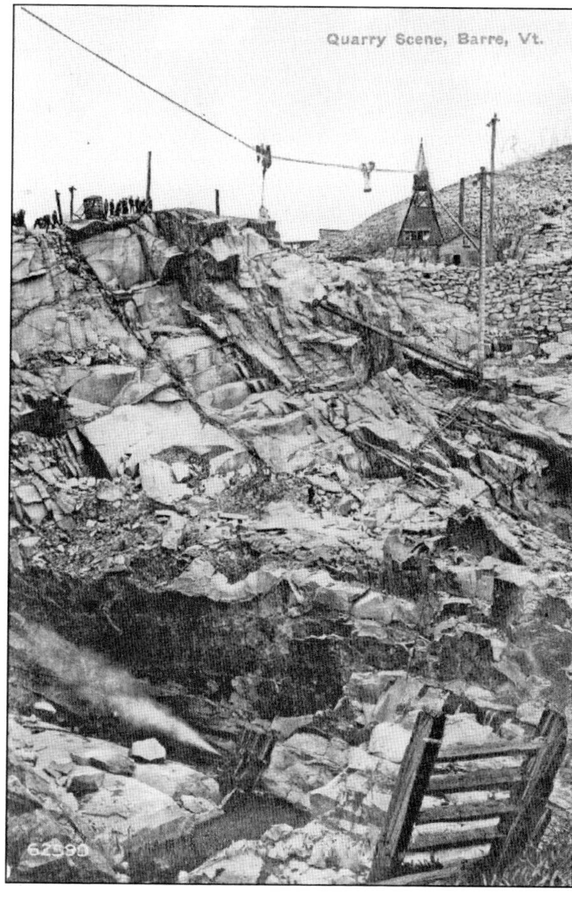

In this 1919 postcard, visitors are looking down from the edge (top, left) of the quarry into the pits. The *Rock of Ages* website states, "By 1924, so many people were coming to look into the 'holes,' BM&V [Boutwell, Milne, and Varnum] included a room for visitors in the floor plan of the new machinists' building." (Courtesy of the Rock of Ages Corporation.)

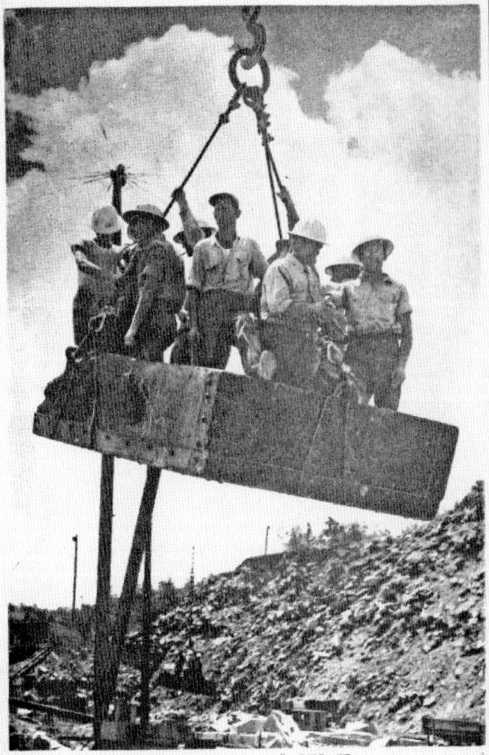

Ready to Descend 350 Feet
ROCK OF AGES

The "Men Going Down into the Hole to Begin Their Workday" image is dated August 1950. Residents would line up on top of the hole to watch the men ride the rock down to the bottom. (Courtesy of the Rock of Ages Corporation, H 444.)

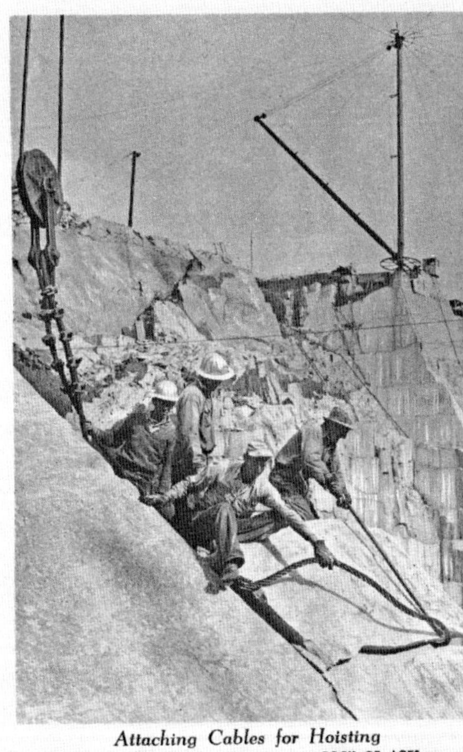

Attaching Cables for Hoisting
ROCK OF AGES

The "Attaching Cables for Hoisting" postcard shows four unidentified men balancing on a 50-ton block of granite while securing steel guy wires around the granite. Around the edges of the quarry were 12 huge derricks, whose masts are three feet in diameter and 110 feet tall. These derricks hoist the huge blocks of granite up to the top of the hole. (Courtesy of the Rock of Ages Corporation.)

A stone carver gazes out the window while he waits for the day's granite. Arthur Wellington Brayley's 1913 book *The History of the Granite Industry of New England*, reported, "At the city terminus of the Barre Railroad may be seen the busy throng of stone cutters engaged in changing the rough blocks of granite, delivered by the cars, into things of beauty." (Courtesy of the Vermont Granite Museum.)

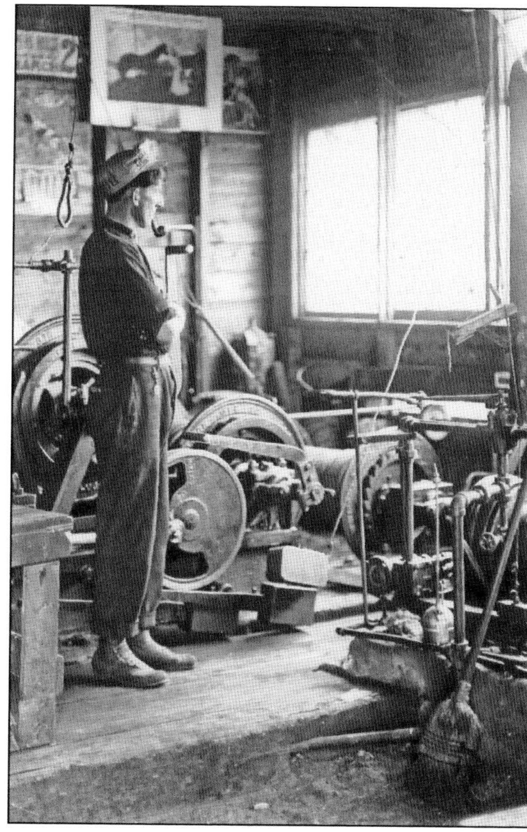

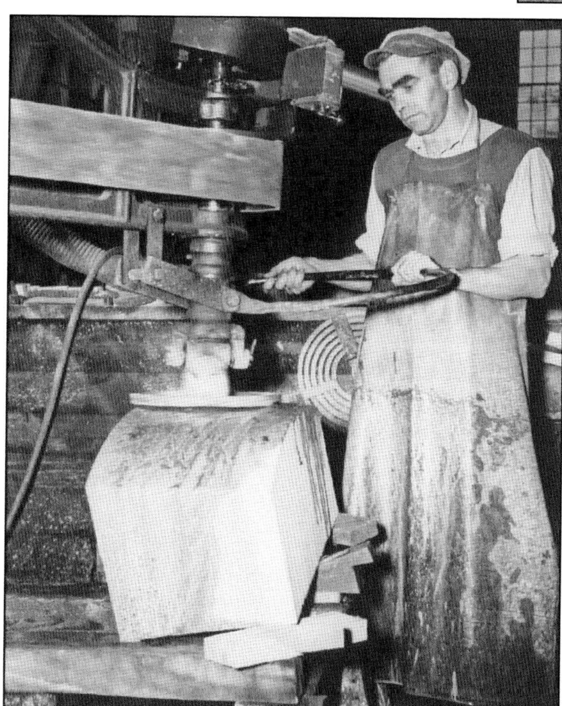

An unidentified man is polishing a large granite block. The finished product would shine like glass. (Courtesy of the Vermont Granite Museum.)

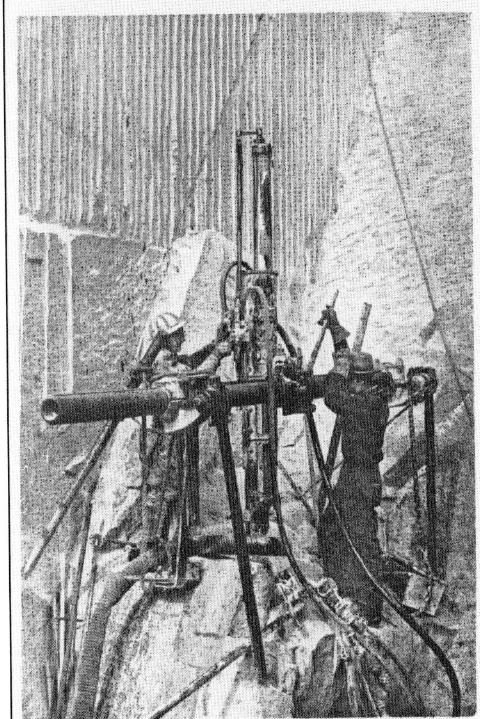

Channelling - 1st Step In Removing Granite
ROCK OF AGES

Cutting deep into the pit using the broach channeling method (1885–1945) is shown in this image. Channeling refers to the process of cutting a continuous vertical channel on the left, right, and rear sides of granite to completely detach it from the bedrock using power tools. The series of closely spaced large diameter holes along the length of the channel in back of the man help the process. (Courtesy of the Rock of Ages Corporation.)

Seven men and one boy pose for their picture while sitting on a huge piece of stone. Only four of the eight men can be identified as Bill McKane, William Donahue, Frank Watson, and John O'Connor. It is unknown which names belong to which men. There is a faint pyramid shaped top of Spruce Mountain in the distant background of this image. (Courtesy of Paul Bagalio, William Roy, and the Vermont Granite Museum.)

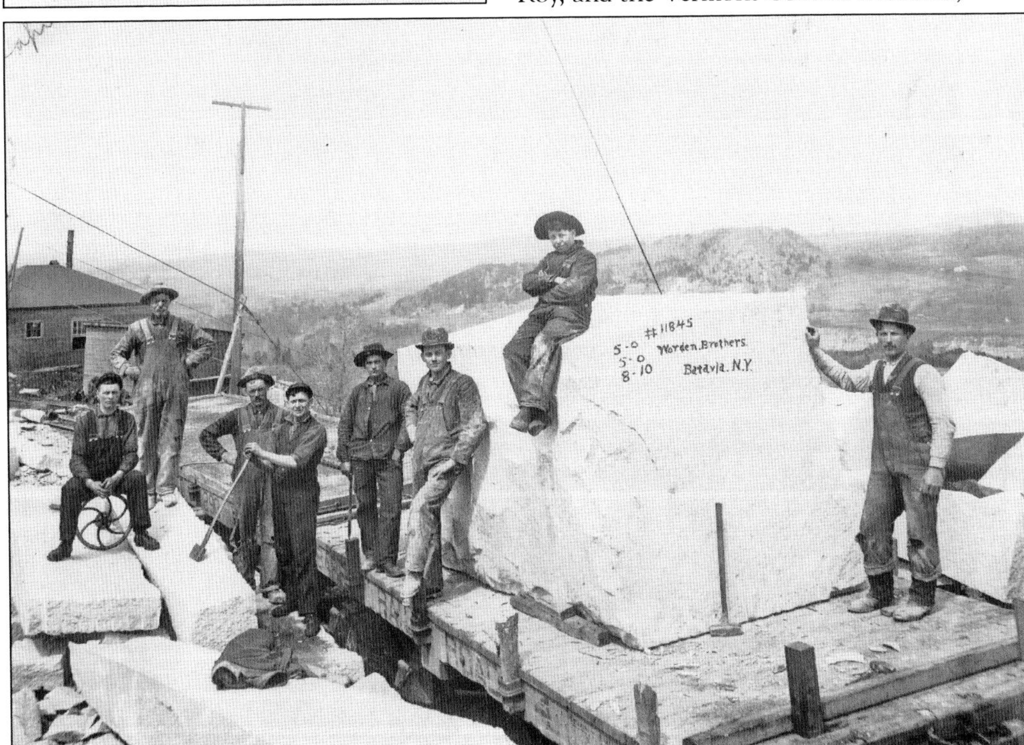

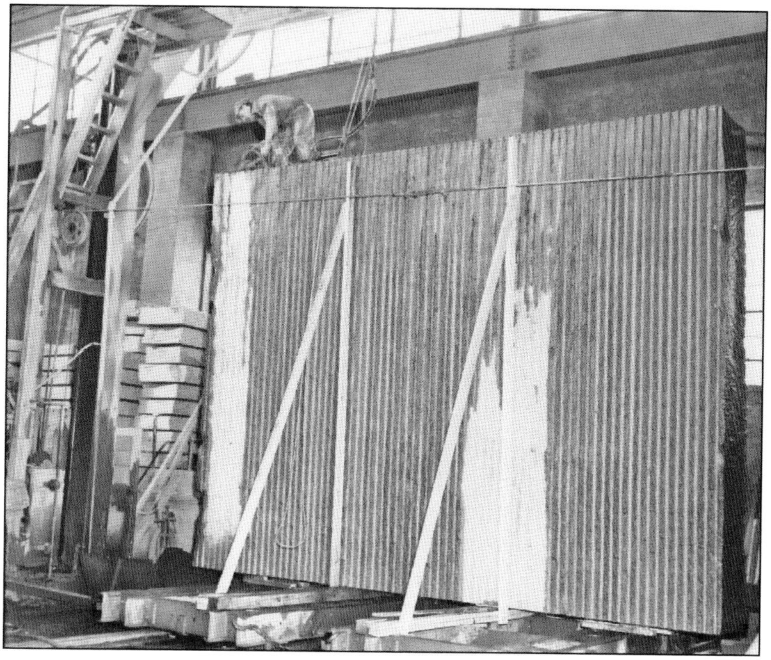

An unidentified man is cutting large granite slabs in the Wells-Lambson Quarry saw plant in this image taken by Arthur Simon. Modern sawing tools, called gang saws, greatly increased the capacity of manufacturers; multiple blades adjusted to desired sizes. Pneumatic hammers and chisels work across the block to produce a hammered finish. (Courtesy of the Barre Granite Association.)

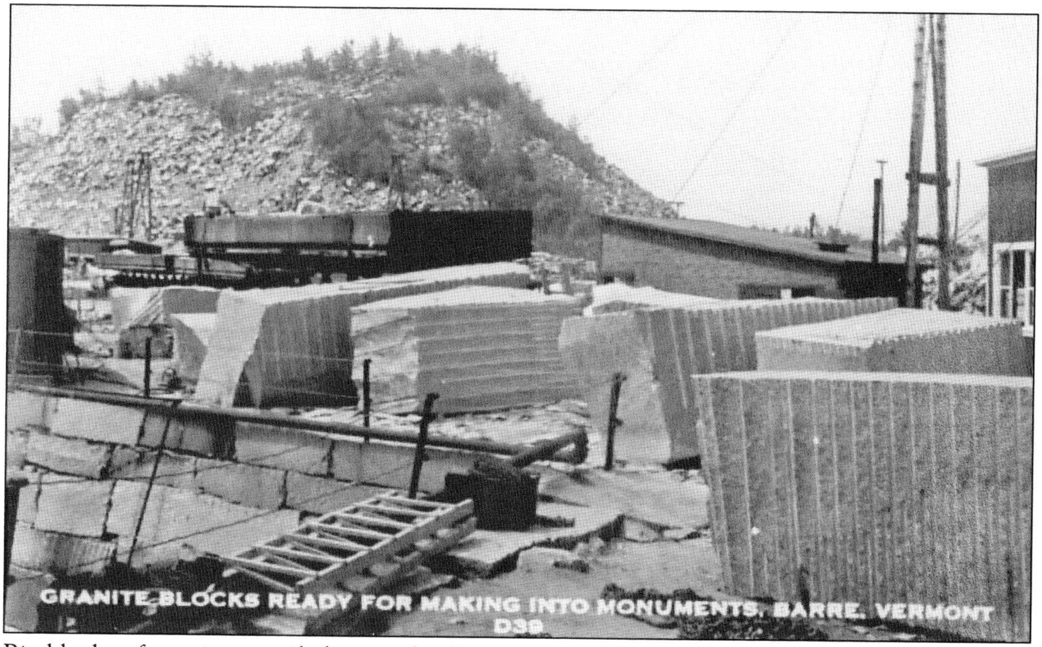

Big blocks of granite are piled up at the Swenson Granite Company yard ready to be sculpted into monuments, fence posts, and other fine products. The *Barre Daily Times*, on November 2, 1932, reported, "One chunk of Barre granite weighed nearly 40 tons to be used as a mausoleum roof. The stone was nearly 24 feet long and 12 feet wide. It weighted 90 tons before being shaped down to the size required."

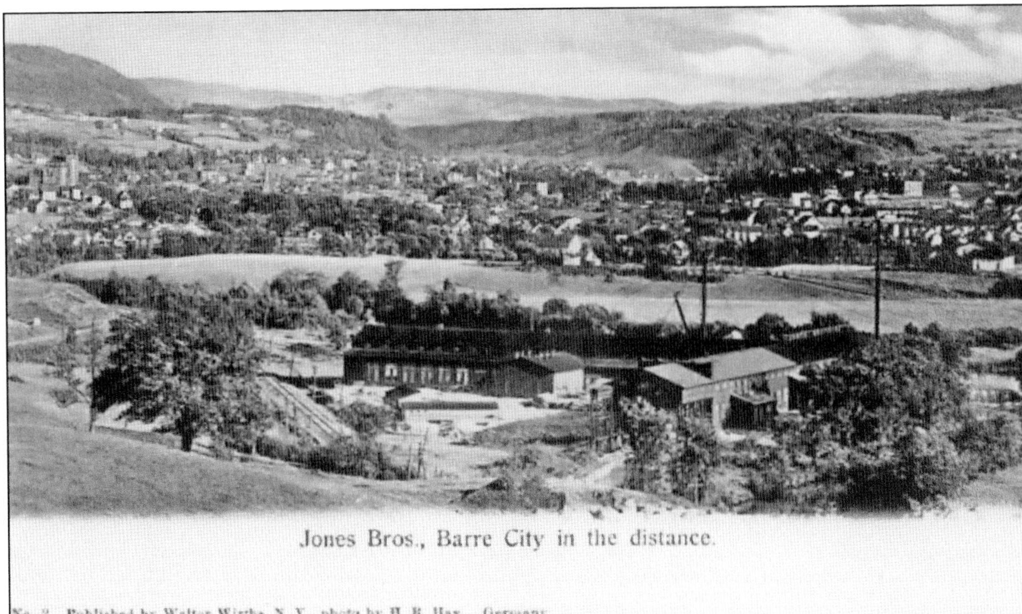

In 1895, Jones Brothers built this quarry shed. They installed a surface cutter, stone-cutting machines, gang saws, cutting and polishing lathes, traveling derricks, pneumatic surface cutters, and pneumatic tools. The tools and machinery were operated by steam and water.

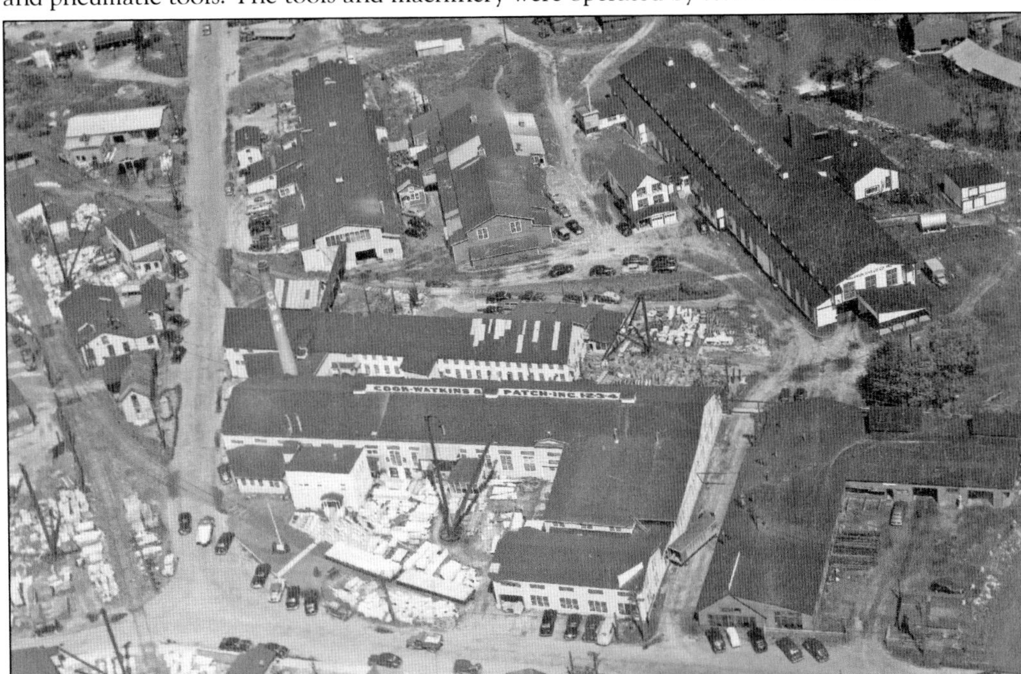

This is a bird's-eye view of Cook, Watkins & Patch, a Barre granite company. (Courtesy of the Vermont Granite Museum.)

Shown is the exterior of the Cook, Watkins & Patch Granite Company where granite is piled and waiting for its time to be shaped into monuments and statues by skilled artisans. Two men are guiding the granite onto the truck on the left. (Courtesy of the Vermont Granite Museum.)

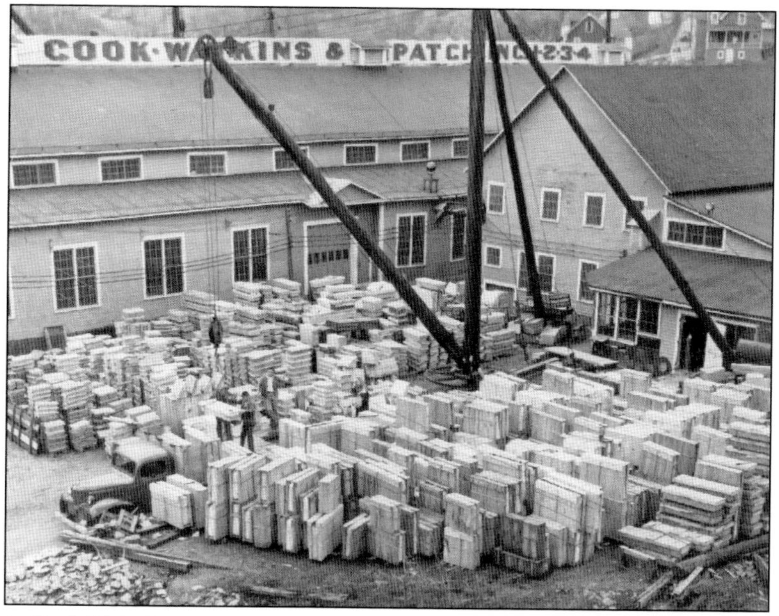

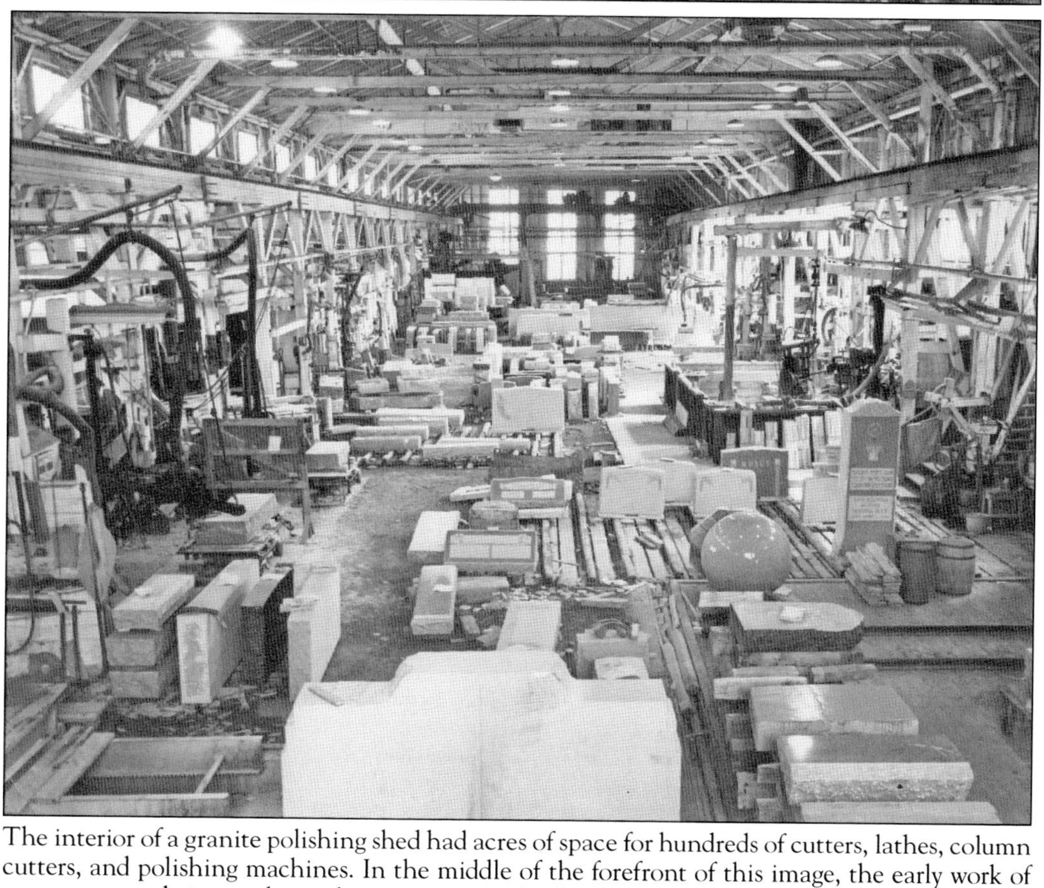

The interior of a granite polishing shed had acres of space for hundreds of cutters, lathes, column cutters, and polishing machines. In the middle of the forefront of this image, the early work of a race car was being sculptured into a memorial. The completed memorial is pictured in Hope Cemetery on page 72. (Courtesy of the Vermont Granite Museum.)

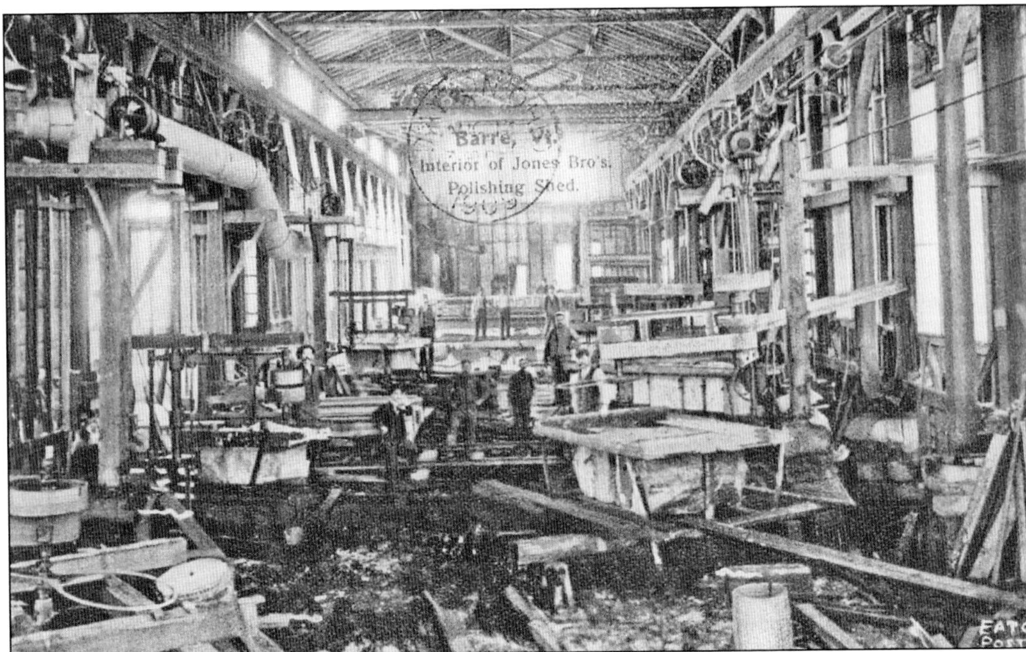

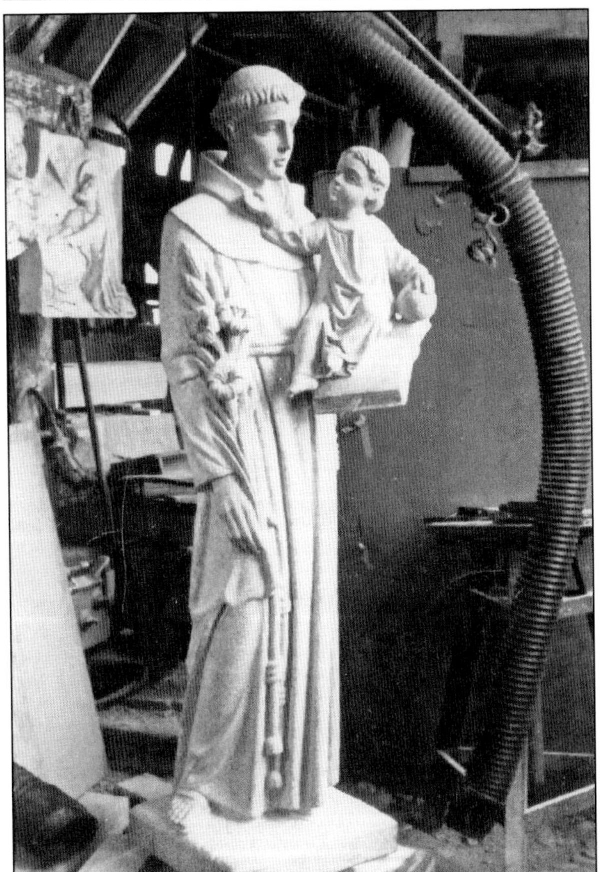

The interior of the Jones Brothers polishing shed, seen here in 1909, is now the Vermont Granite Museum and Stone Arts School. The opposite side of the postcard says, "Finest granite center in the world. It's also a fine thriving burg." They were the largest dealers of Barre granite in the market and exported most of their granite products to Boston.

Before the invention of the air filtering system, shown to the right of the statue in 1962, granite dust destroyed many workers' lungs, and many died at an early age. (Courtesy of the Vermont Granite Museum and Stone Arts School.)

The hands of a skilled stone carver are over roses, symbolizing love and wisdom, on a block of granite. The polished finish was conducted in the following stages: steel shot, coarse emery, fine emery, and polishing emery under a felt disk. The template was created with a pneumatic sandblasting machine. (Courtesy Barre Granite Association.)

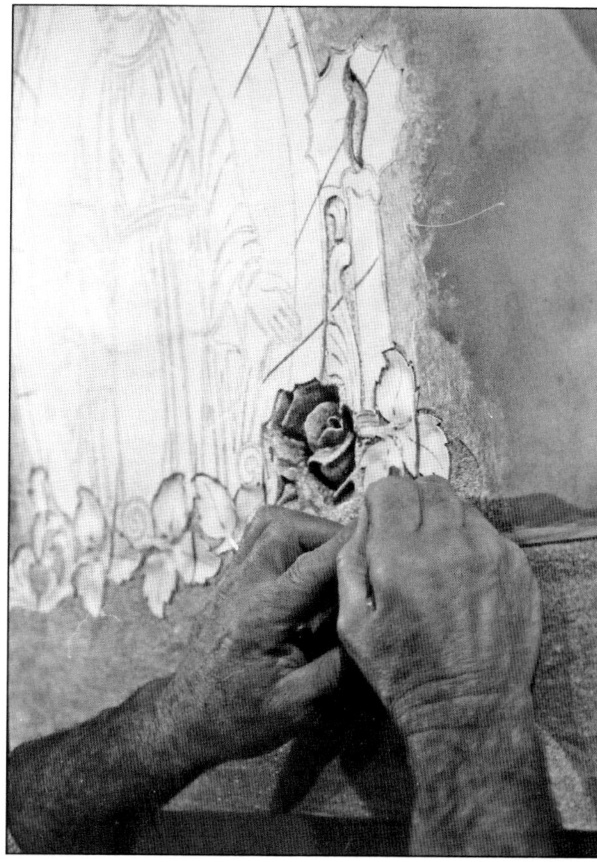

These are elegant decorative plaster models of architectural column capitals in an 1895 image by F.W. Sherburne. Stone carvers create large sculptures from plaster casts made from maquettes, or small preliminary models of an envisioned sculpture created by the sculptor. Maquettes were used to visualize and test shapes and ideas without experiencing the cost and effort of producing a full-scale result. (Courtesy Barre Historical Society.)

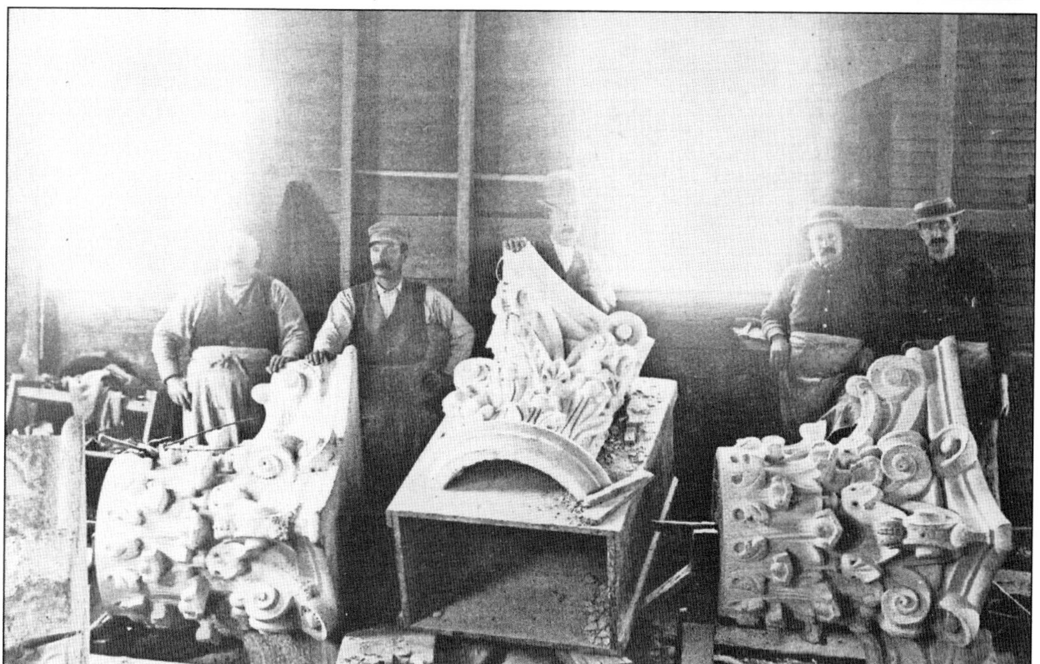

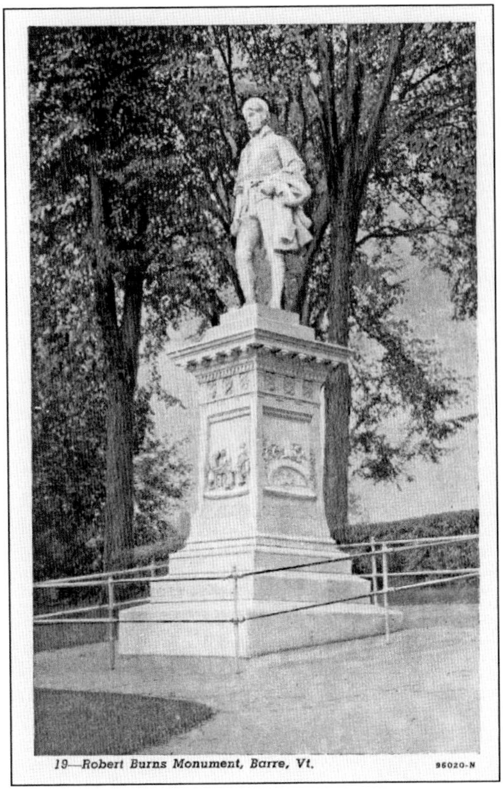

At the entrance to Spaulding Graded School stands a statue memorializing the Scottish poet Robert Burns. Dedicated in 1899, it overlooks the town common. *Barre in Retrospect 1776–1976* states, "It embodies the skills of two national groups, Italians and Scots, who immigrated in large numbers to Barre in the 1880s and 1890s." This postcard is dated 1919.

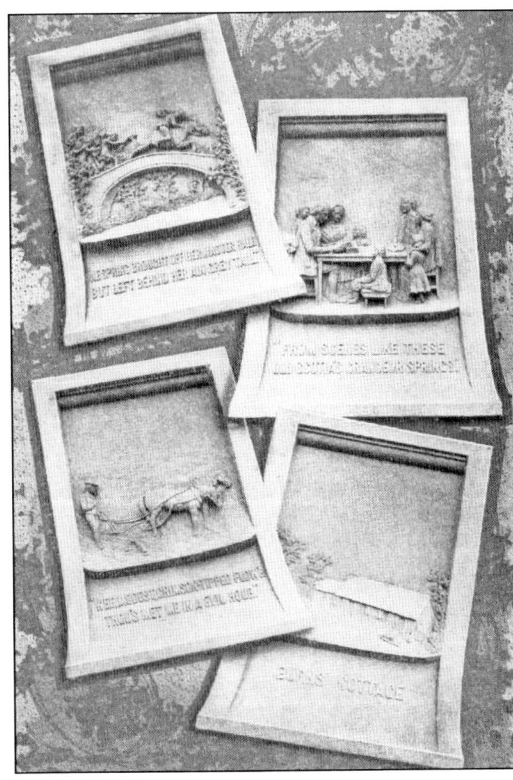

The four panels from the Burns Monument were carved by a young Italian named Elia Corti. The panels depict scenes from Robert Burns's life and his poems.

The 1919 Soldiers and Sailors Monument was created by a German-born American sculptor from New York named C. Paul Jennewein. It was the winning design in a contest called "Youth Triumphant." A semicircular granite bench surrounds the statue, and the carvers Gino Tosi, E. Yuri, and A. Dementi were from Barre.

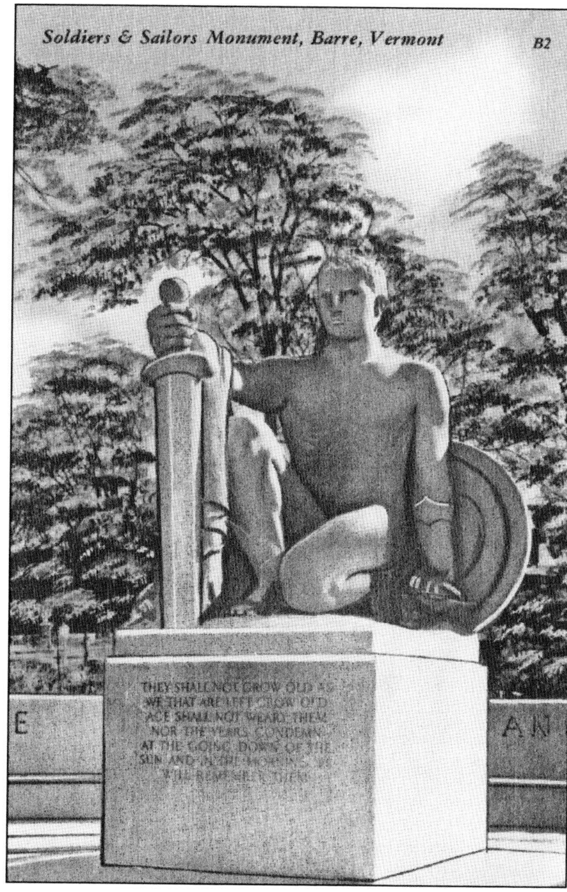

This is the entryway to Hope Cemetery in 1915. Donald G. Allen's *Barre Granite Heritage* reports, "Italian Carlo Abate designed the entryway. Louisa Ambrosini Fuller served as the model; Enrico Mori and Gino Tosi were the granite carvers." Many of the memorials are engraved with symbols and emblems, indicating membership in an organization or society.

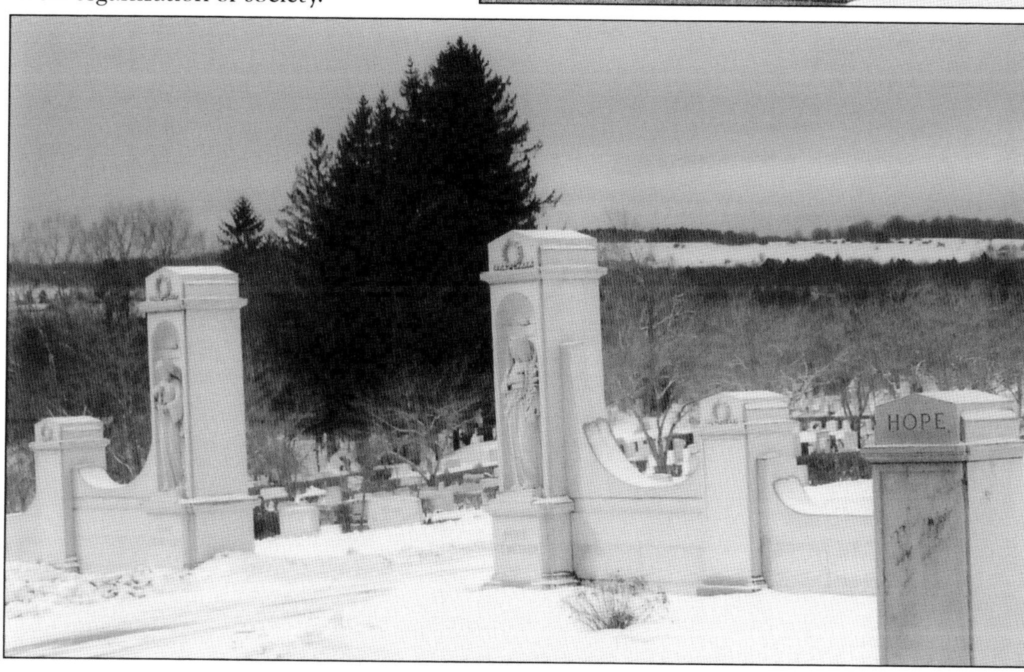

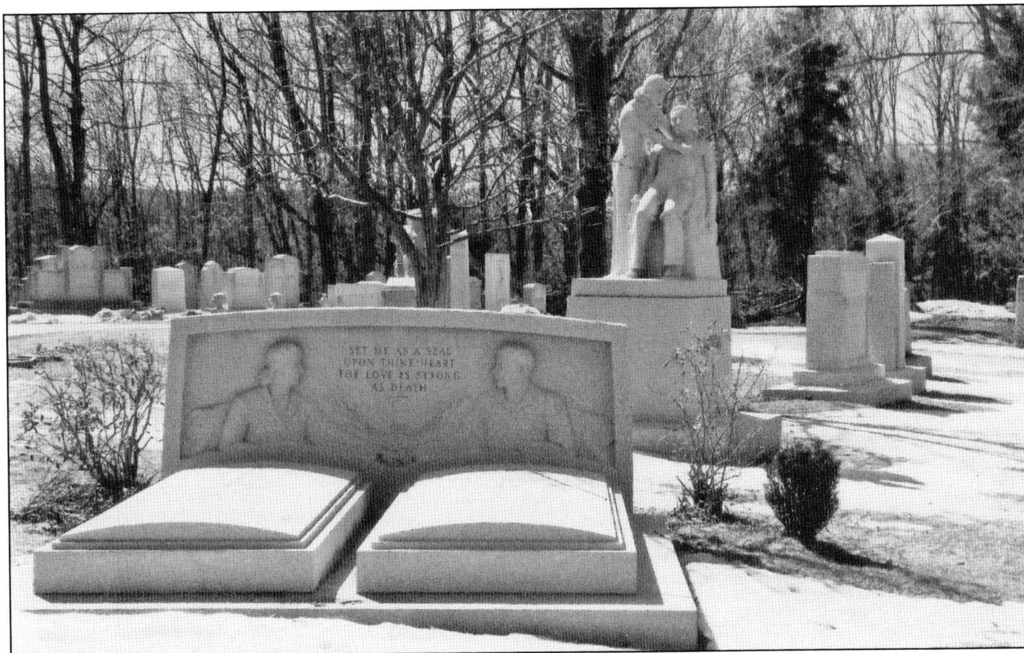

In Hope Cemetery on the memorial of William and Gwendolyn Halvosa, they are shown in two beds while holding each other's hands (foreground). Italian-born Louis Brusa (1886–1937) carved his own monument the year before he died (background). His wife holds him as he lay dying of silicosis. He died the same year the granite sheds started to use modern dust-filtering systems.

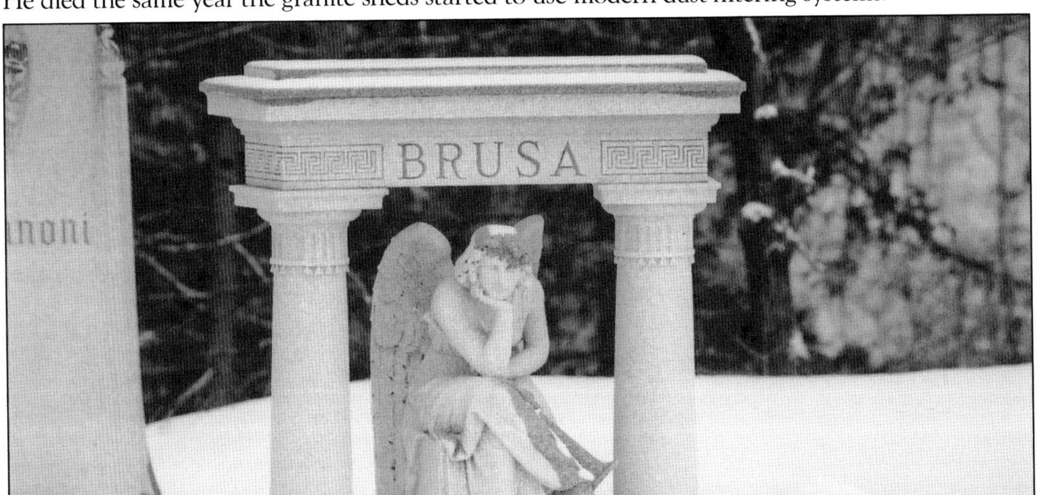

The Italian stone carvers that came to work in Barre were highly educated and political. They were also artists and business-minded. In 1920, Louis Brusa carved the Cesare Brusa monument known as the bored angel in Hope Cemetery. Italians John and Louis Brusa started the Brusa Brothers quarry business in 1906.

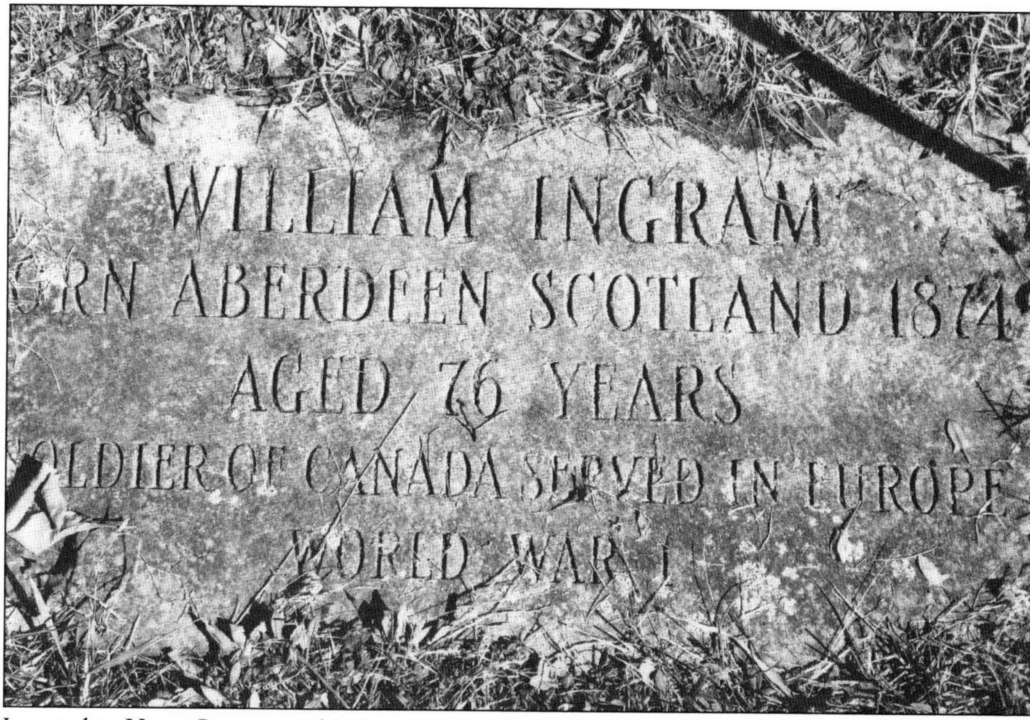

Located in Hope Cemetery, this is a memorial for William Ingram, who was born in Scotland.

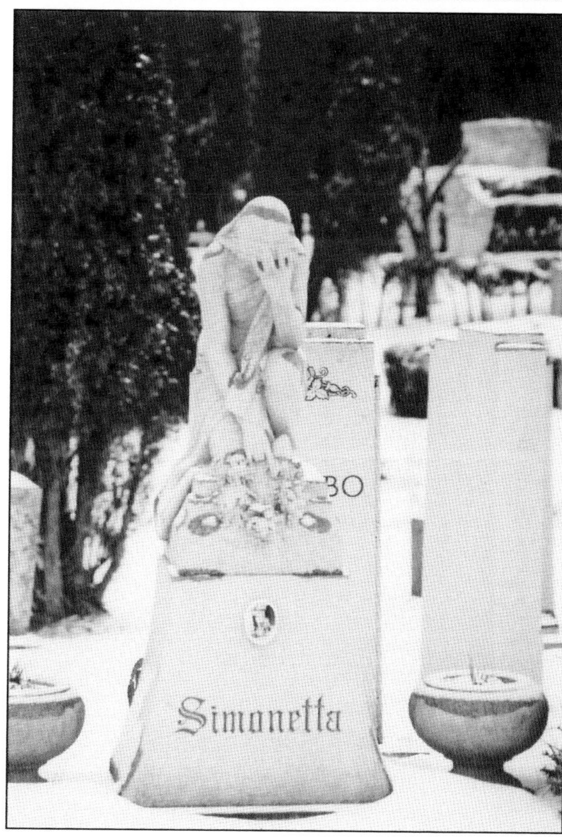

A weeping angel that was carved in granite by Alcide Fantoni was erected in Hope Cemetery. The memorial was sculpted for Italian-born granite cutter Paul Simonetta (1887–1935).

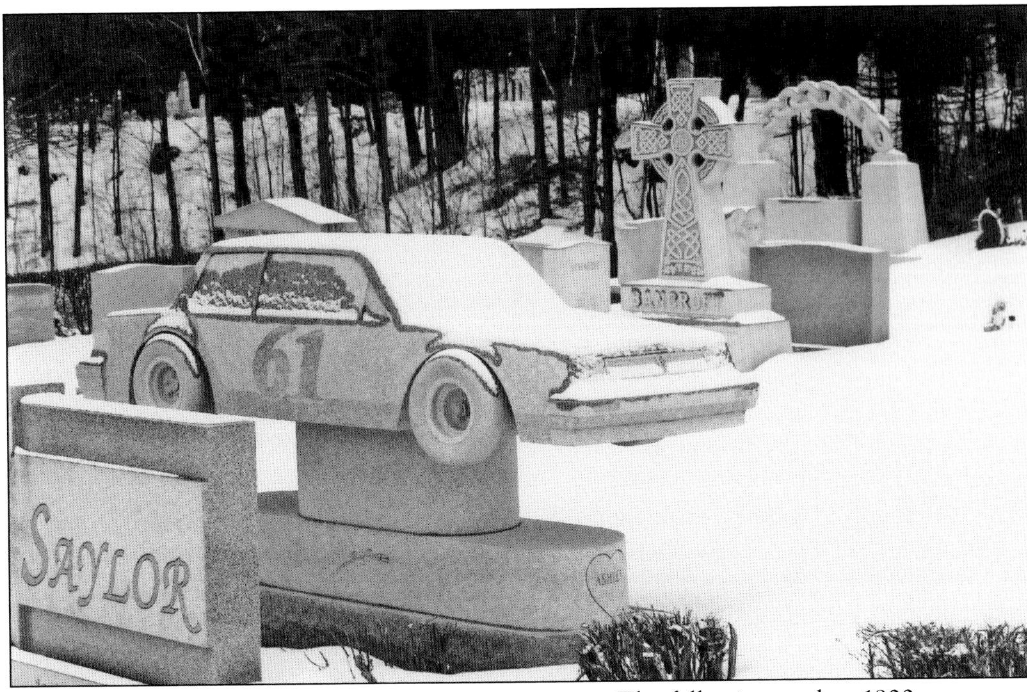

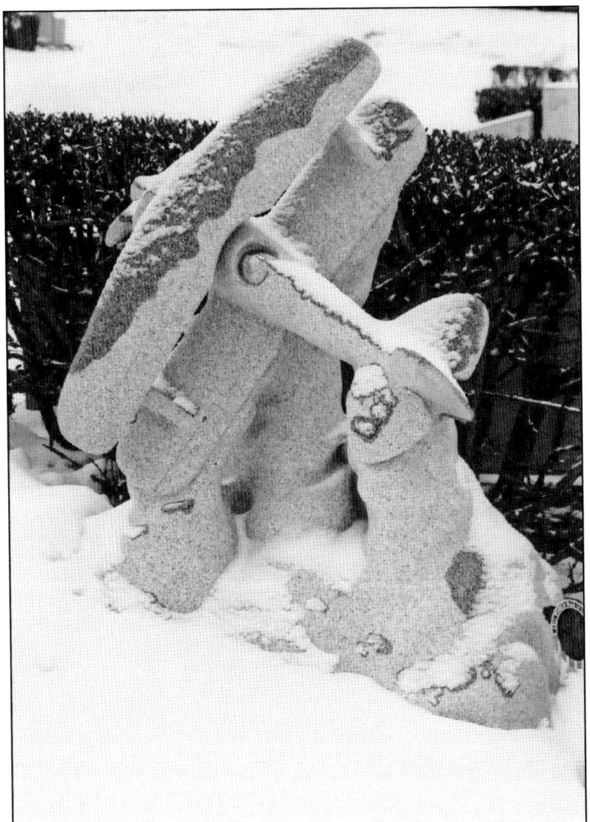

The following are late-1900s memorials: Saylor (front), Laquerre's reproduction of his own race car, and the Bancroft memorial carved in the Celtic Cross, a symbol meaning immortality.

The image taken in winter shows the Leo LaCourse (1963–1994) granite biplane memorial erected in Hope Cemetery to show Leo's love of flying.

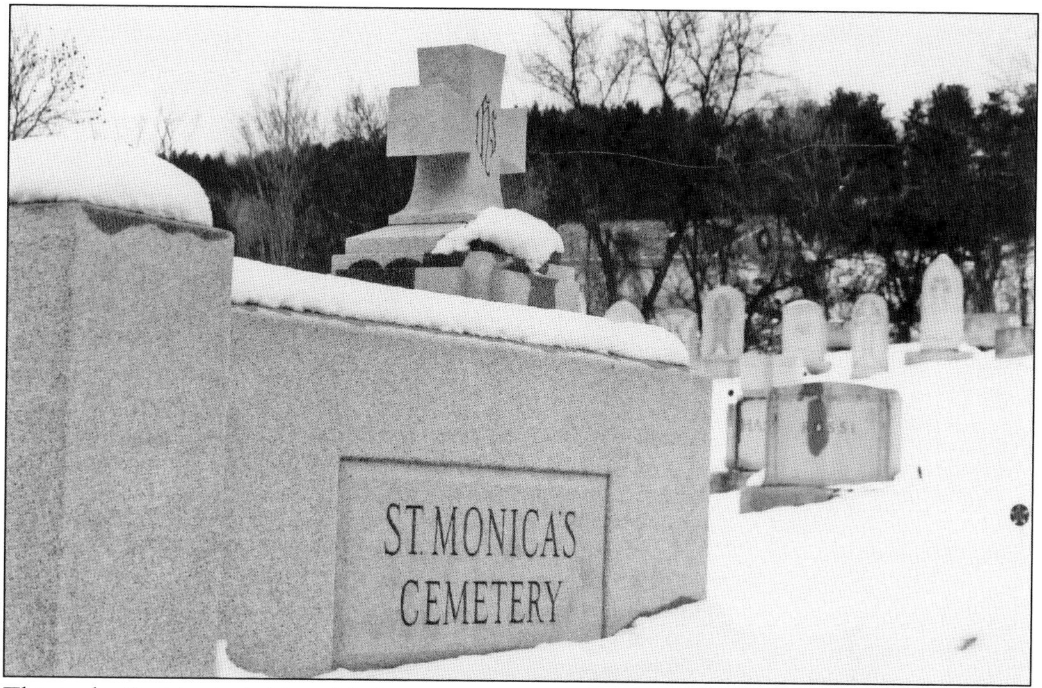

This is the St. Monica's (church) Cemetery entryway. Many priests and nuns from the Catholic Church are buried here, as well as Lebanese immigrants.

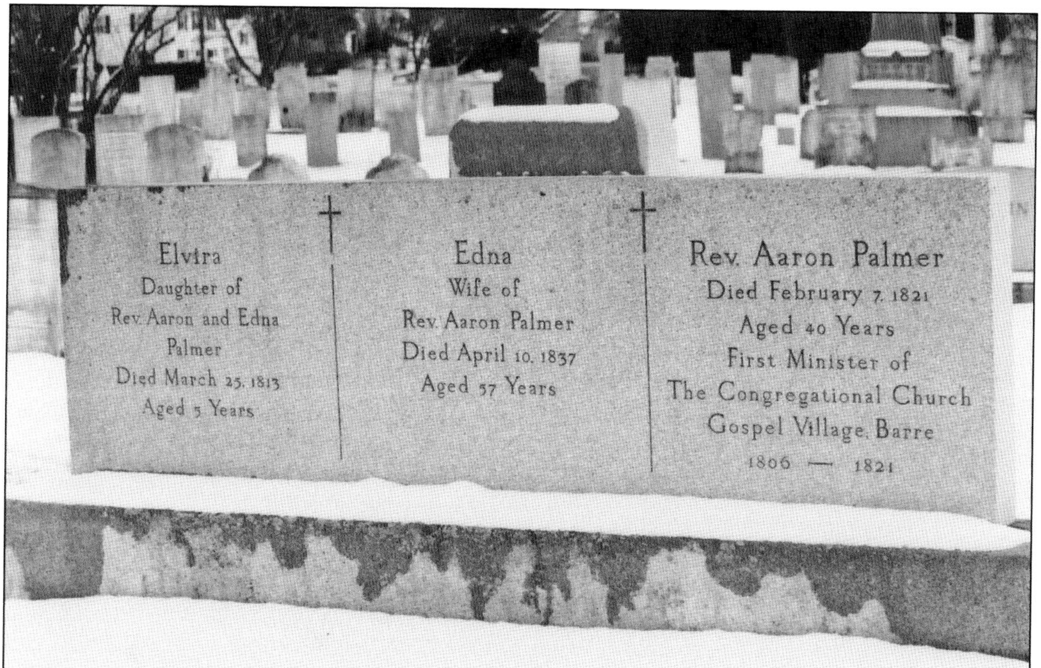

Ezekial Wood donated a parcel of his land for Elmwood Cemetery. Pictured is the simple monument of Elvira Palmer (left), Edna Palmer, and Rev. Aaron Palmer, first minister of the Gospel Village Church.

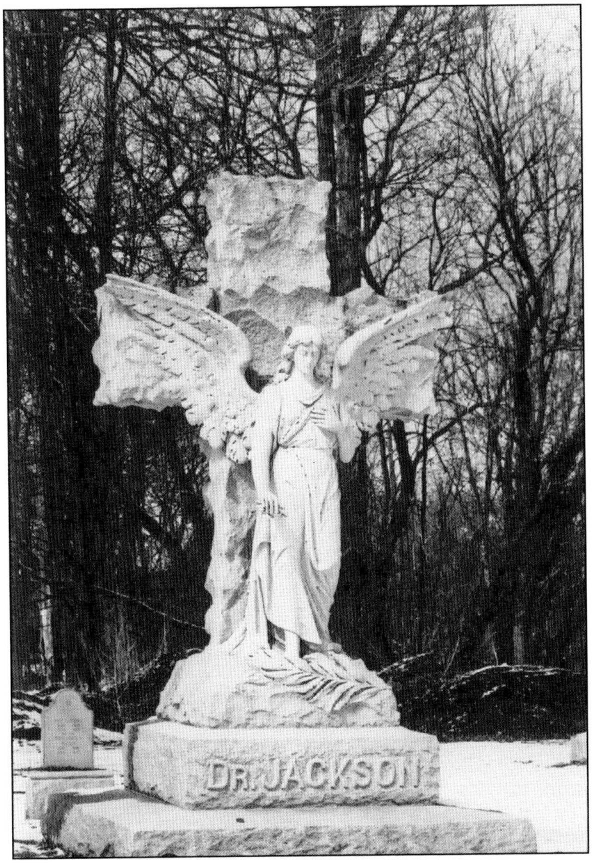

Dr. Jackson's monument was erected in Elmwood Cemetery. As discussed in Donald G. Allen's *The Barre Granite Heritage, With Guide to the Cemeteries*, "at the turn of the century Dr. Jackson was perhaps Barre's leading intellectual . . . he prevailed in politics, education and culture . . . Augusto Sanguinetti carved the cross of shell-rock or rock-pitch finish."

Both the William Barclay monument (left) and the George B. Milne Mausoleum are in Elmwood Cemetery. Barclay and Milne emigrated from Scotland to Barre.

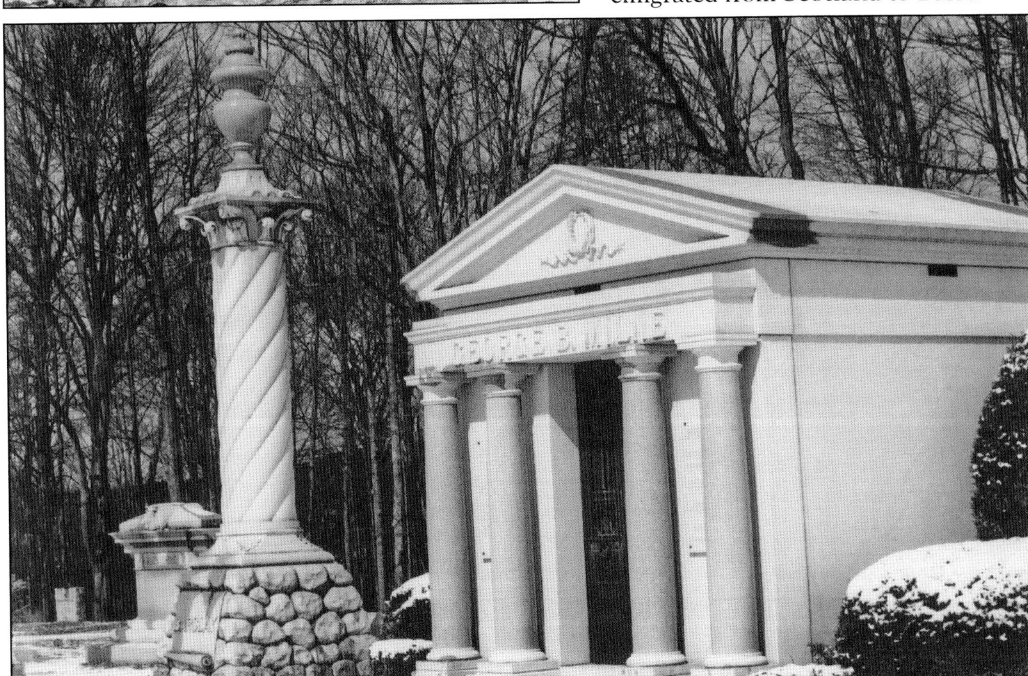

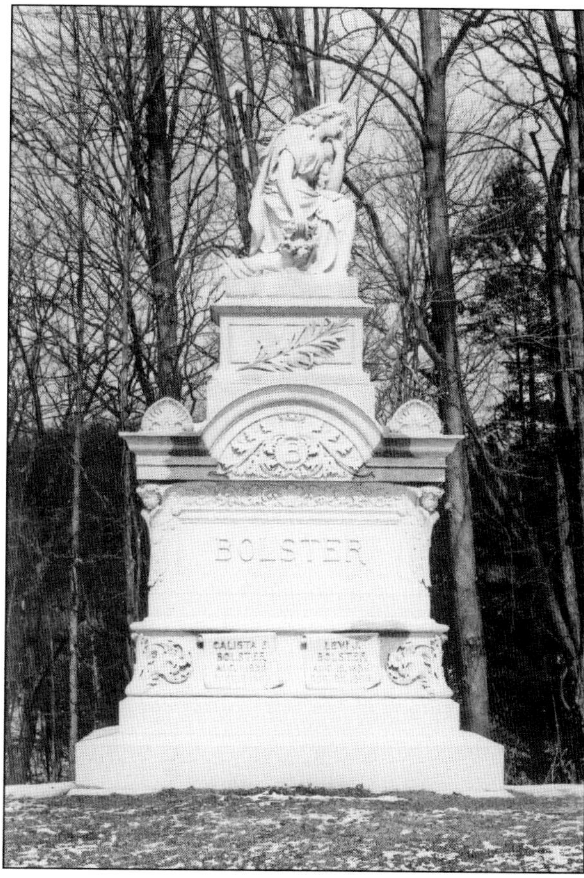

The Levi and Calista Bolster memorial (1836–1908) was erected in Elmwood Cemetery. Levi was a businessman in Barre City. There are cherubs on the corners and palm branch, a symbol of peace.

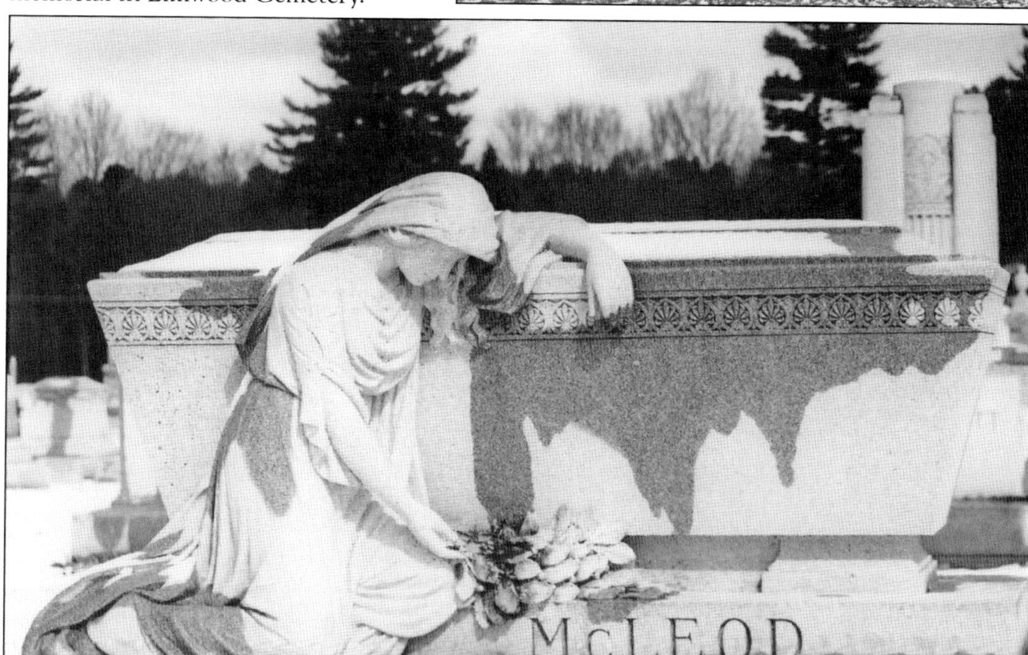

The sarcophagus, designed to remain above ground, is ornately carved with a mourning woman placing roses—symbolizing love and wisdom—on the grave. It is John G. McLeod's (1867–1929) memorial in Elmwood Cemetery.

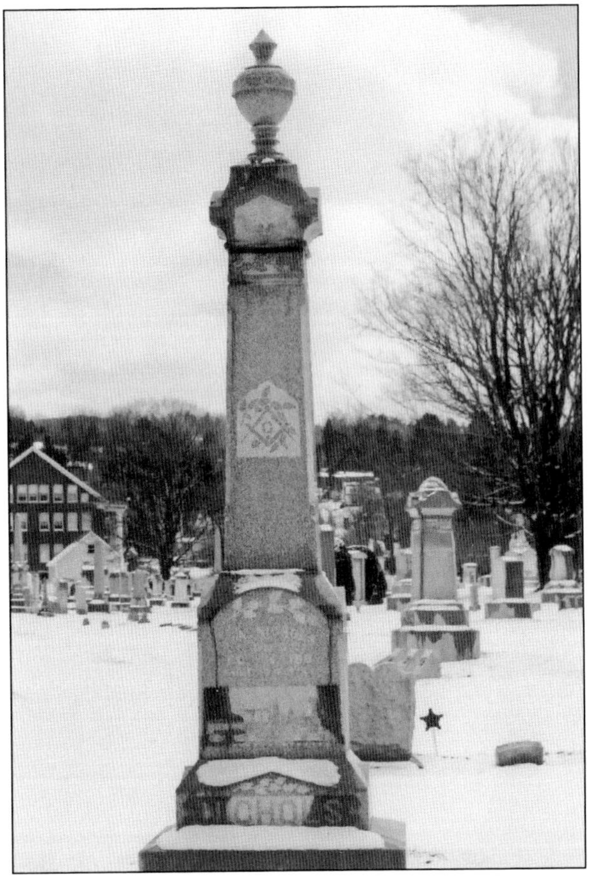

There is a train elaborately etched on the bottom of Robert Nichols's (1844–1888) memorial in Elmwood Cemetery. Nichols was a locomotive engineer and died in a train accident.

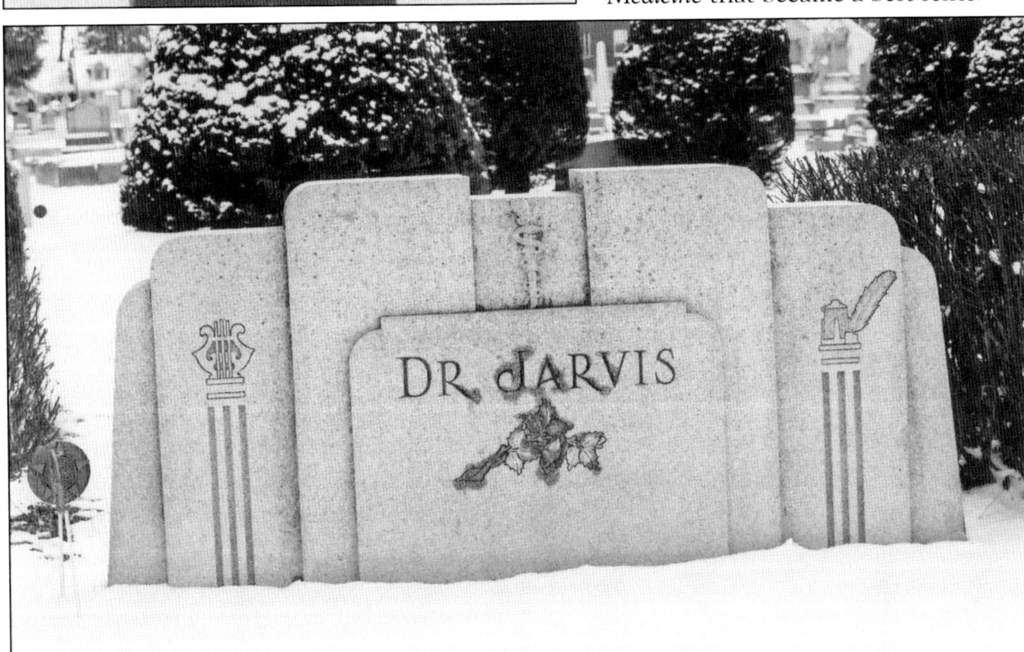

Dr. DeForest Clinton Jarvis (1891) specialized in the treatment of the ear, eye, nose, and throat and had an office in the Howland Building in Barre village. His memorial is in Elmwood Cemetery in Barre. He authored a book named *Folk Medicine* that became a best seller.

Donald G. Allen's *Barre Granite Heritage: With Guide to the Cemeteries* reports, "William LaPoint [1870–1933] was a mayor of Barre, playwright and friend of labor. This is the only monument in Elmwood Cemetery with a life-sized bust of the man memorialized."

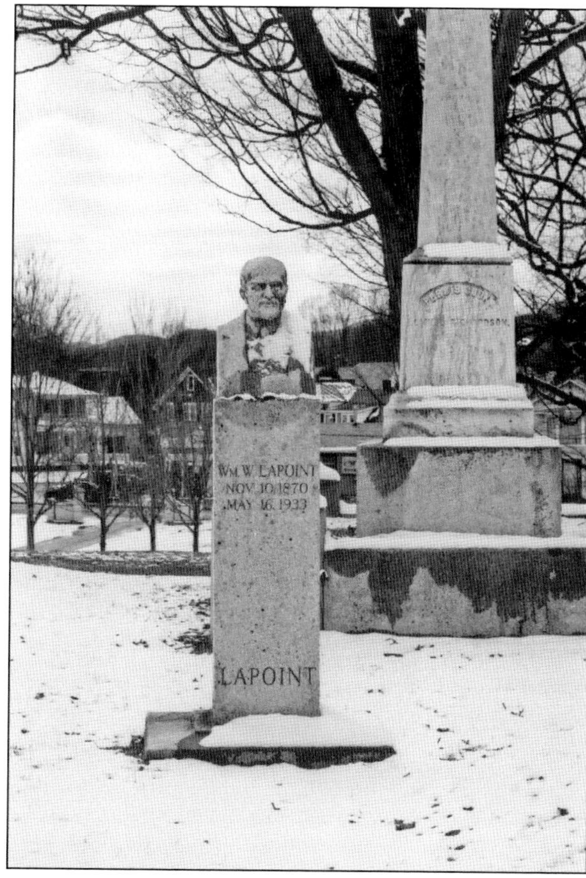

The Lincoln School (middle) and the obelisk (the tall, four-sided, narrow tapering monument which ends in a pyramid-like shape at the top) memorial of Leonard Frost Aldrich in Elmwood Cemetery are pictured here. Known for his love of education, Leonard Frost Aldrich donated funds to build a free public library that was named the Aldrich Library in his memory.

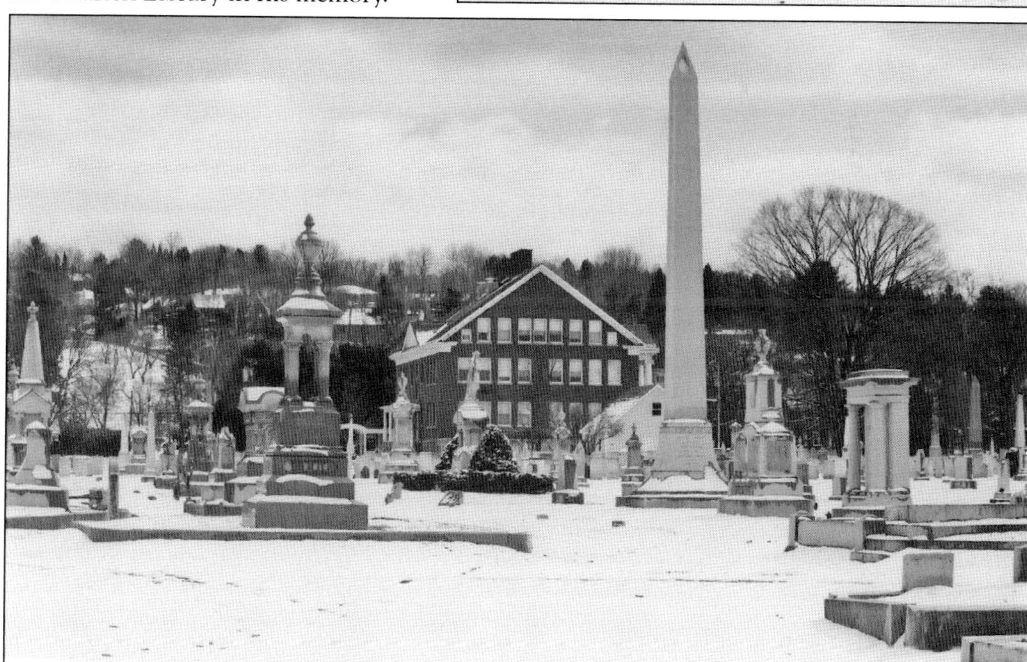

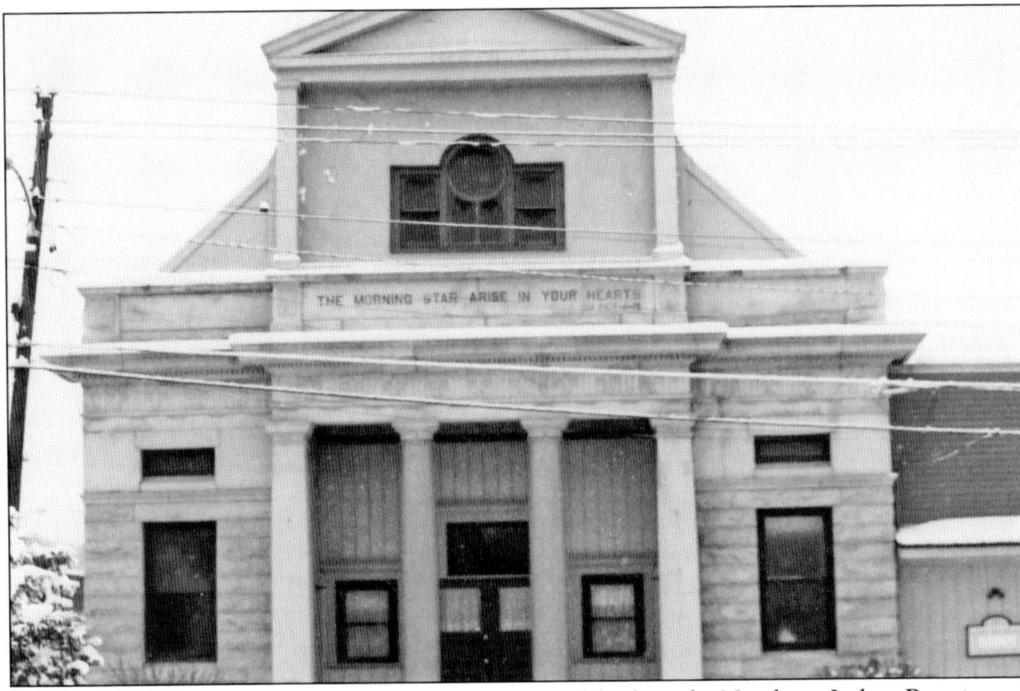

Pictured here is the Italian Baptist Church (1906–1908) built in the Northern Italian Renaissance style of architecture of the 15th and early 17th centuries. Italian-born Ariel Bellondi, the church's first minister, influenced the architecture, as is evidenced by the beautiful pilasters that were integrated into the entryway. Currently, the Morning Star Fellowship uses this building.

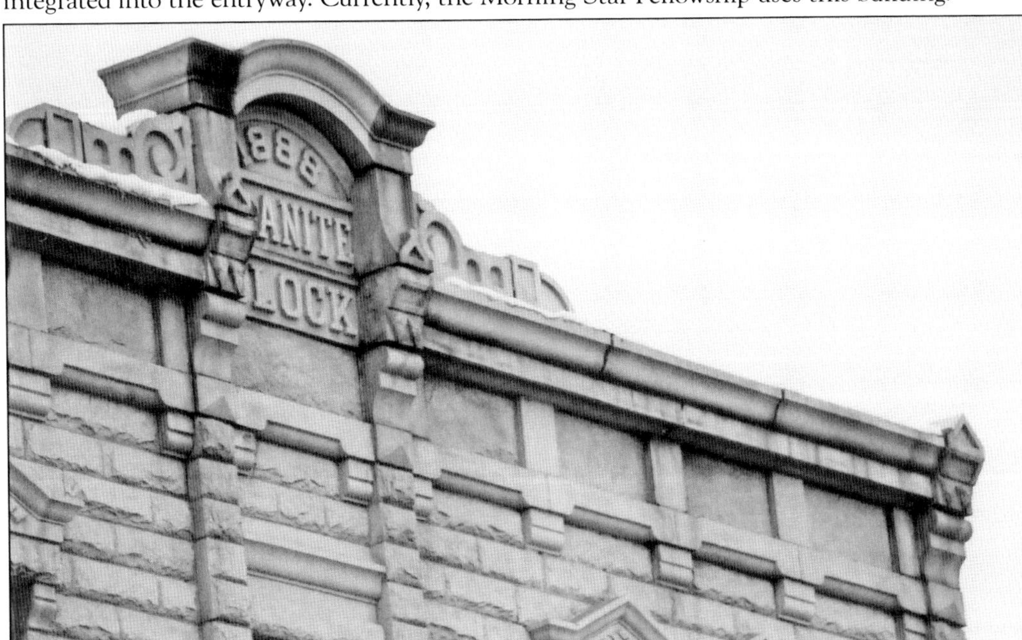

Downtown Barre is a showpiece of granite craftsmen. One example is the Granite Savings Bank that was built in 1888. It was constructed of rock-faced granite blocks with the facade that boasts peaked granite cornices on the upper-story windows.

Five

TIMES OF UNREST AND CHANGE

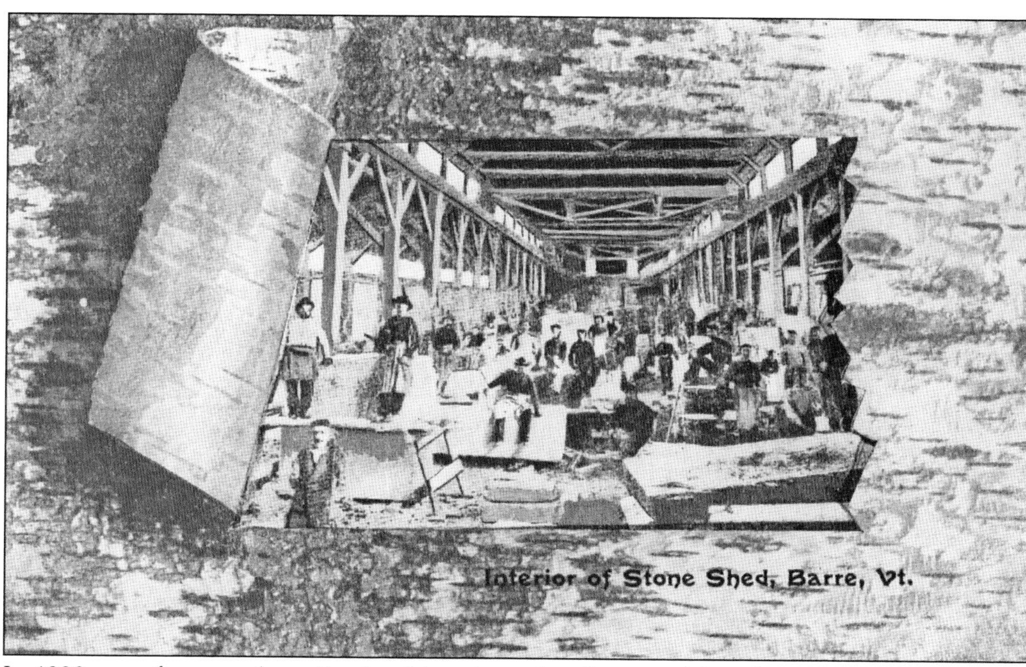

In 1880, men from northern Scotland immigrated to Barre and found work in the quarries and sheds. Hard-working Scots labored in the sheds about 10 hours per day, six days a week. After joining the Granite City National Union, they fought for and won increased wages and shorter working hours. By 1900, there were 15 labor unions claiming membership in the granite industry.

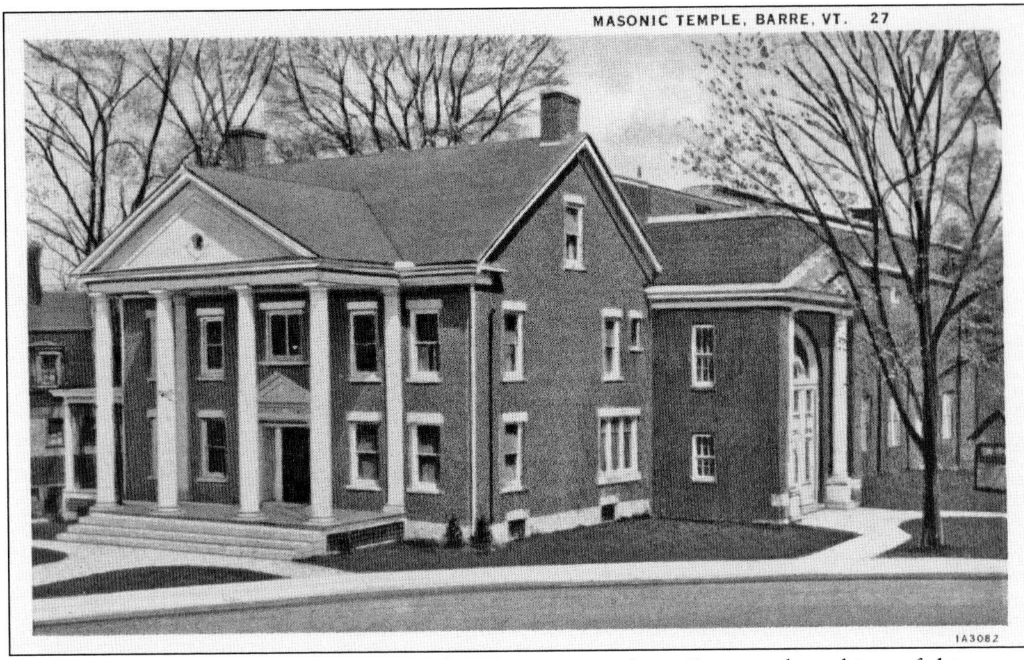

The Masonic temple in Barre is the subject of this postcard. The anti-Masonic movement (1826–1836) was a time of great upheaval as the movement started as a conflict between sharply divided religious groups—Baptists, Universalists, and Christians—and the Masons. Freemasons helped thousands of people through their Scottish Rite charities.

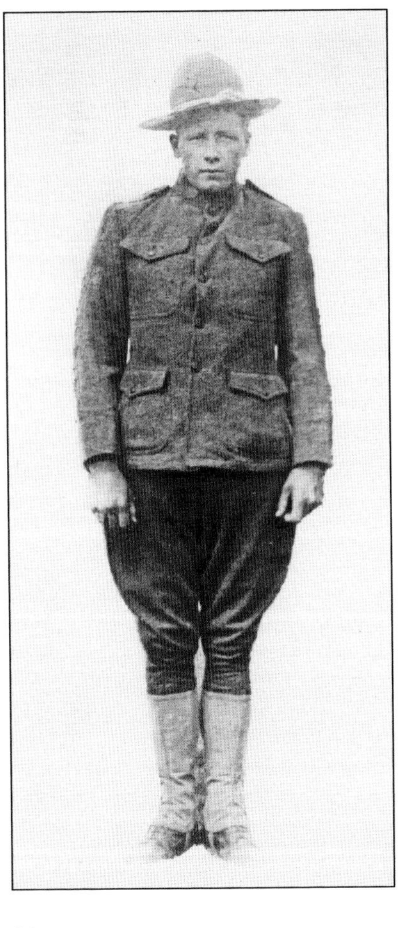

An unidentified World War I (1914–1919) Barre soldier is wearing an olive drab uniform, an Army service hat (worn by officers in the field and all enlisted men of the Army), and widely flared breeches with aced tapered legs at the bottom. (Photograph by Rockward.)

Pictured is the medallion with the resistance hammer on the Socialist Block, now known as the Old Socialist Labor Party Hall. The building was completed in 1900 by members of the Italian community. They took pride in their heritage and were ready to stand up for what they believed in. Many concerned themselves with the poor or destitute.

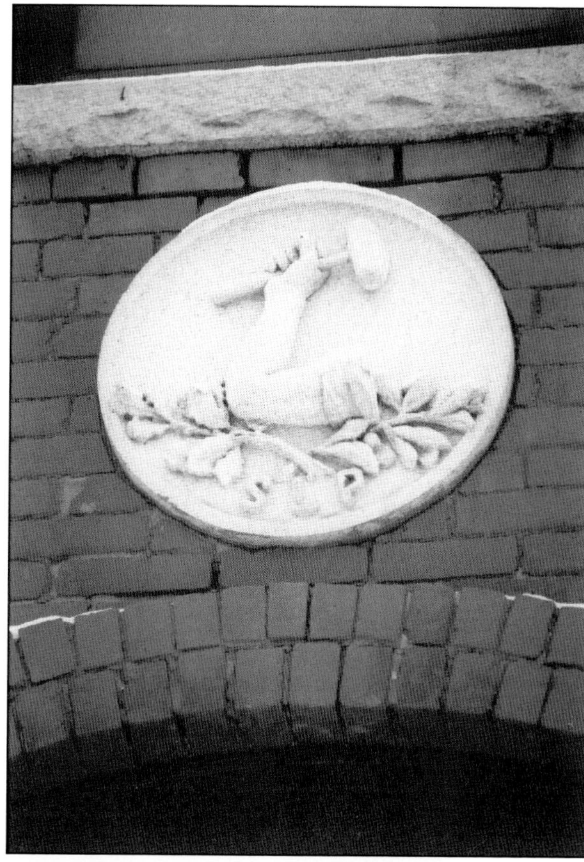

Dances, boxing, and wrestling matches were held in the Socialist Labor Party Hall. Italians were originally affiliated with the Socialist Labor Party before affiliating with the Industrial Workers of the World. In 1916 and in 1929, the city elected a Socialist Party candidate as the mayor of Barre.

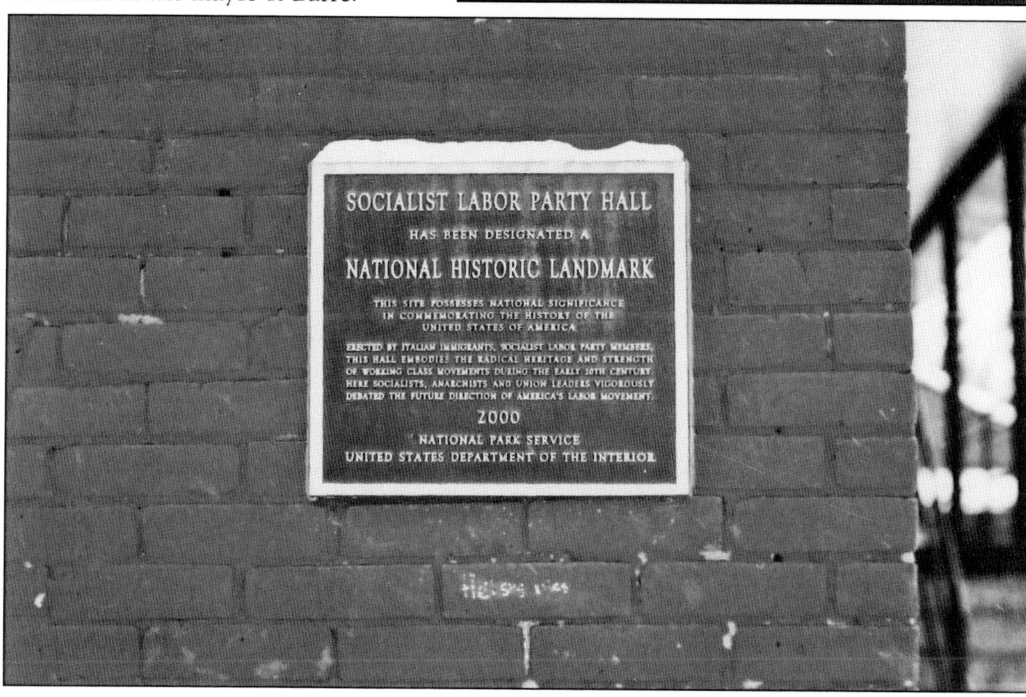

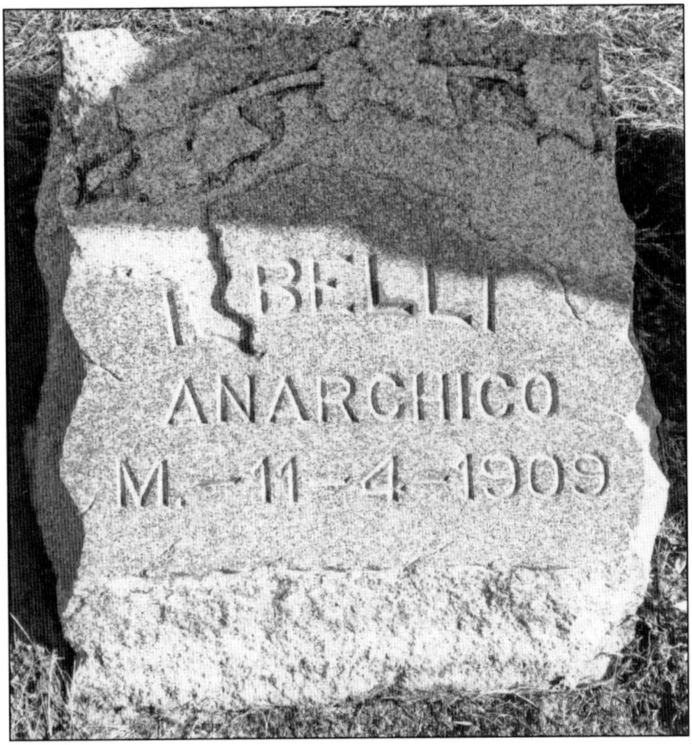

Italian born, Innocente Belli's *Anarchico* "anarchist" memorial is visible here in Hope Cemetery. In Paul Heller's article in the April 30, 2010 *Barre Times Argus* he says, "Belli was arrested in 1900 for participating in a nearly successful assassination attempt on Barre's chief of police, Patrick Brown."

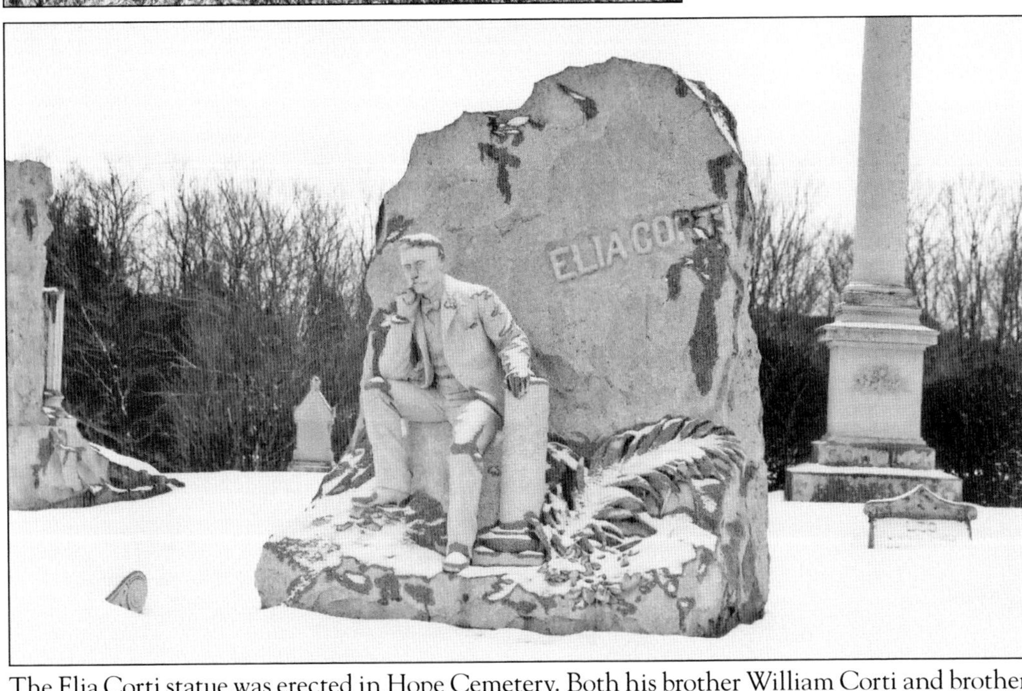

The Elia Corti statue was erected in Hope Cemetery. Both his brother William Corti and brother-in-law John Comi carved it. The *Barre Daily Times,* on October 5, 1903, reported, "Eli Corti was shot and killed at a meeting in the Socialist building where both socialists and anarchists were present . . . Italians were quite divided in their political loyalties. Andrew Garetto was charged with the shooting."

The death rate was very high for the granite stonecutters due to silicosis. The winter scene on the stonecutter monument of the Italian worker, an apron-clad figure of a sculptor with chisel and hammer in hand, was erected in Dente Park in 1985. It was later dedicated to Carlo Abate (1860–1941), a sculptor and educator, who was born in Italy.

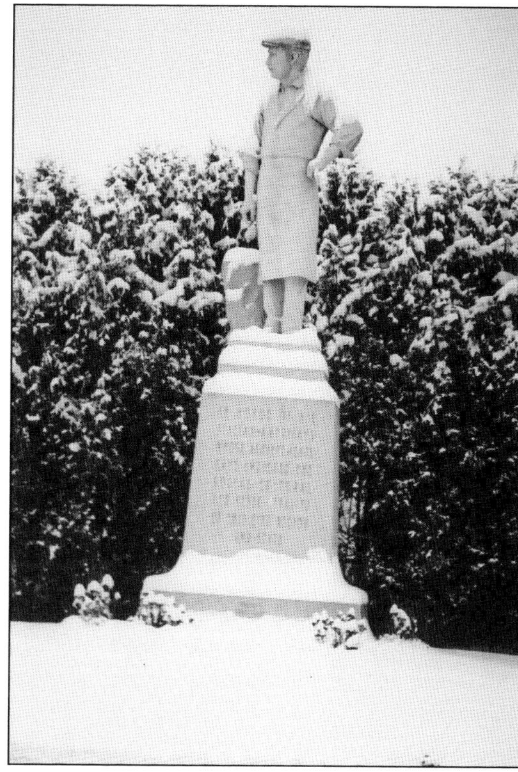

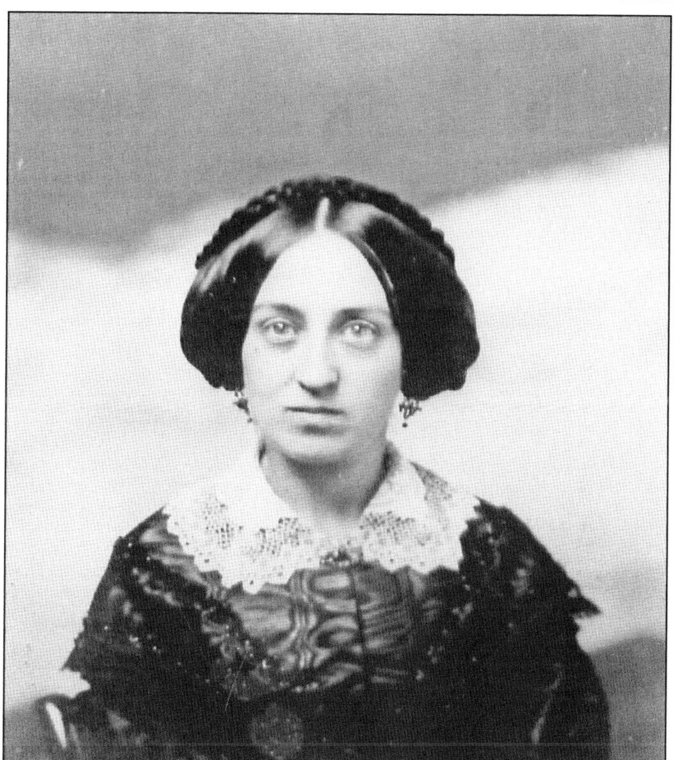

Life was dreadful for the stonecutters' widows and their children; most were left to their own means of supporting themselves. Widows took in guests as lodgers to support their families and they evolved into drinking houses where neighbors gathered together to socialize. An unidentified Italian-born woman who lived in Barre is visible in this 1864 image.

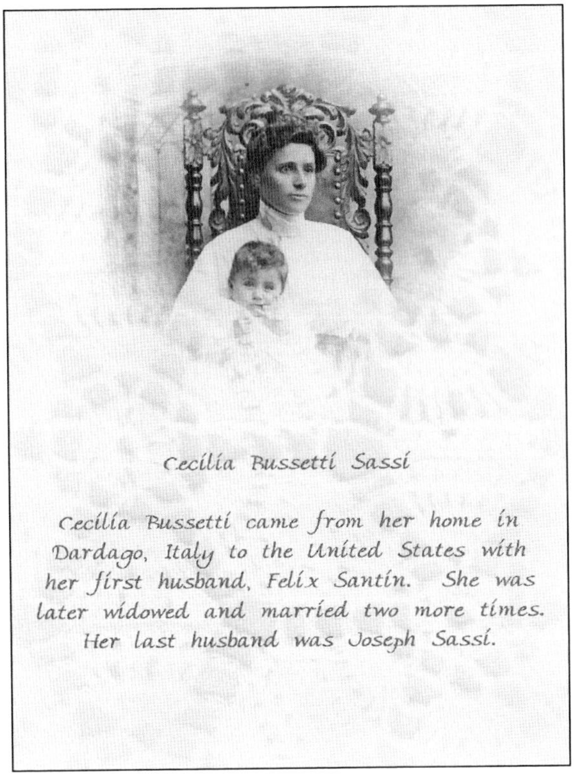

Cecilia Bussetti Sassi was one of Barre's widows. (Courtesy of the Vermont Granite Museum.)

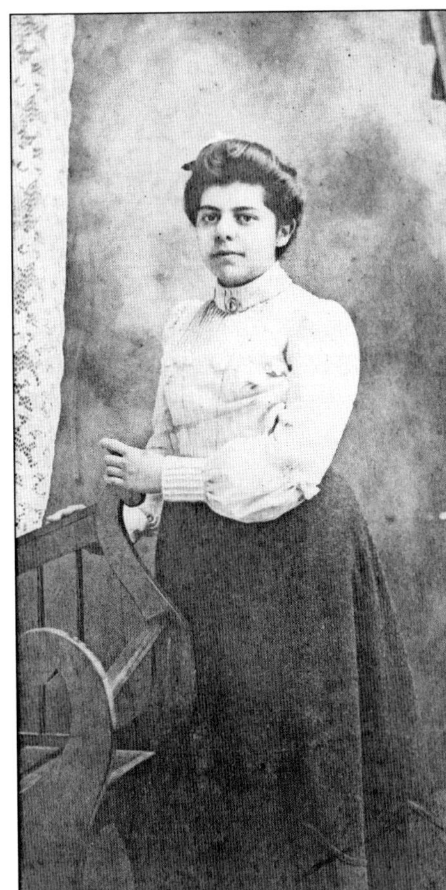

There were numerous reports in the local newspapers of drunken mayors, businessmen, ministers, and parents—sparking an interest in the temperance movement. The 1901 Barre directory reported the following temperance societies: Neal Dow Lodge, No. 75; IOOF; Prohibition Alliance; and the Woman's Christian Temperance Union.

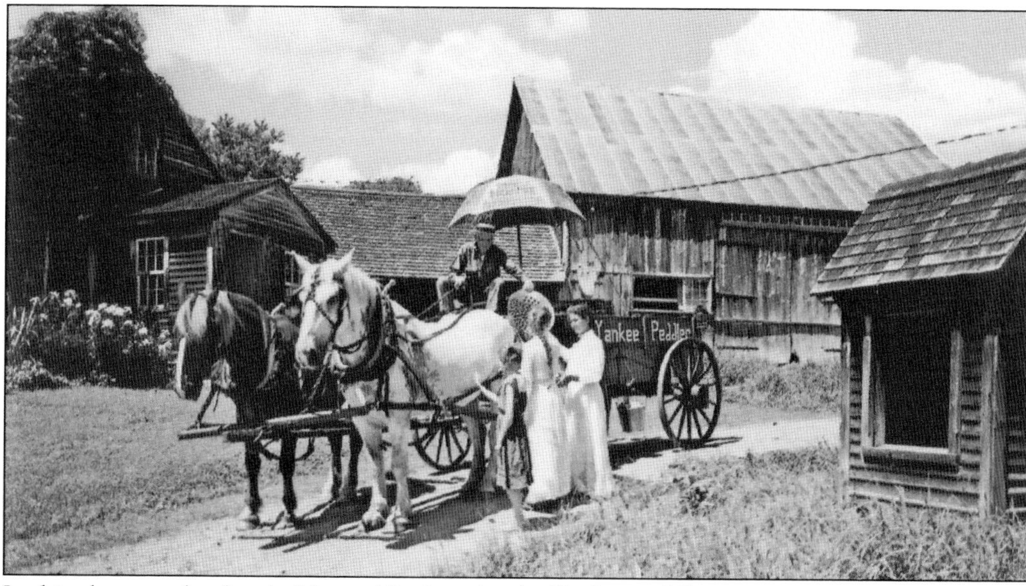

In this photograph taken by Howard Rutkowski, the Yankee peddler is carrying potent medications packed full of potions, herbs, combs, and cure-alls for ills ranging from snakebites, nervous diseases, lung diseases, and melancholia. Many cure-alls were made with alcohol. The wanderer also sold horse products.

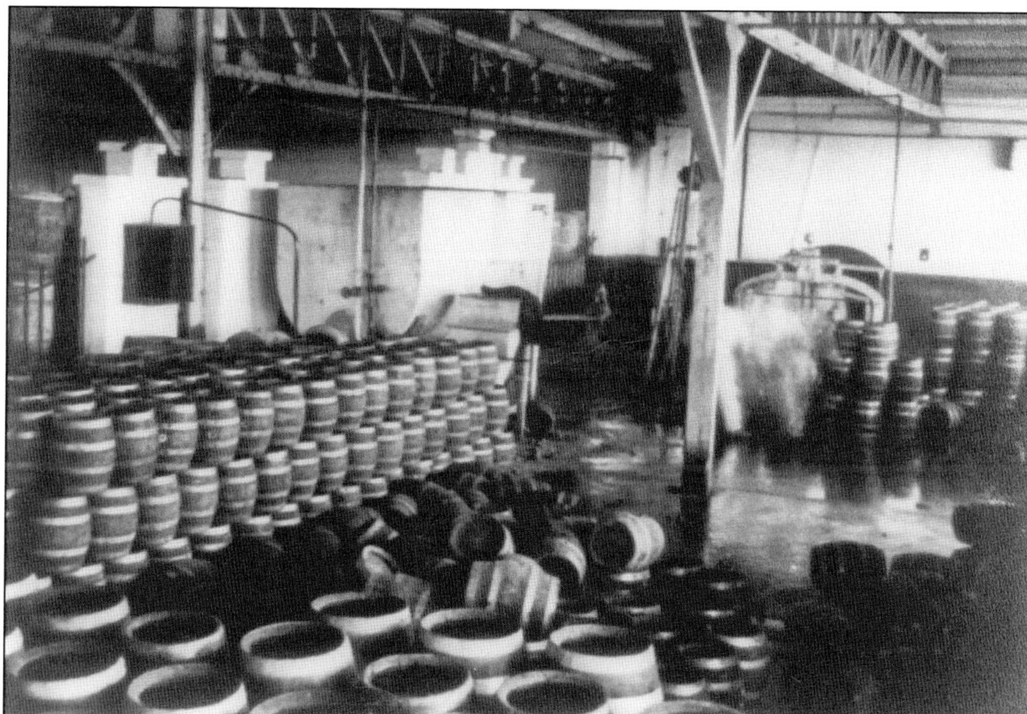

Clarence Morse's *Good Money in Bad Times* recounted that liquor was warehoused at the Labounty Line House (split between Canada and Vermont). "Some people went there to drink, and many to pick-up loads of booze destined for Barre." Morse recalled that Barre served as the depot for much of the alcohol. (Courtesy Library of Congress.)

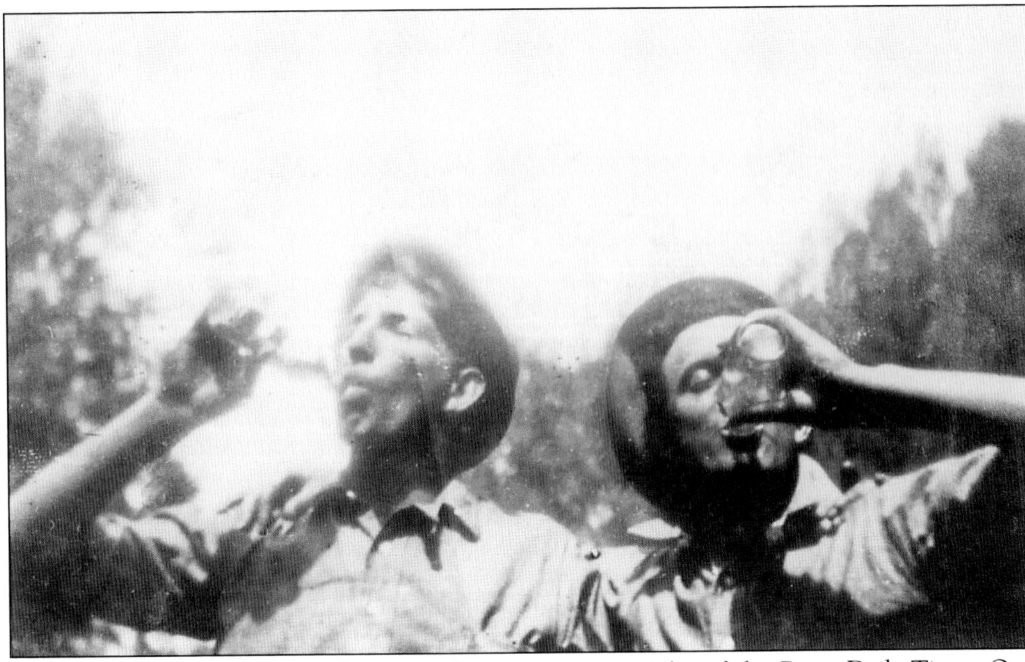

In the 1930s, stories about raids appeared in numerous articles of the *Barre Daily Times*. One report on Saturday, August 16, 1930, read, "Big Mopping Up of Liquor Done in Barre, Officers Raided Five Separate Places. Last night. Seizure included one still, forty-two bottles of wine and grappa [a milk bottle filled with high wine]." (Courtesy the Library of Congress.)

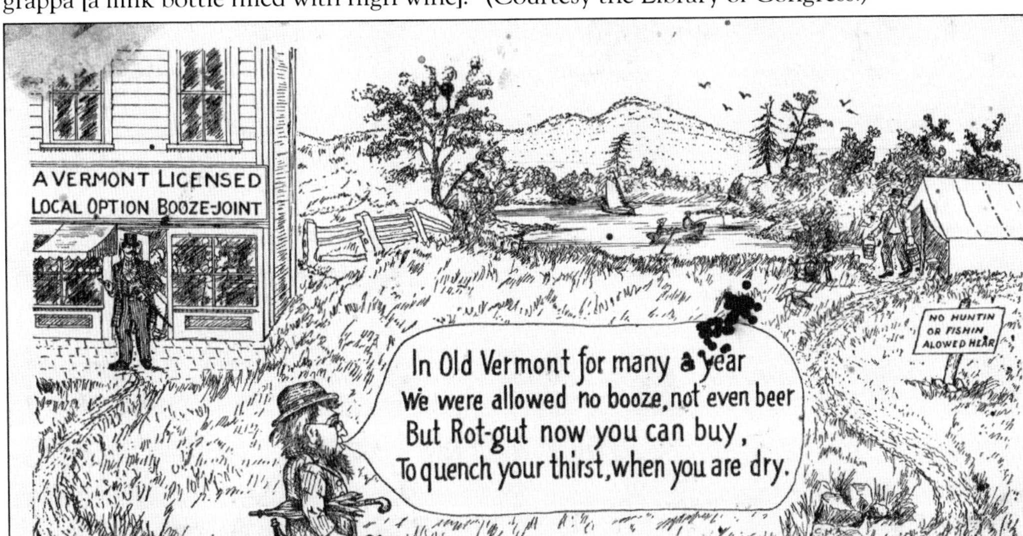

When the prohibition laws loosened and licensed taverns were permitted to sell liquor, drinking houses that unlawfully sold alcoholic beverages continued to sell them illegally. The Union Card Company of Montpelier published this humorous postcard. (Courtesy W.E. Shattuck.)

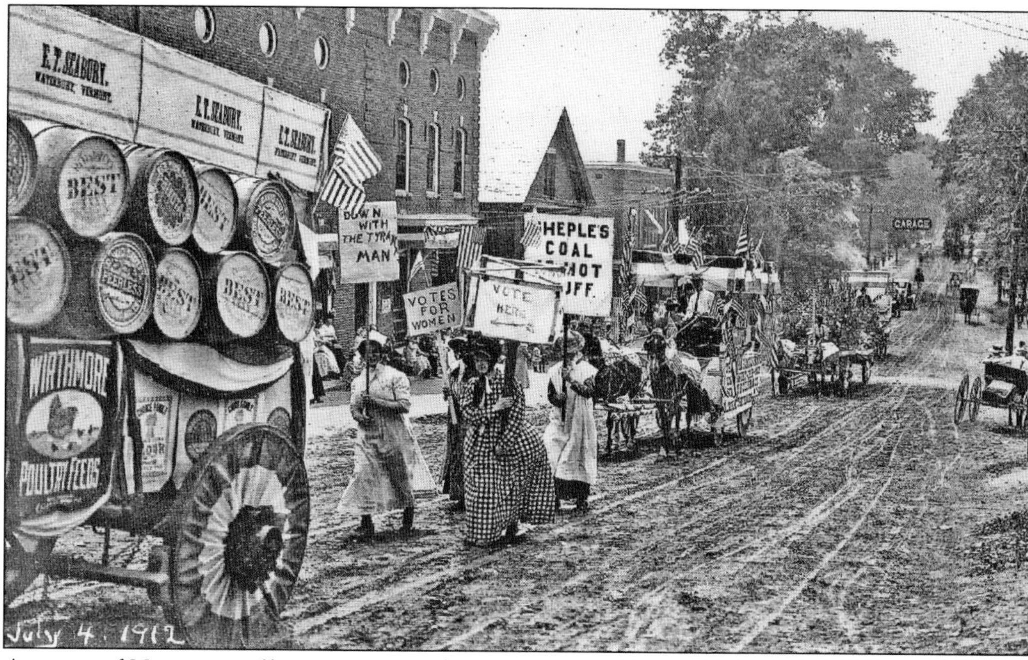

A group of Vermont suffragettes is marching in a Waterbury parade in 1912. Suffragists had a long struggle because Vermont was the last state to ratify the amendment on women's rights. The other side of the postcard says, "Had a great time, Love and kisses. Dee, Barre, VT."

The temperance movement had an impact on the women's rights suffrage movement. Both Ellen Hoar (1887–1963) and Effie McCollum Jones (1869–1952) of Barre were active in the fight for the female right to vote. Suffragettes adopted a style of clothing that presented an innocent public image to add integrity to their cause.

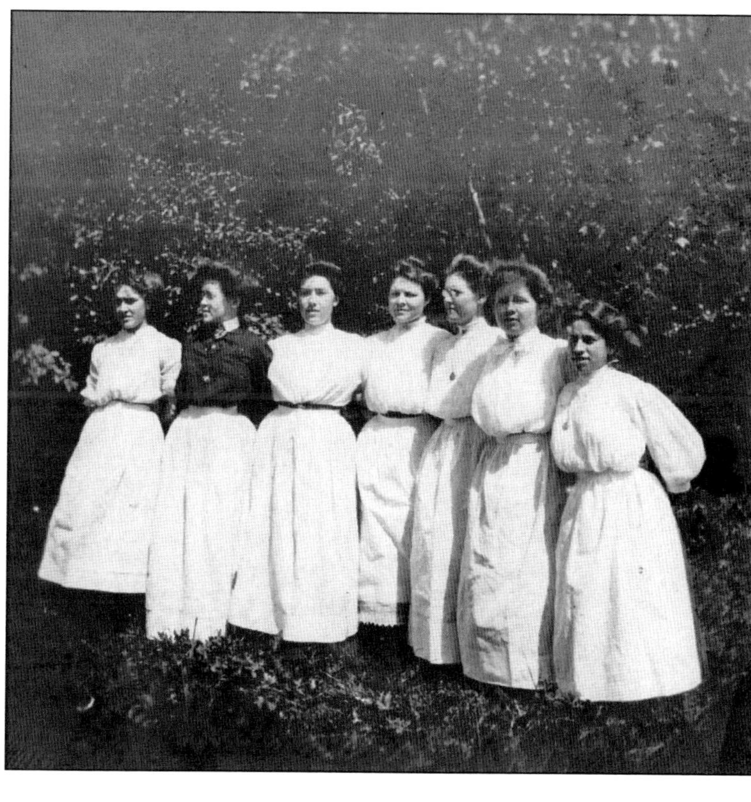

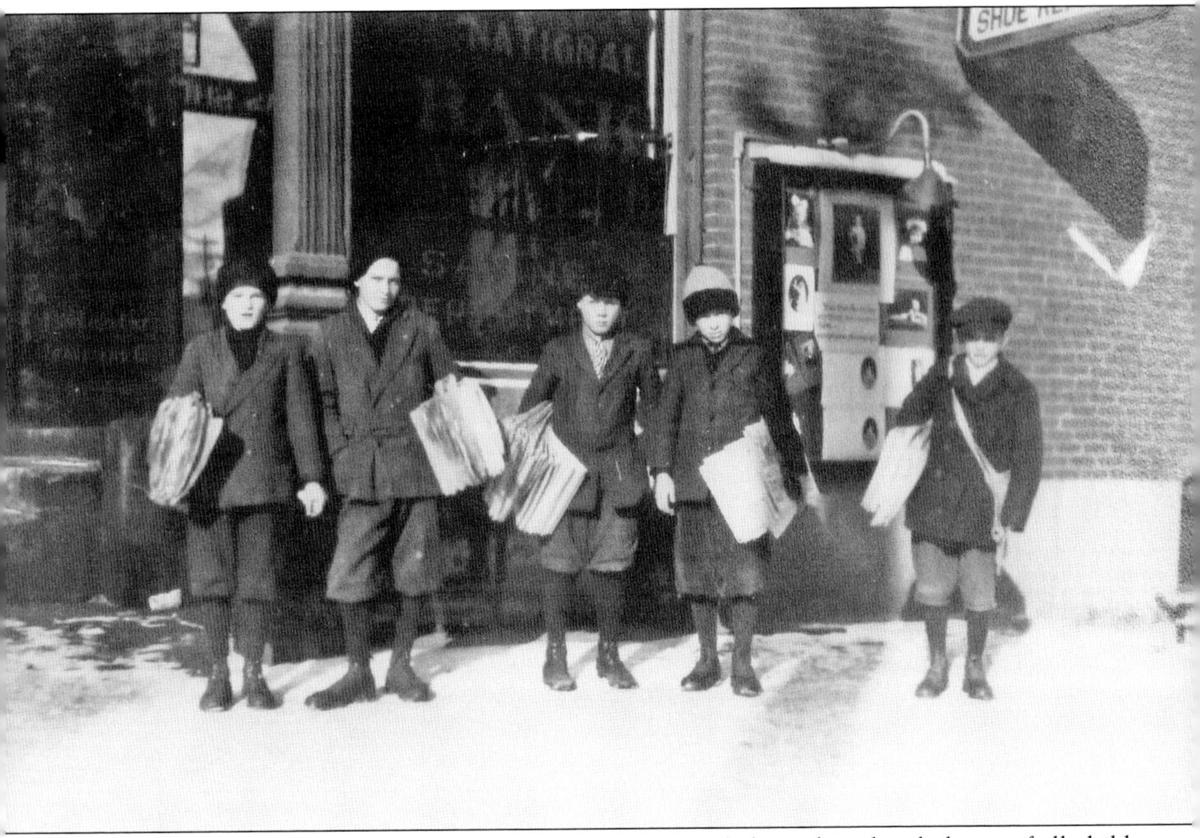

The National Child Labor Committee, an organization dedicated to the abolition of all child labor, was formed in the 1890s. These five child workers in this photograph by Lewis Hine were from Barre. Unable to attend school, these children were expected to work long hours, often in unsafe conditions like granite sheds, factories, and farms. Women's reformers helped get the Child Labor Amendment passed. (Courtesy Library of Congress, LC-DIG-nclc-03981.)

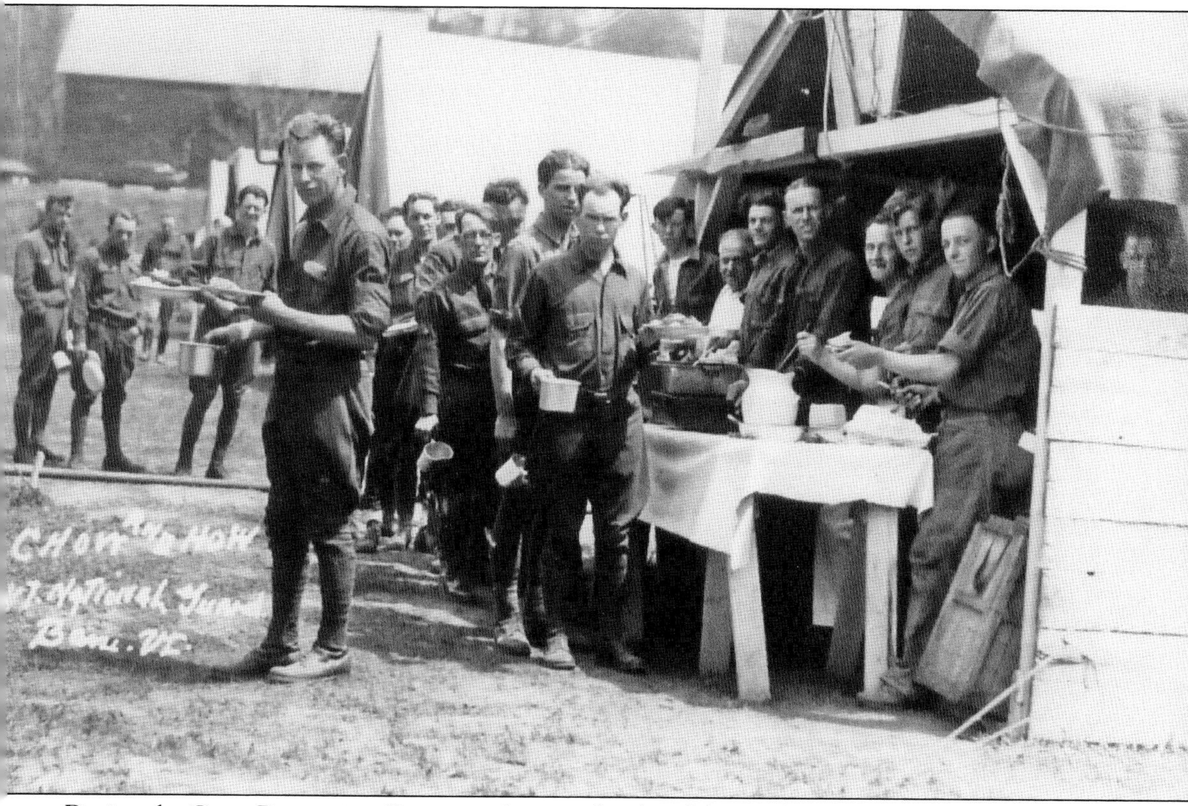

During the Great Depression, Barre was the site of violent labor strikes. Working conditions were hard, long, dangerous, and unhealthy, and wages were low. The 1933 Vermont National Guard was sent to Barre during one of the granite industry strikes, and air handlers were installed in the sheds as a result of the strikes.

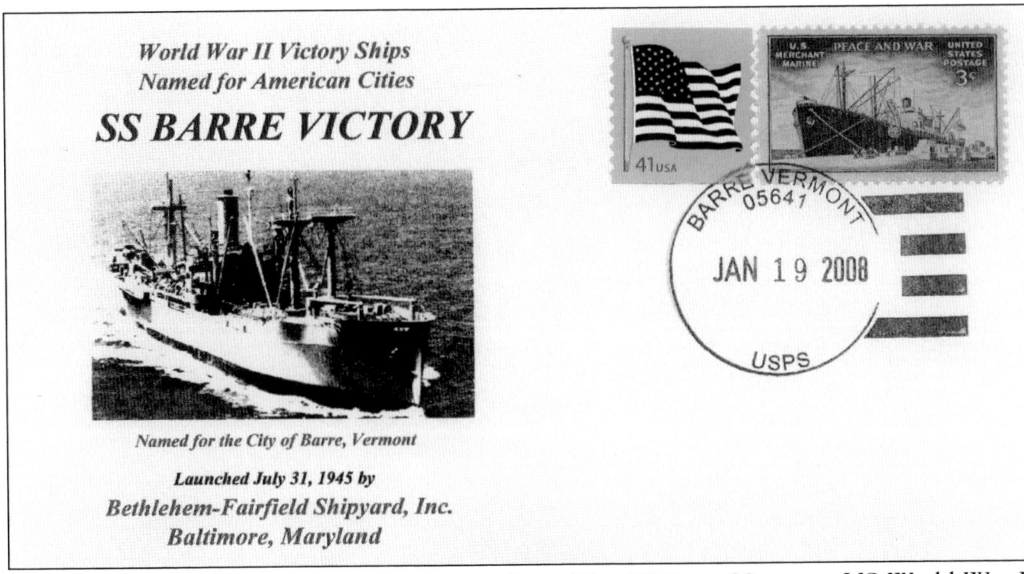

North American shipyards built 531 Victory ships. The SS *Barre Victory*, a US World War II cargo ship, was launched in 1945. In 1993, the *Barre Victory*—named for the city of Barre—was scrapped in China.

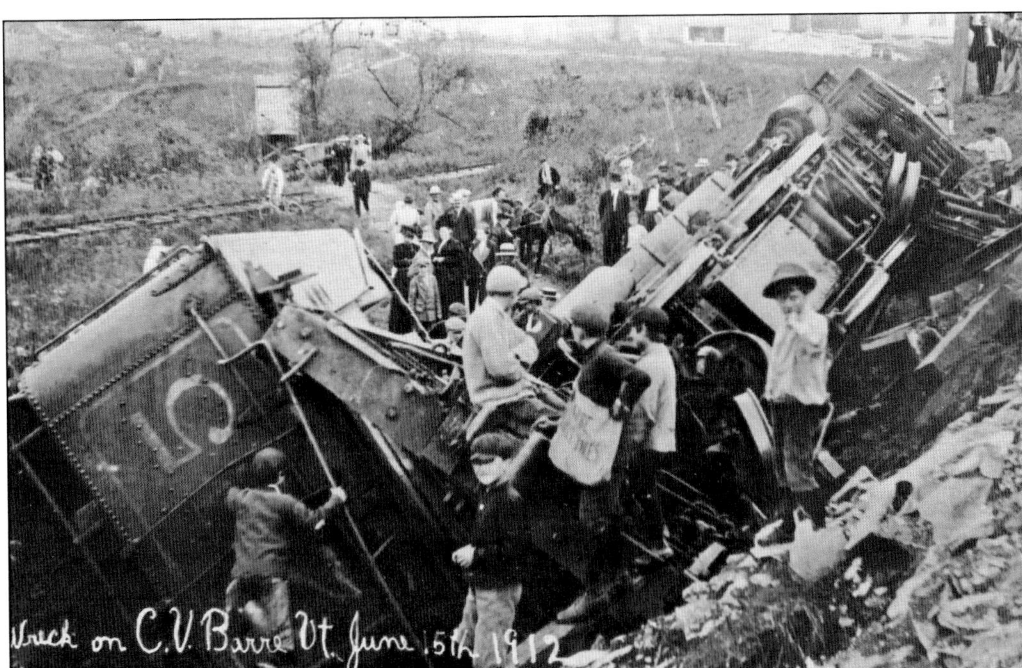

On June 15, 1912, Engine 205 derailed near Wiley Street in Barre on the Central Vermont Railroad. (Courtesy of Aldrich Public Library, Barre, Vermont.)

Six

Firehouses and Fires

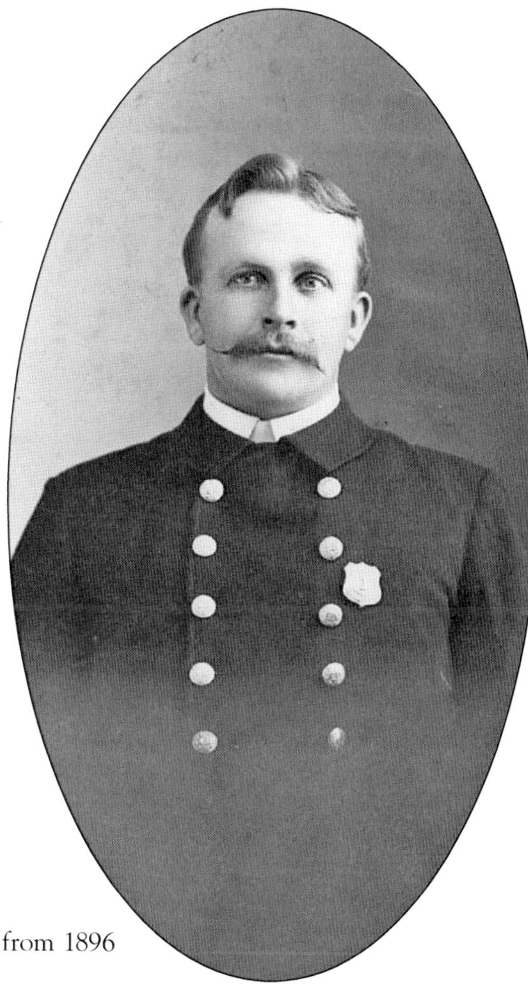

Nelson Phelps served as the Barre fire chief from 1896 until 1901. (Courtesy of Valerie Beaudet.)

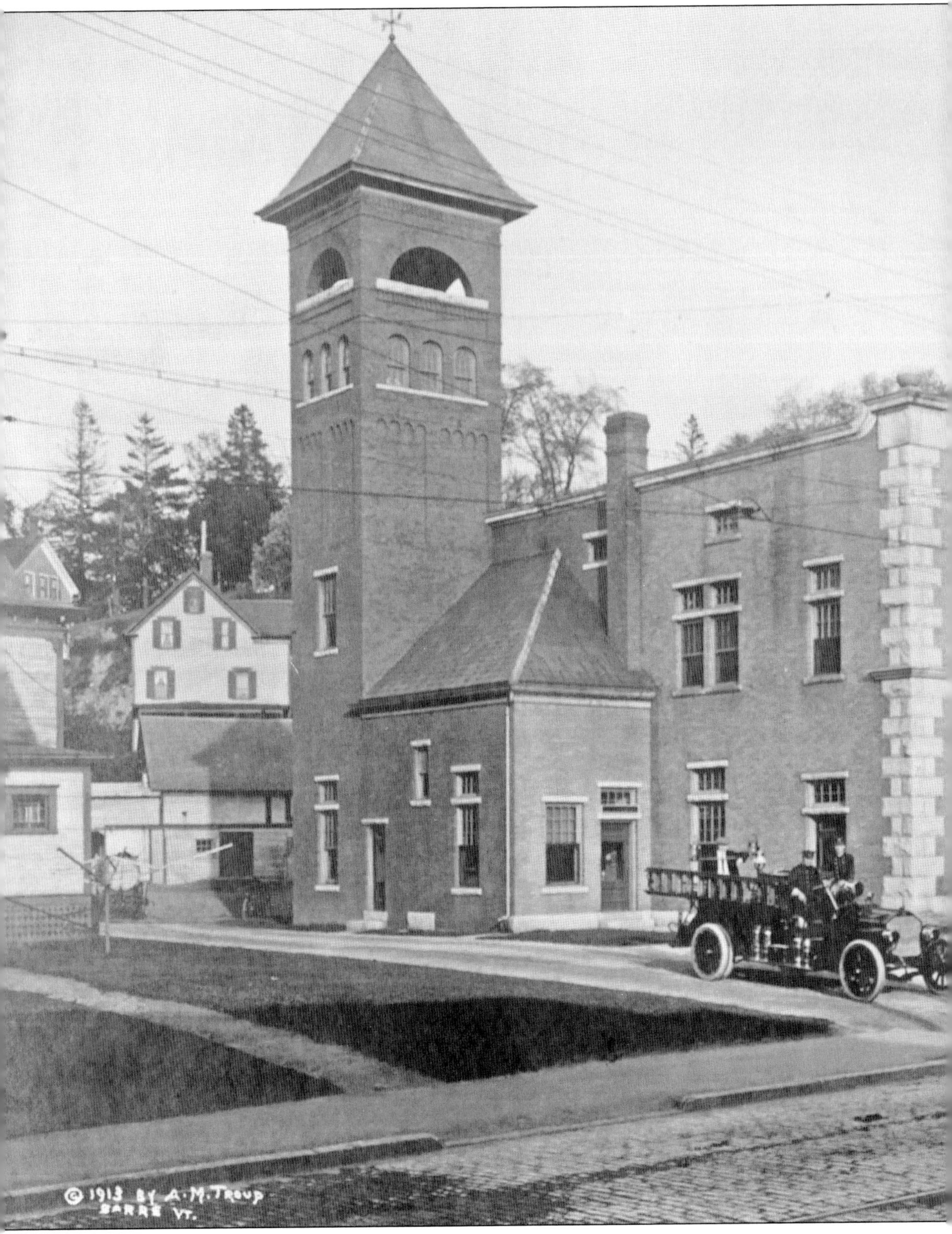
© 1913 BY A. M. TROUP
BARRE VT.

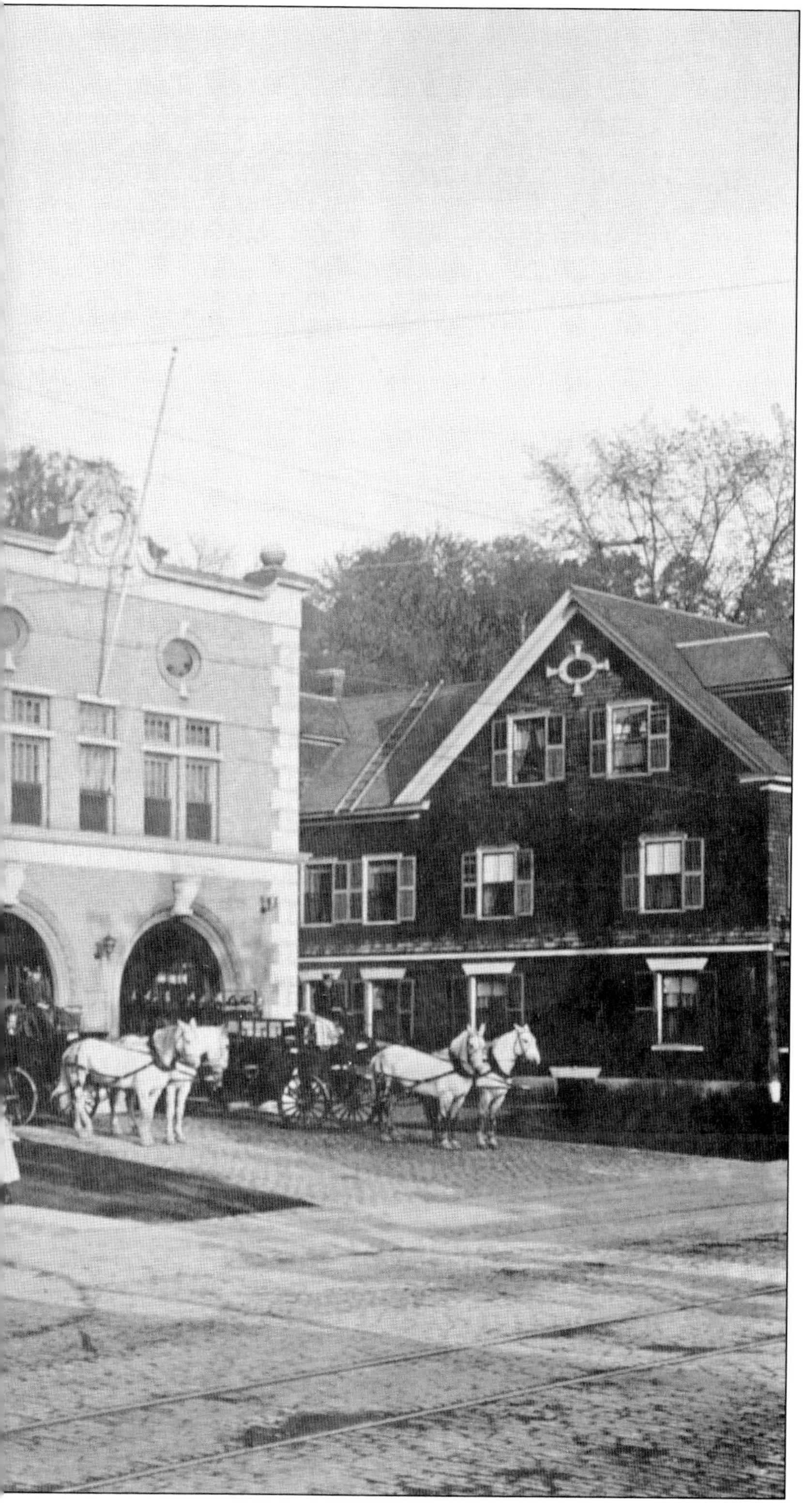

Barre City outgrew the firehouse located in Depot Square so in 1904 construction began on a new firehouse. Barre City's annual report remarked, "The new building featured eight horse stalls, a club room, reading room and sleeping quarters for the best men anywhere in New England, outside the city of Boston." Steam-driven, horse-drawn pumps for the firehouse were the start of a new era in the municipal fire service. This Troup photograph is dated 1913. (Courtesy Valerie Beaudet.)

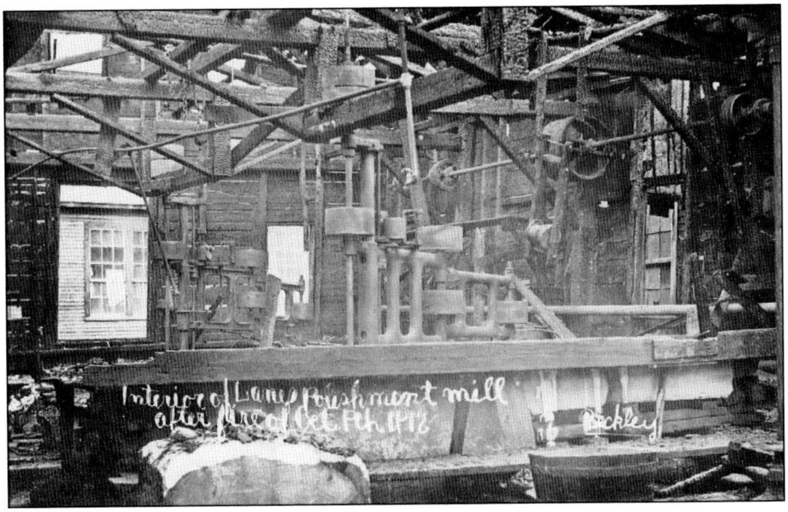

An interior view of the Lane's Polishing Mill in this Beckley photograph shows what it looked like after the fire of 1912. Willis A. Lane (1861) was the proprietor of the polishing machine shop. He invented the Granite City Polishing machine that was used all over the world.

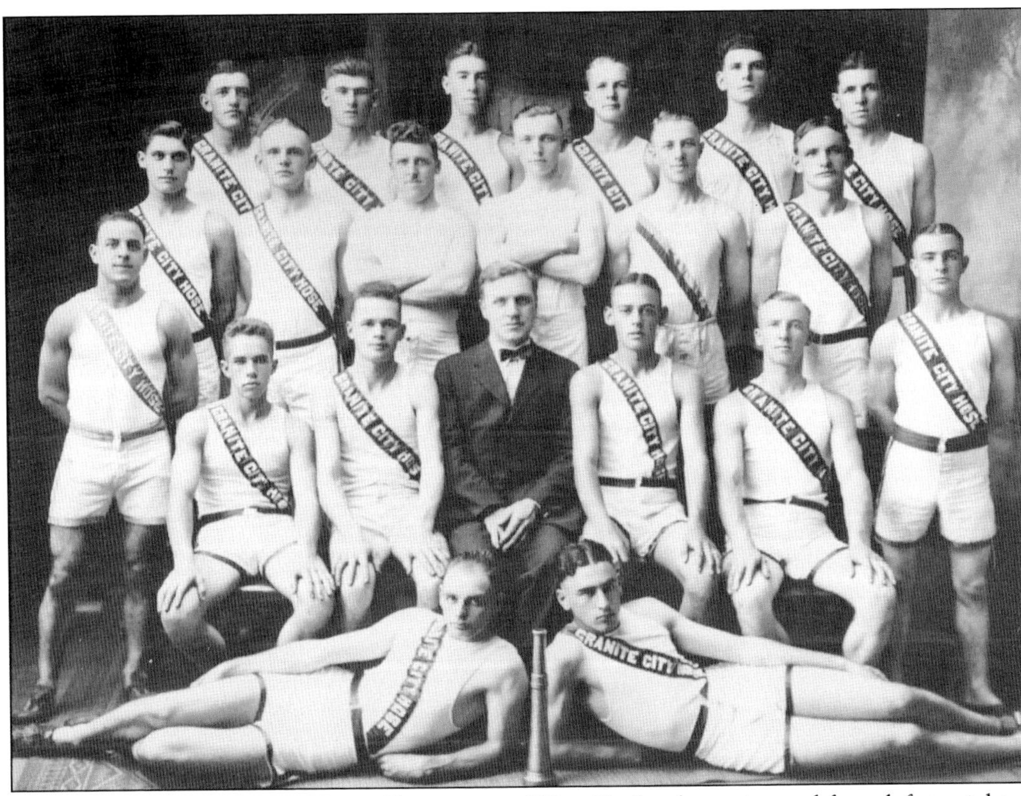

The 1922 Grand City Hose Team Champions of New England are pictured from left to right as follows: (on floor) W. Guernsen and H. Wescott; (first row) S. Sierre, G. Mile, Capt. J. Glass, W. Nelson, M. D'Hern, A. Dowers, and R. Massie; (second row) J. Aime, H. Johnson, B. Philip, P. Angwin, J. Shepard, and T. Burnett; (third row) A. Paquet, A. Caccivio, W. Burke, R. Kendell, A. Christie, and L. Ladd.

The Capitol Savings Bank, identified by the ice-covered clock, was totally engulfed in flames when the Barre firemen arrived on a frigid winter day. Firefighters fought the flames, but the building was completely destroyed. The photograph was taken in the mid-1900s. (Courtesy of Aldrich Library, Barre, Vermont.)

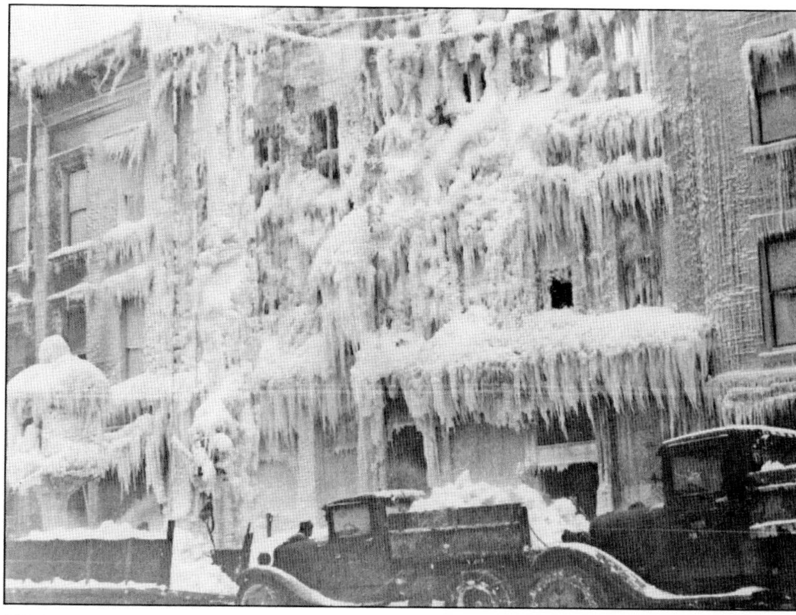

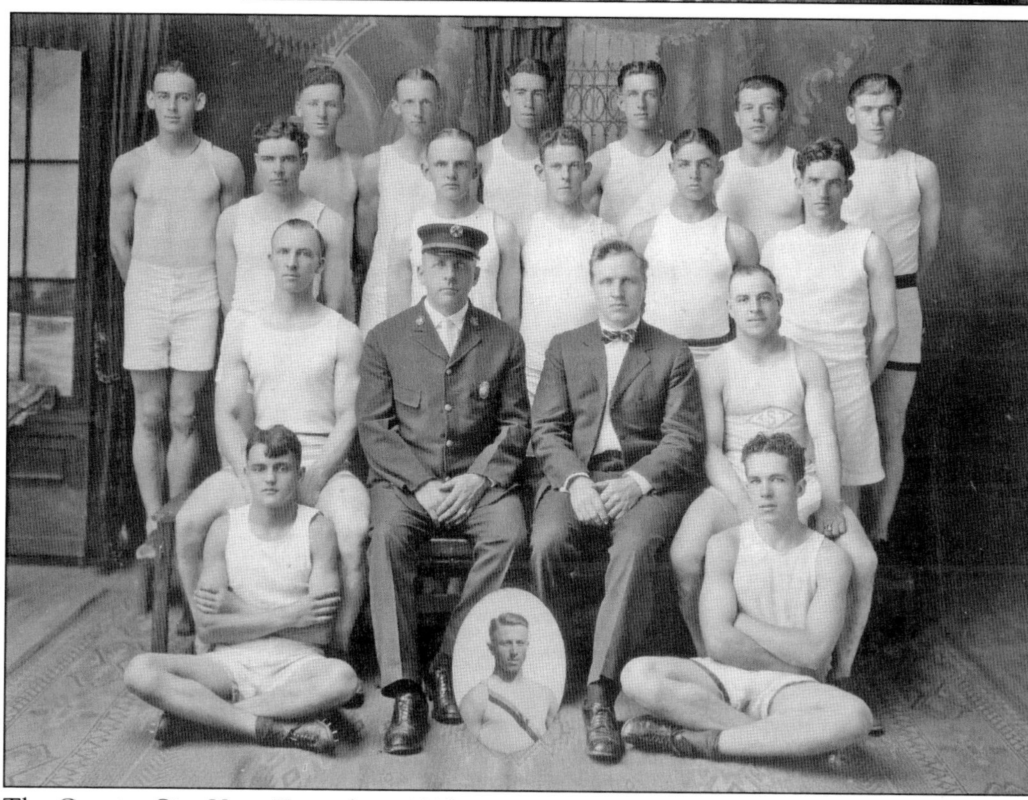

The Granite City Hose Team from 1925 are pictured here. From left to right are (sitting on floor) L. Rossi, J. Shepard (inset), and J. Milne; (first row) A. Dowers, J. Heney (chief), W. Nelson (manager), and S. Sierra; (second row) ? Mcnulty, H. Johnson, L. Kavanage, T. Roman, and A. Ironside; (third row) M. Ohern, F. Mitchell, L. Bjorn, W. Burke, T. Booth, F. Jenson, and A. Caccivo. (Courtesy Valerie Beaudet.)

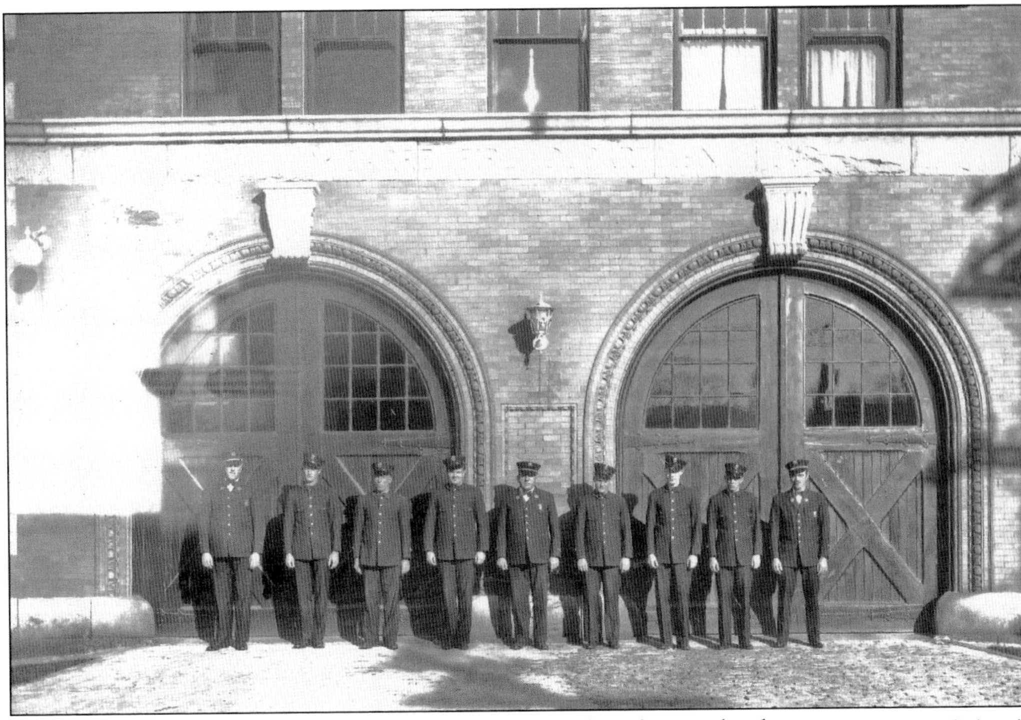

Firefighting was a highly procedural skill that required professionals who spent years training in both general firefighting techniques and specialized areas of expertise. This 1940s picture shows how prideful firemen were to serve the citizens and protect their cities. Barre was the scene of several great fires, and firefighters were always ready for action. (Courtesy Valerie Beaudet.)

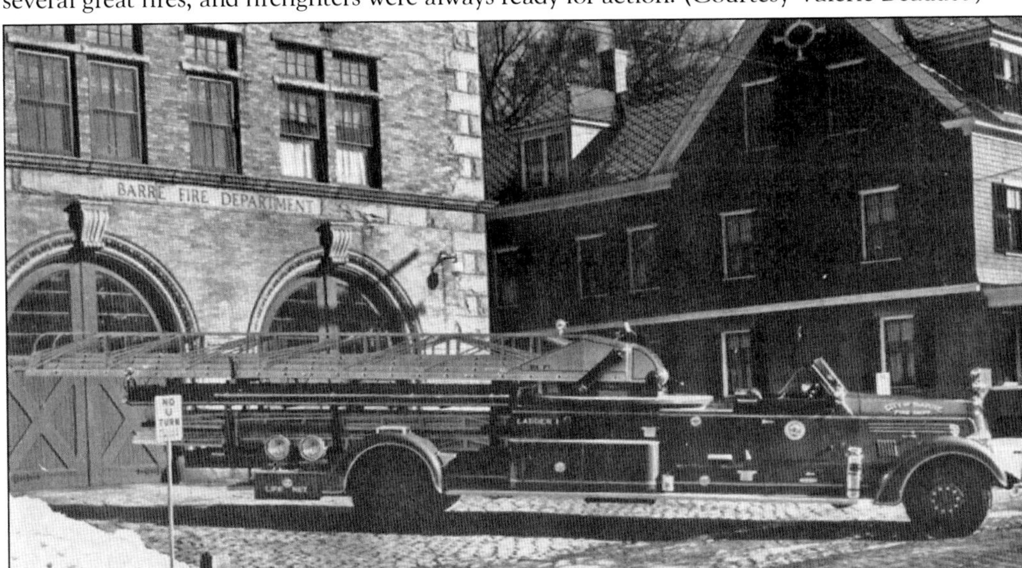

In the 1930s, fire trucks had to have ladders, which was important because the sizes of buildings were increasing and the firefighters needed to reach higher floors. These ladders allowed firemen to reach heights of up to 150 feet. (Courtesy Valerie Beaudet.)

Seven

Fun, Festivities, and Attractions

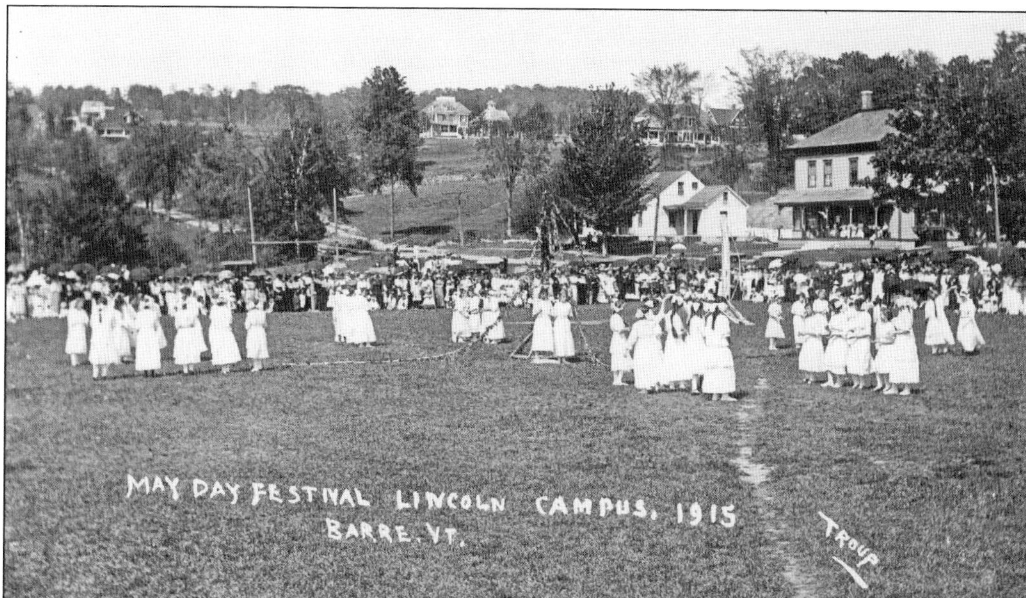

The 1915 May Day festival took place in the baseball field behind the Lincoln Elementary School. May Day festivals celebrate spring and rebirth after the long winters. May Day is known for its tradition of ribbons connected to a maypole and dancing around the pole in a circle. The celebration ends by the crowning of a May queen. The maypole in this photograph by A.M. Troup is a good example of the long ribbons.

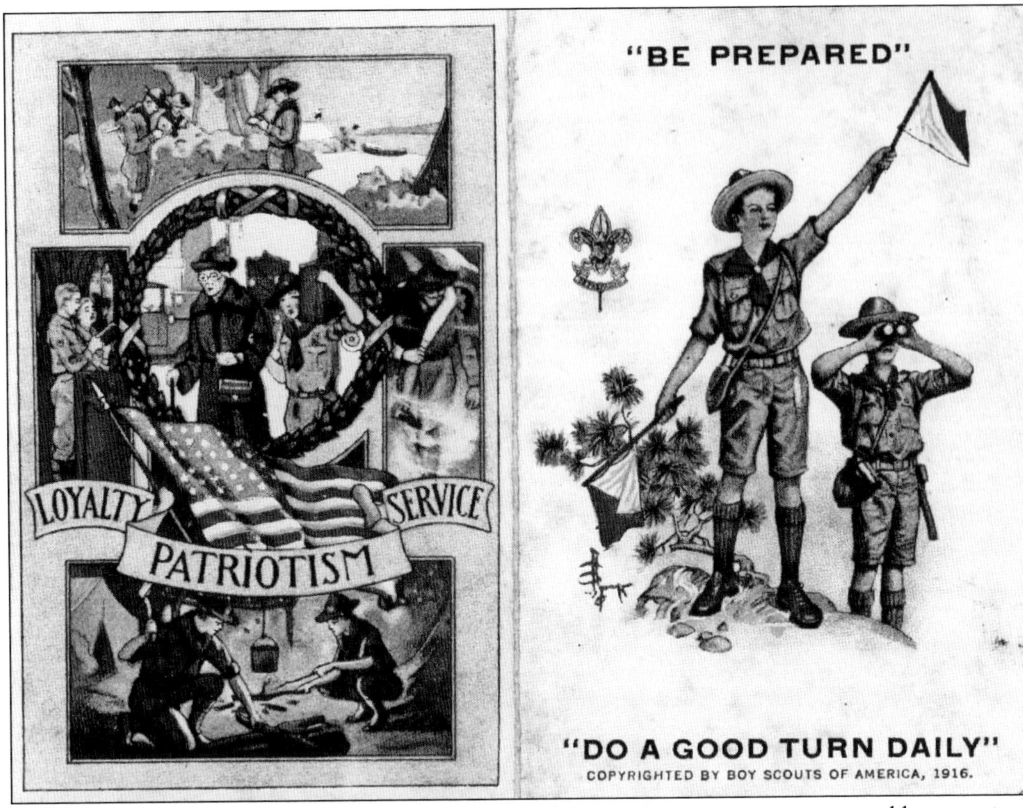

This Boy Scouts registration card has survived from 1916. In 1907, William Foster Milne (1885–1920) organized the First Boy Scout Troop in America. Milne was a stonecutter who emigrated from Scotland to Barre. (Courtesy of Boy Scouts of America.)

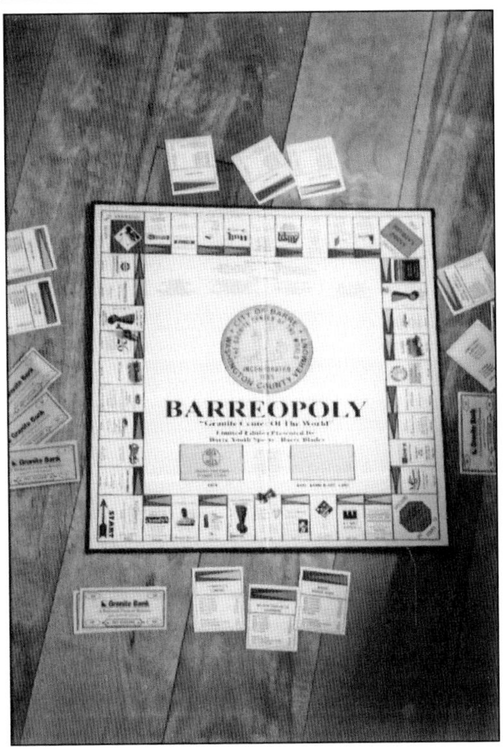

The game Barreopoly: "Granite Center of the World" was created for the Barre Blades Youth Sports fund drive. The all-volunteer organization started in 1972 is dedicated to the betterment of communities through youth participation in sports. Barreopoly came complete with Granite Savings Bank money, Rock of Ages playing cards, and tiny metal tokens.

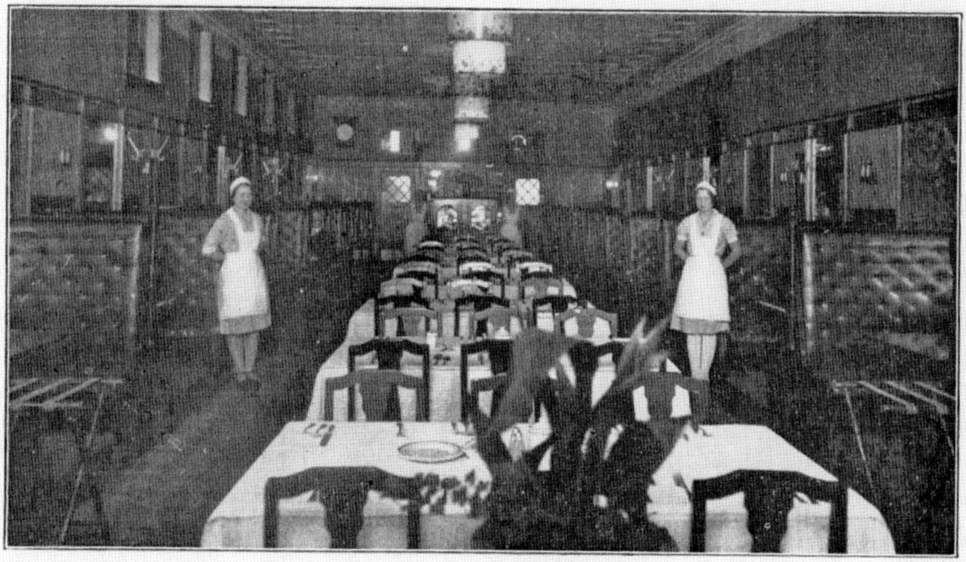

BARRE RESTAURANT, 158 NORTH MAIN STREET, BARRE, VT.

This 1942 image shows the inside of the Barre Restaurant. The street side of the restaurant had an eye-catching neon sign used to lure customers to the restaurant. Neon signs were popular in the United States from about 1920–1960.

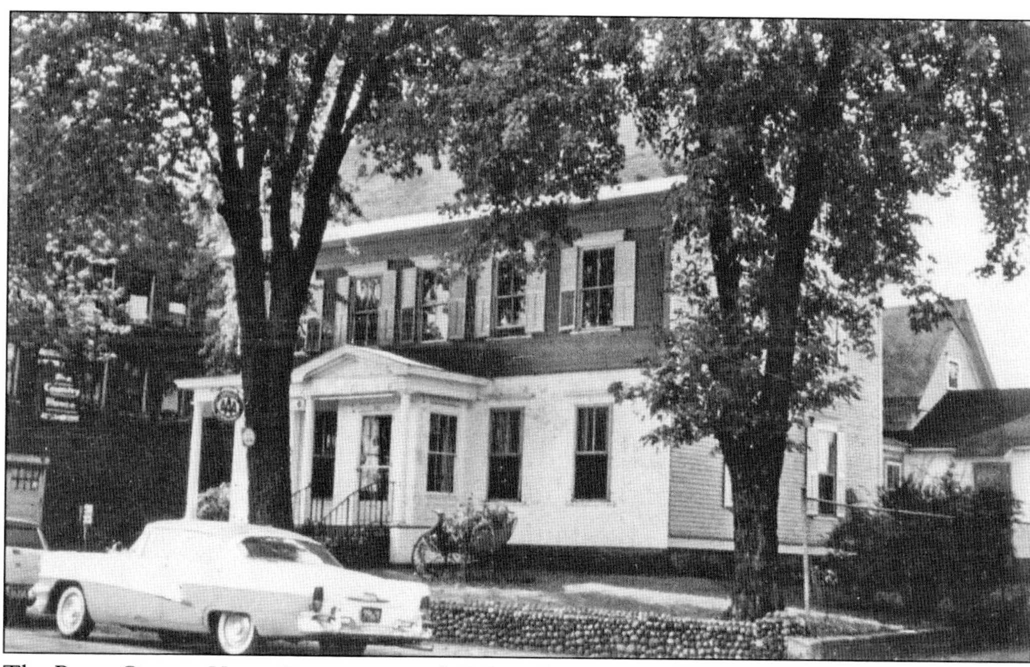

The Barre County House Restaurant and Oxbow Lounge was built in 1873 as a residence. It was renovated into an Italian restaurant in 1949.

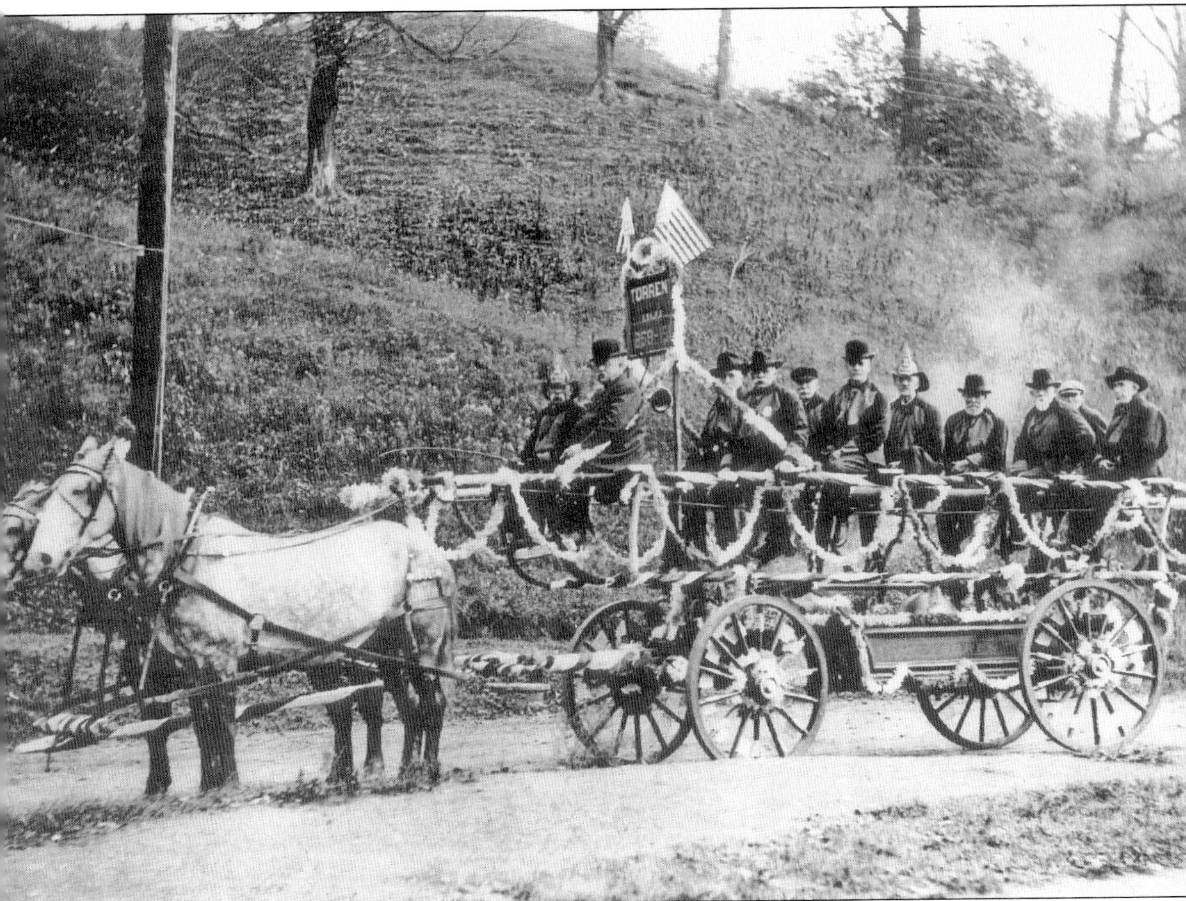

Payette Cutler is at the reins of this horse-drawn decorative wagon during a parade. The Barre Fire Department firefighters are riding in the wagon. (Courtesy Valerie Beaudet.)

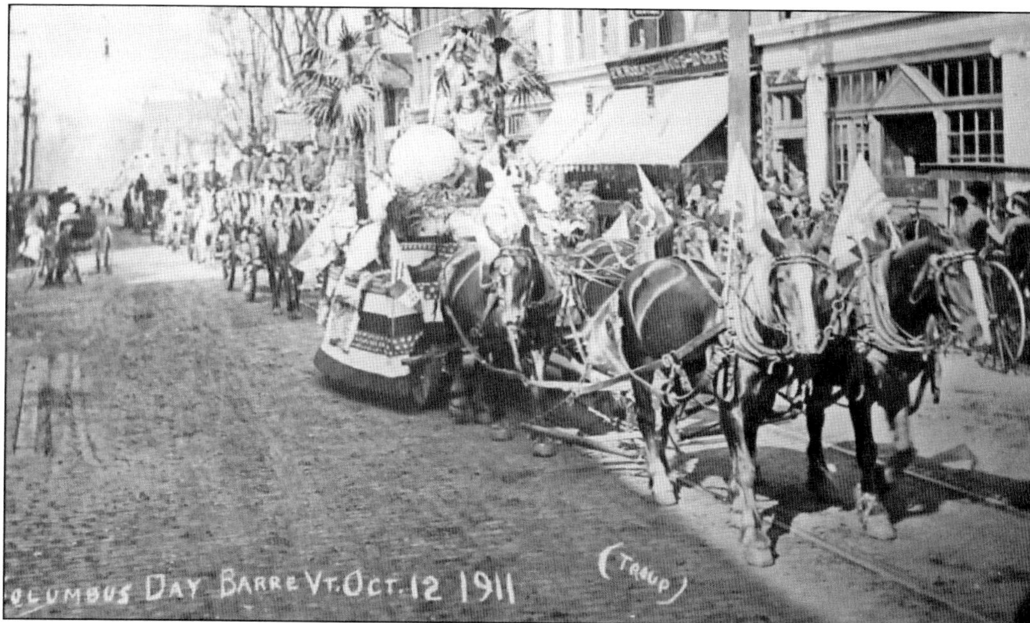

This 1911 Columbus Day Parade ground float is being towed by four horses carrying flags. The parade is longer than the viewer can see with many decorated floats. The float is elaborately decorated with palm trees and flags. Note that the horses are following the trolley tracks. (Photograph by Troup.)

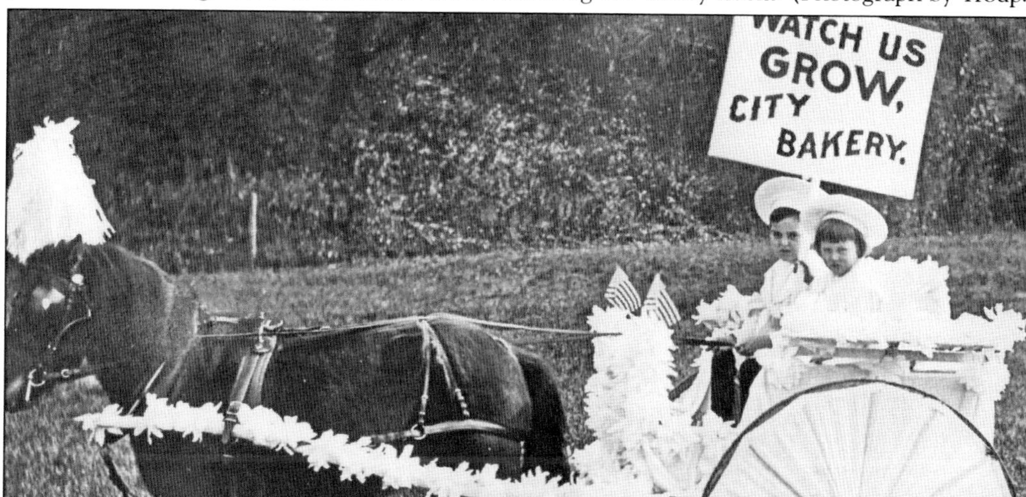

The 1911 Columbus Day Parade City Bakery float was being pulled by a pony but paused for a photograph. The wagon is elaborately decorated with paper ruffles, and the pony wore a pointed tassel in this Troup photograph. (Courtesy of Aldrich Public Library, Barre, Vermont.)

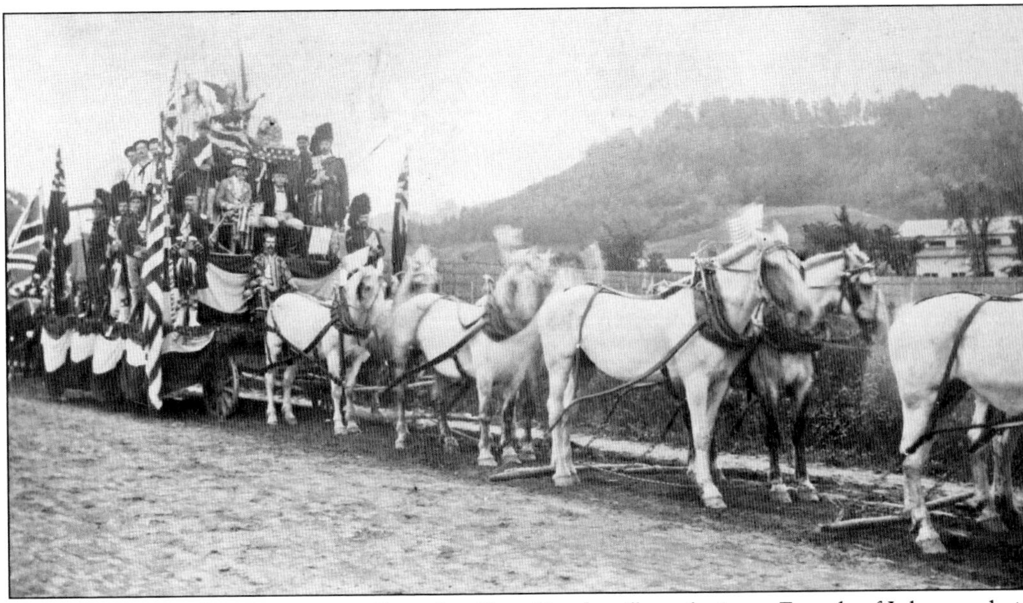

A team of eight white horses is pulling the Clan Gordon float during a Fourth of July parade in an unidentified year. (Courtesy of Aldrich Public Library, Barre, Vermont.)

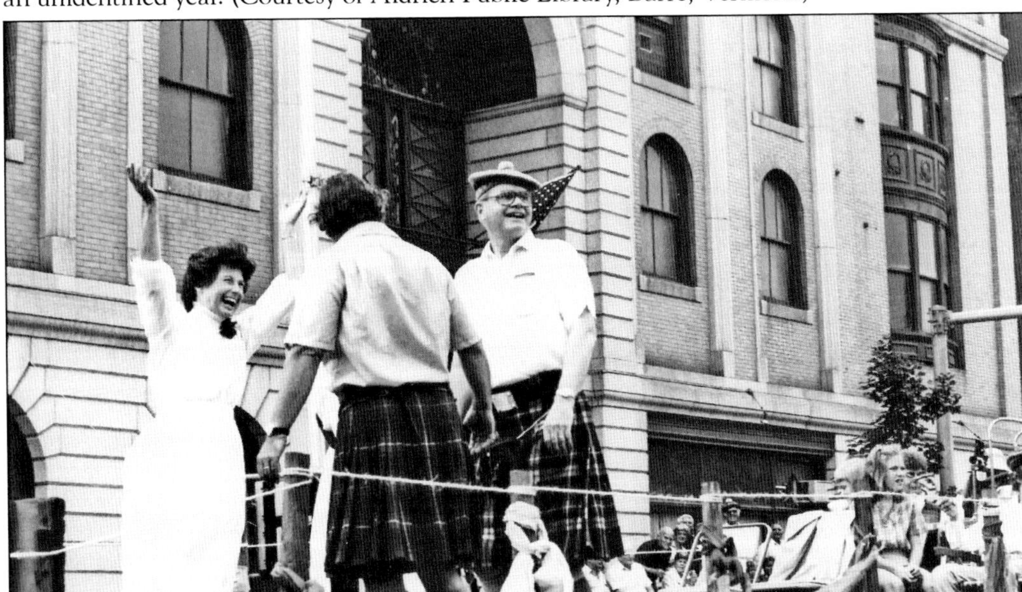

Early on in Barre's history, ethnic societies like the Societa' di Mutuo Soccorso and the Clan Gordon No. 12 of the Order of Scottish Clans were organized. Clan Gordon No. 12 grew to be the largest Scottish society in this country, with upwards of 500 members. A late-1900s Barre Heritage Festival Old Homes Days float is shown. (Courtesy of Barre Granite Association.)

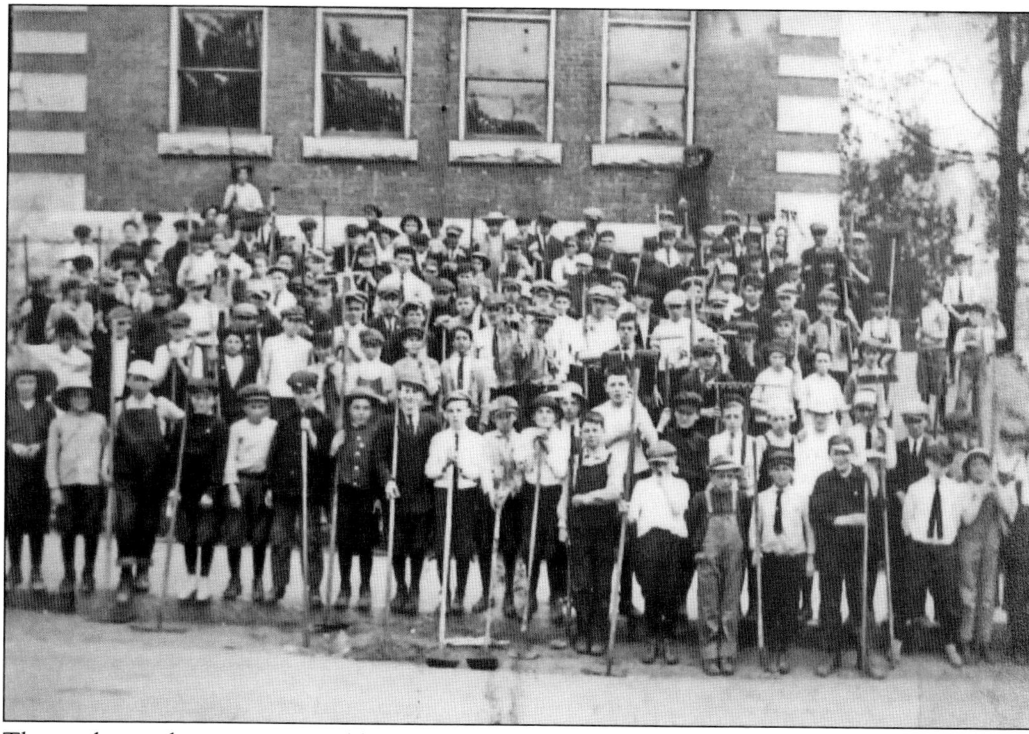

The student volunteers pictured here are ready to begin their work during Green-Up Day. The Green-Up Day movement, which advocates a day when people gather together to clean up all the roadside litter, has continued each spring with the hope of leaving behind a generation that is memorialized in tossed plastic bottles, Styrofoam cups, and aluminum cans. The image is dated 1914.

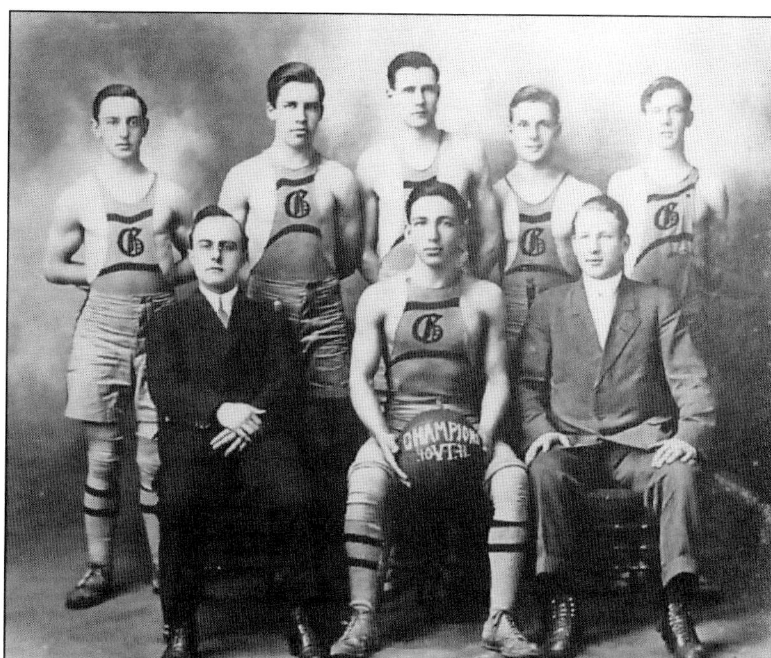

The Barre basketball team (1910–1911) is shown with the championship basketball in a photograph by H.W. Shores Stacey.

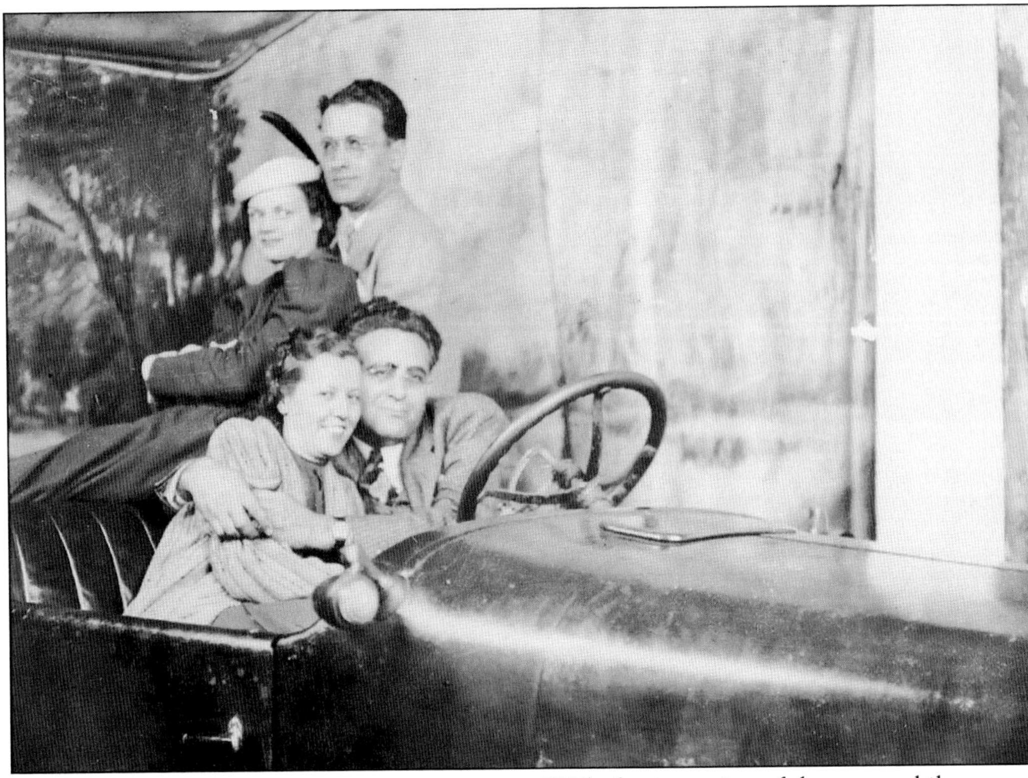

With the invention of the automobile, residents could go on special sightseeing excursions like journeys to the beach, amusement parks, and lover's lane.

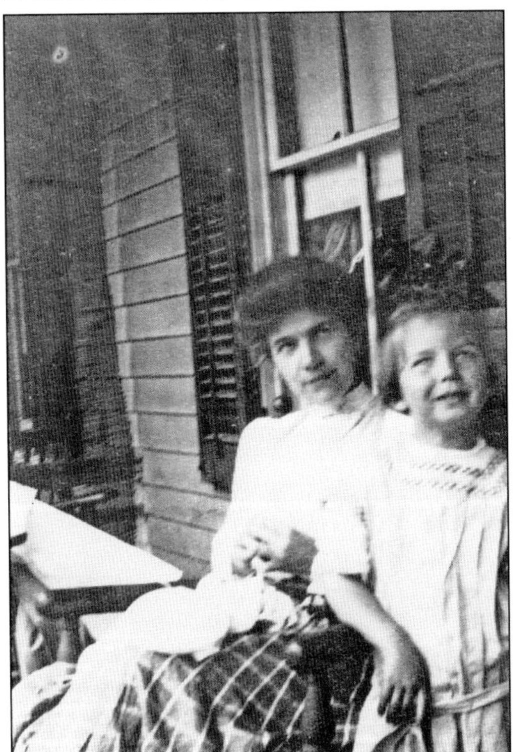

Life's simple pleasures included watching wildlife in the backyard. The back of this image says, "Watching the cardinals, Aunt Grace and Shelby – June 1908."

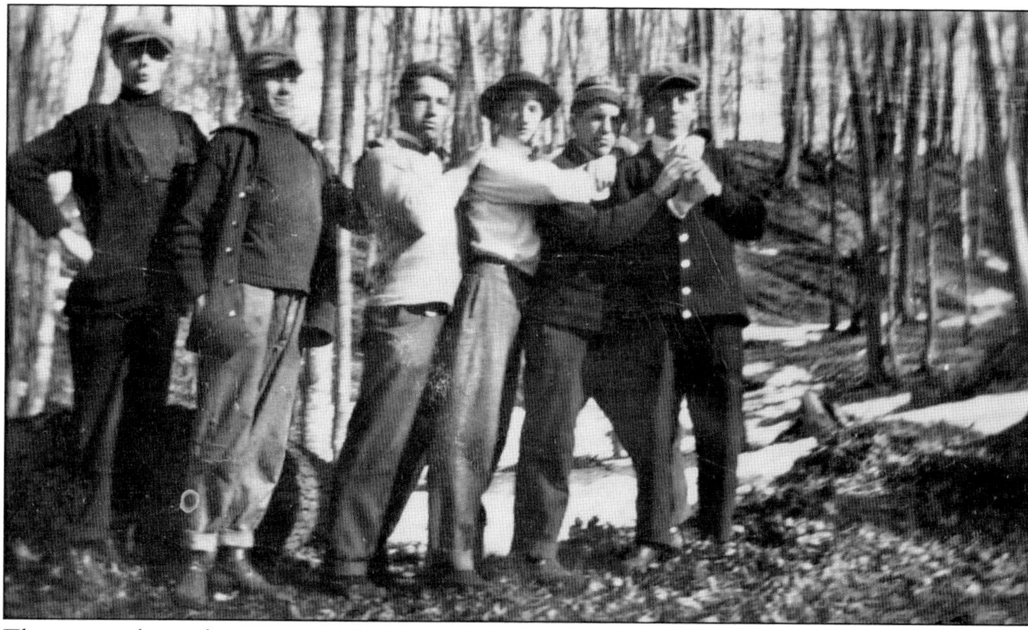

The image above shows six friends enjoying each other's company. The unidentified man on the left is wearing a casual newsboy cap that was popular in the late 19th and early 20th centuries.

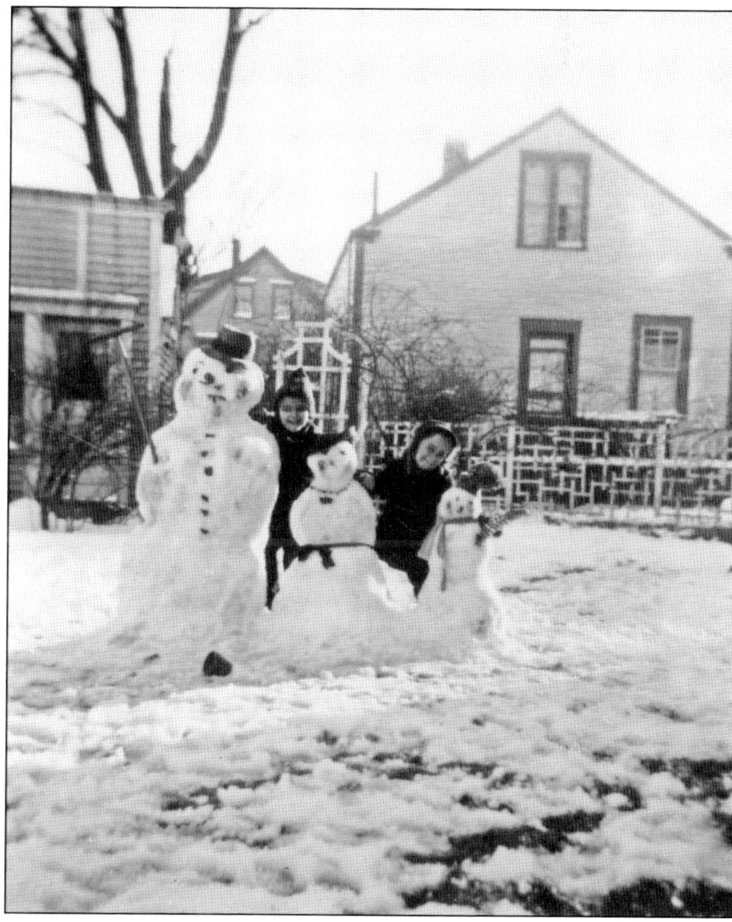

On this fine winter day in 1941, Margaret and Judy peek behind three snowmen.

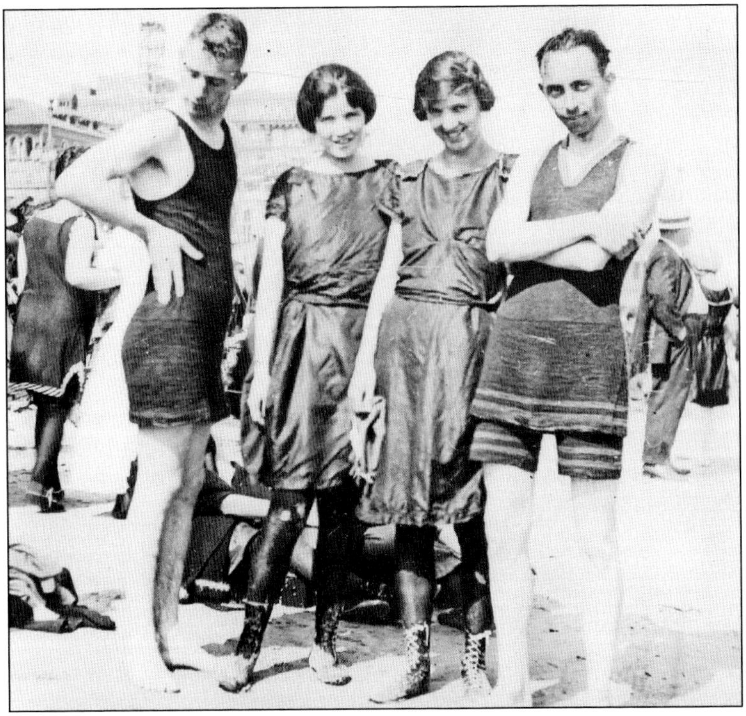

With the invention of the horseless carriage and train, Barre residents could head to Cape Cod for a cool dip in the salt water.

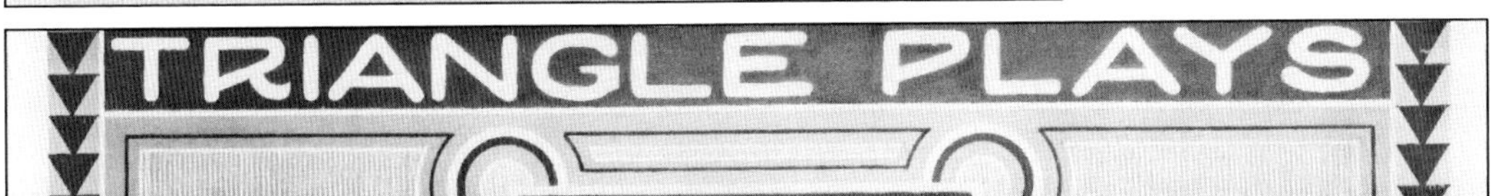

Barre Opera House seated 1,000 patrons and offered space for professional and local events including boxing, speeches from anarchist Emma Goldman, and many wonderful plays. This poster advertised the Triangle plays performed at the Barre Opera House.

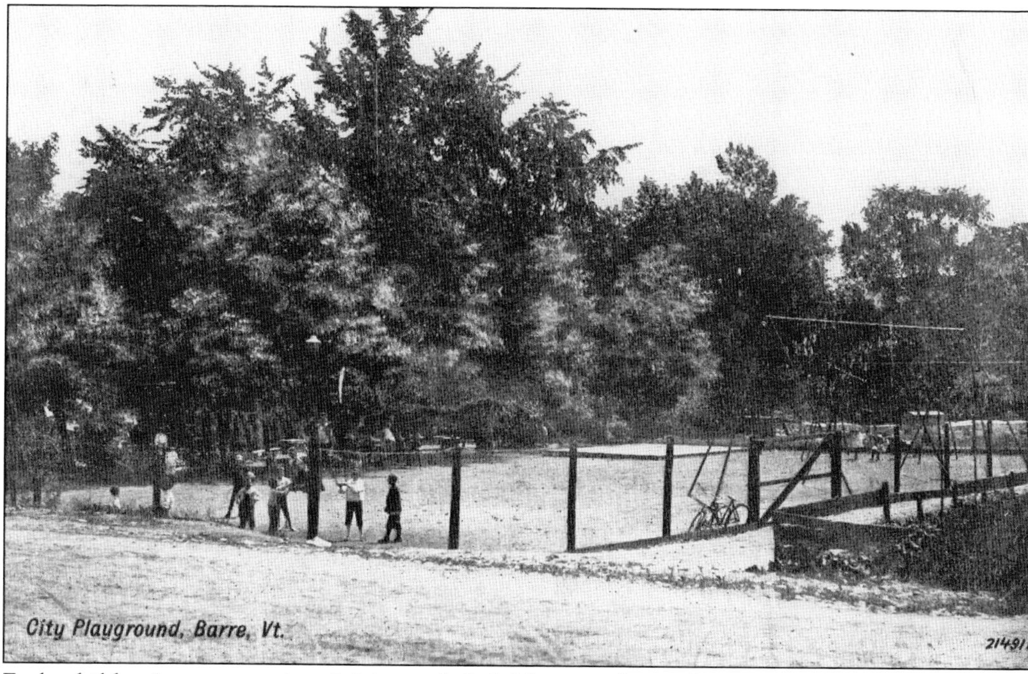

Early children's games and activities included fishing, stilts, jacks, yo-yos, checkers, hopscotch, kick the can, paper dolls, marbles, hide-and-seek, ice skating, sliding in the snow, baseball, and taking trips to the store for penny candy or for ice cream. These activities often occurred at the city playground pictured here in 1911.

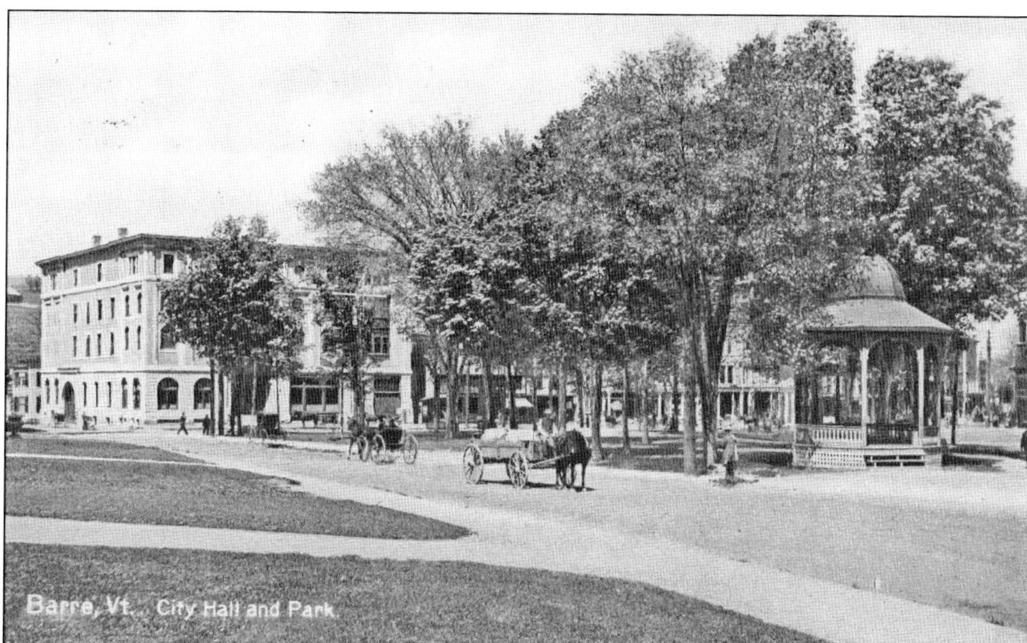

This late-1800s postcard shows the old bandstand in Barre City Common (now City Park). The Cornet Band, Scot Bagpipe Band, Italian-American Trans Band, and the Barre Summer Band all played in the park's gazebo.

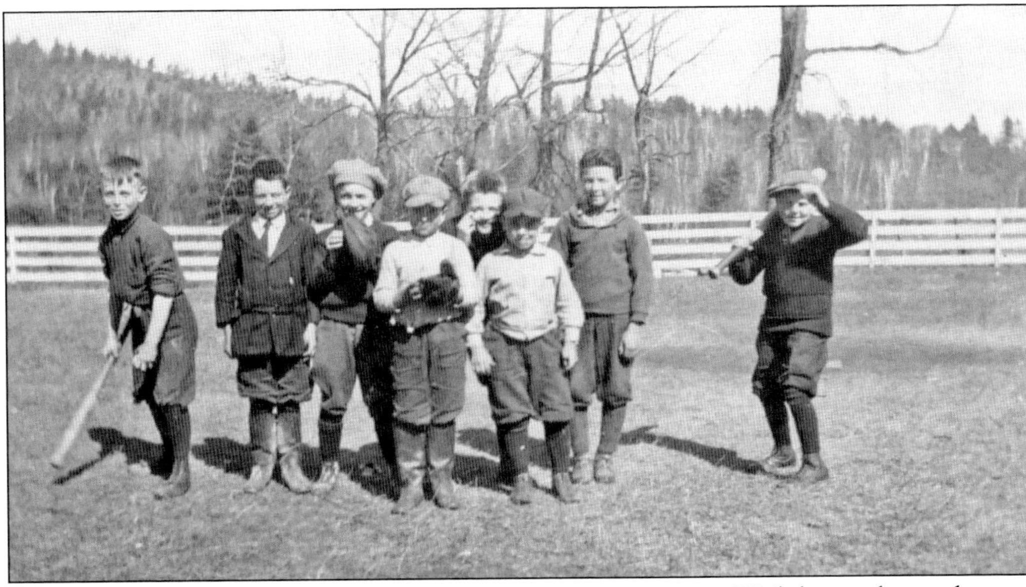

With bats as big as the boys, eight unidentified youths dressed in knickers pose for the camera while imagining their next homerun.

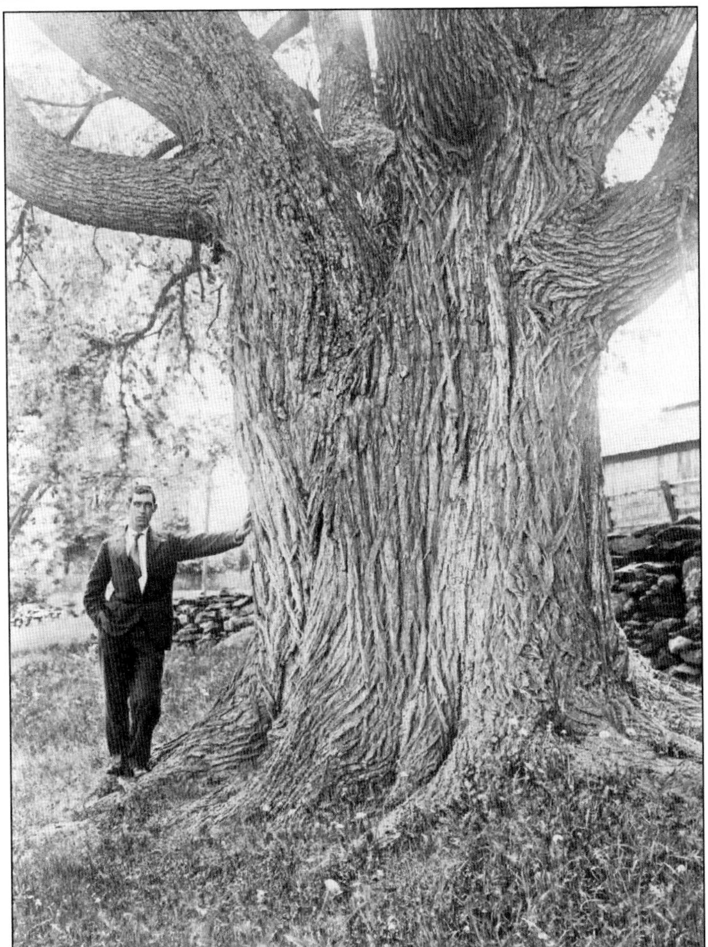

William Robertson poses at John Averill Farm under an enormous elm tree in 1913. Barre planted many elm trees along roadsides and around the park during the 19th century, but most of Vermont's elm trees died from Dutch elm disease. (Courtesy of Aldrich Public Library, Barre, Vermont.)

Eight

Changing Fashions

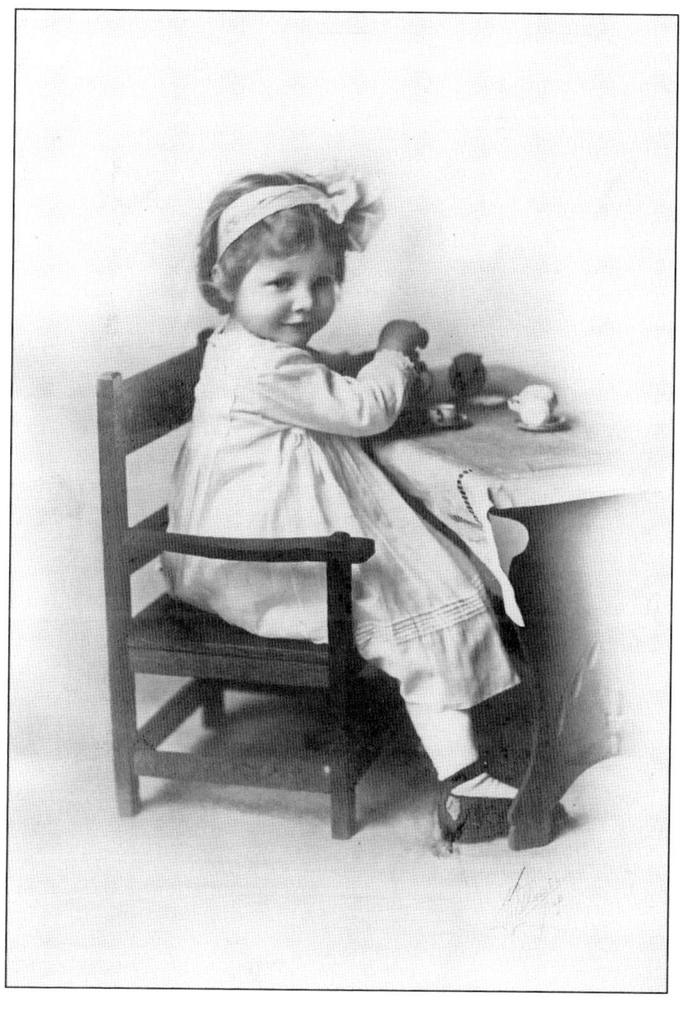

Tastes and trends in clothing and accessories changed over time. The 1914 image is of an unidentified little Barre girl with her toy tea set. She is wearing a big bow and black patent-leather shoes with a single strap and buckle, which was popular during this time period.

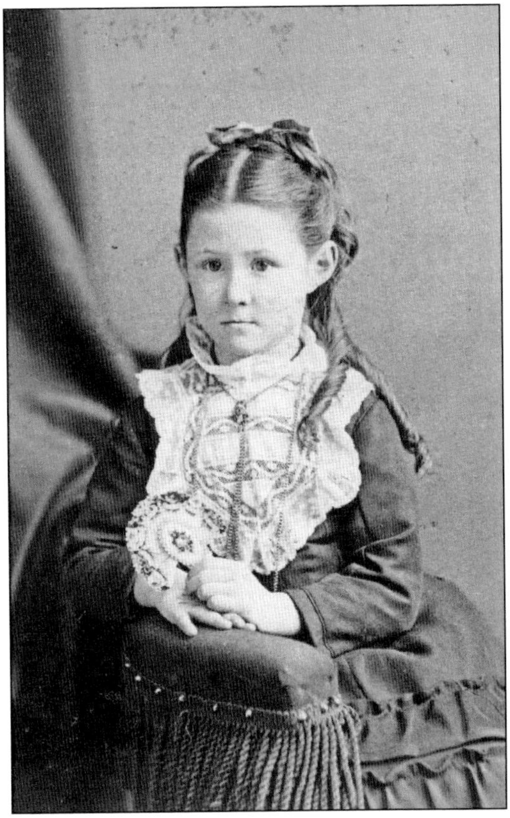

From 1854 through 1885, girls' dresses were heavily decorated with frills, pleats, and trims. A separate skirt was worn beneath the overskirt, and the neckline was high and trimmed. The frilling or pleating was repeated on other parts of the dress, especially on cuffs and the skirt. The long corkscrew curls at the nape of the neck on this little girl are a good example of the hairstyle worn during this time period.

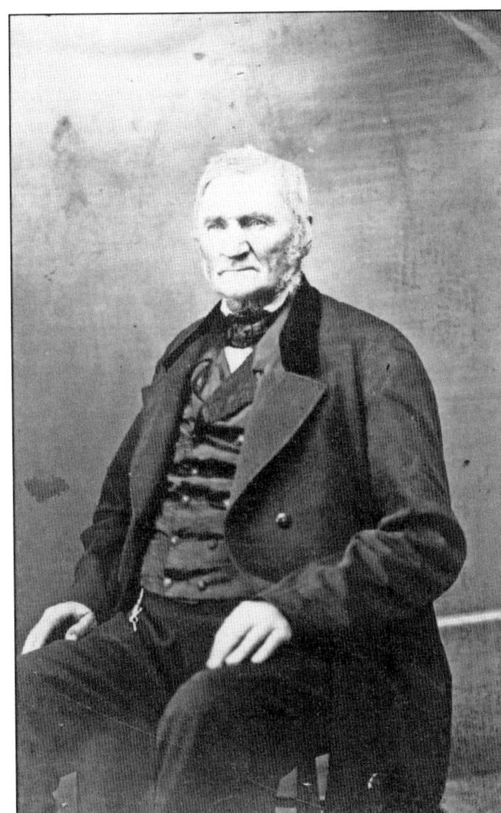

A carte de visite photograph by Azel N. Blanchard dates this image between 1865 and 1879. The wide lapels almost touching the shoulder seams dates the matching coat, trousers, and waistcoat ensemble as possibly being purchased at an earlier time period.

An unidentified woman is wearing a pre-1820s Empire-waist-style dress, which is long and loosely fitting but skims the body. It is often worn in white to signify a high social class.

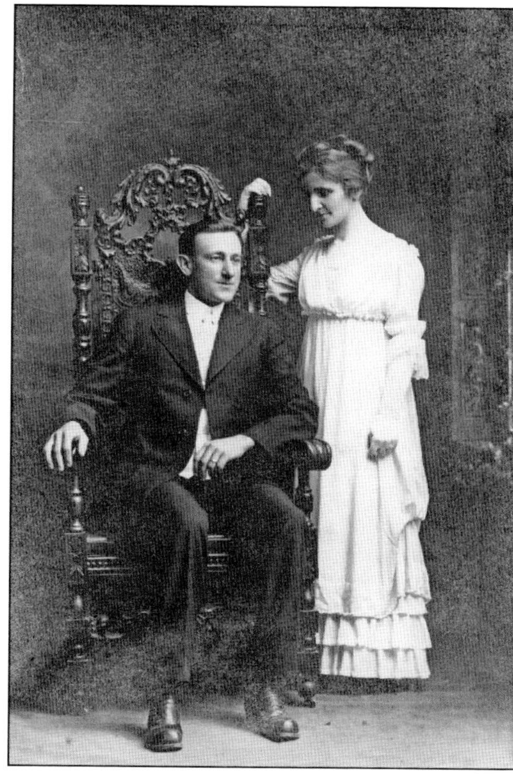

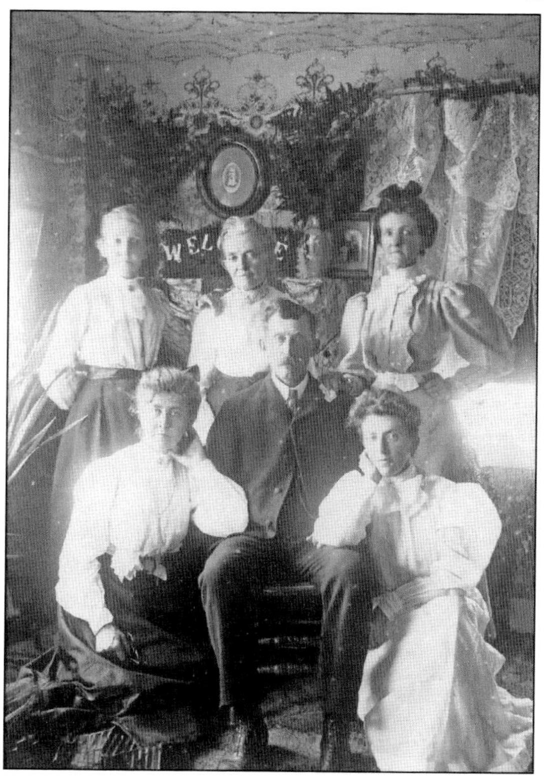

In the early 1890s, corseted floor-length skirts and dresses were used to form tiny waists to produce what was known as the hourglass figure, and high collars with lots of trim and lace characterized women's wear. The styles started to change by the end of 1890s when women started wearing white blouses in contrast with darker skirts and started to enjoy more natural waistlines. The unidentified woman on the right in the back row has a characteristically small waist.

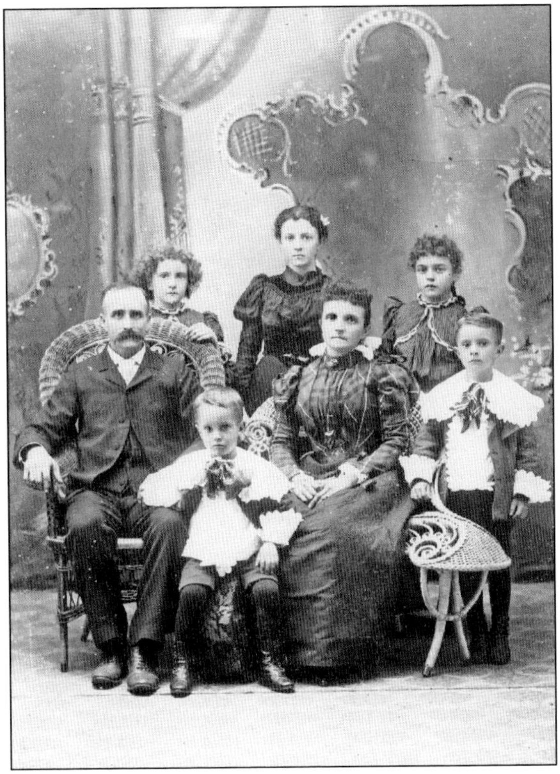

During the Victorian era, wealthy children's clothing was frilly, formal, and uncomfortable. Both boys are wearing suits adorned with an elaborate style of giant Vandyke collars popular with mothers in the 1880s and 1890s.

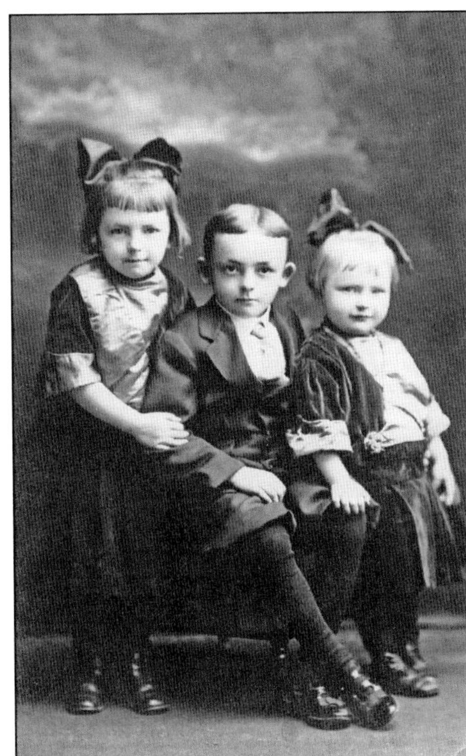

Big bows were a very important fashion during 1910 when this photograph was taken; after the 1920s bows became smaller. The opposite side of this postcard says, "Dear Grandma. From the children."

An Italian-born married couple is visible in this image dated 1902. The woman's hair was pinned into a roll or low bun at the back of the neck, while corseting continued. The man's loosely fitted, mid-thigh-length sack coat continued to slowly replace the frock coat for less-formal business occasions. The mustached gentleman is also wearing a high-neck shirt and a stylish narrow necktie. (Courtesy of the Vermont Granite Museum.)

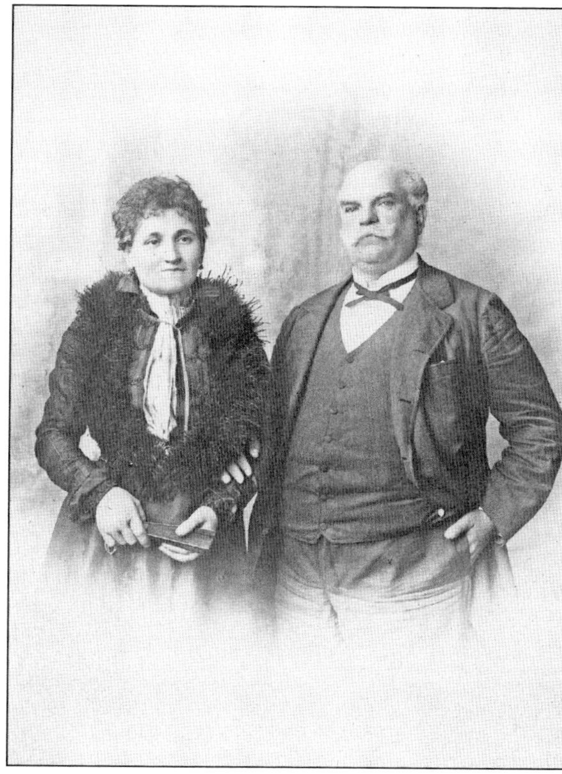

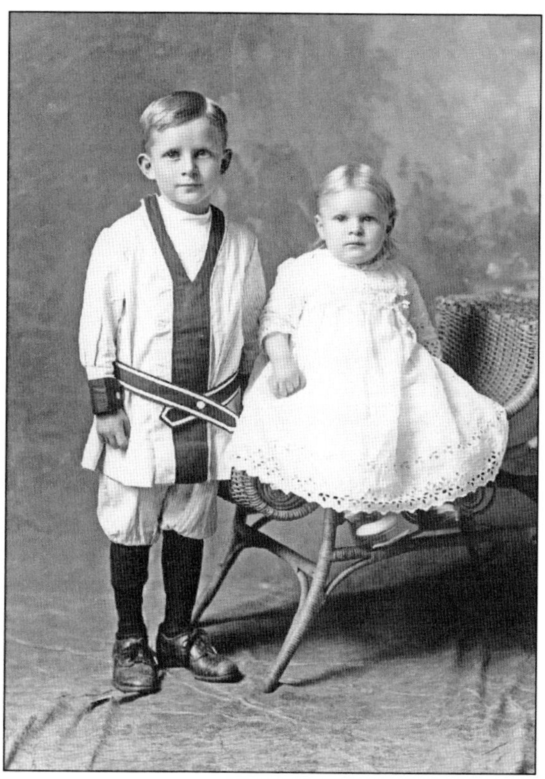

Posed for their portrait taken by Shores Studio are George Daniels (left) and his sister Helen Daniels, who is wearing typical baby clothes for the late 1800s. The long white gown would prevent a baby from crawling too far away. George is wearing pantalets, because during this time period it was not proper to leave children's legs uncovered.

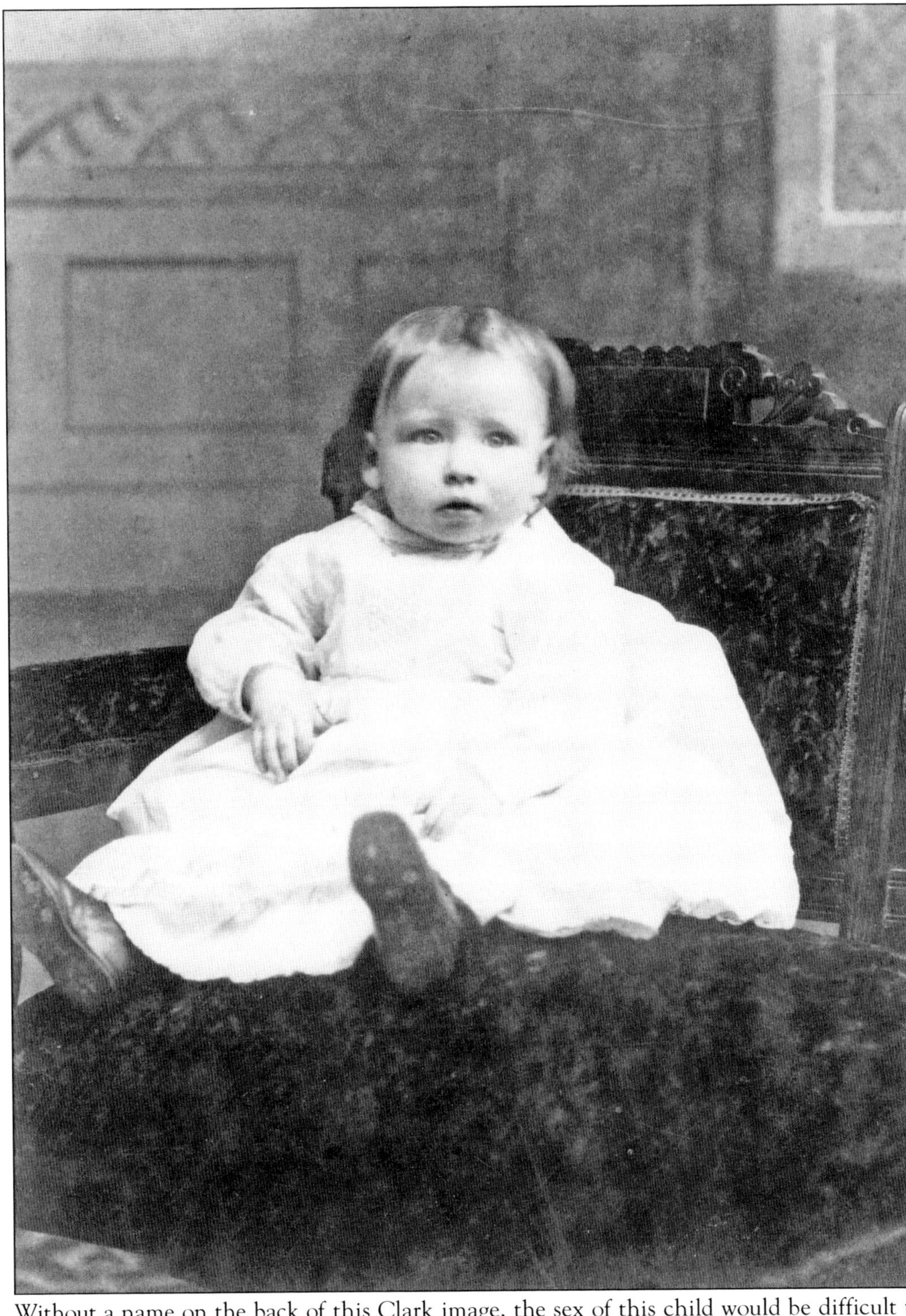

Without a name on the back of this Clark image, the sex of this child would be difficult to determine because in 1871 nearly all infants, regardless of gender, wore dresses. Luckily, the other side of the photograph identifies the child as "Jack."

In 1902, the Buster Brown suit was made popular by the comic strip with the same name. It required a double-breasted tunic or jacket worn with a large round collar, wide floppy bow, and knickers. Usually, Dutch-boy bangs and long hair made the look authentic. The photograph was taken by R.E. Bertherman.

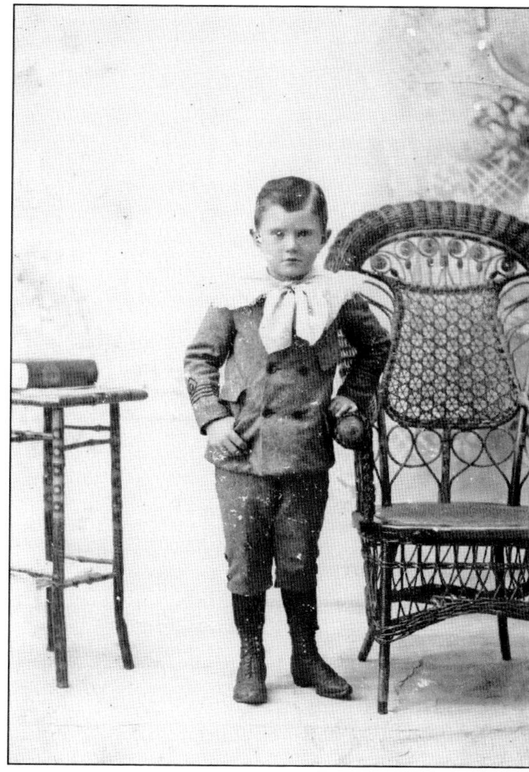

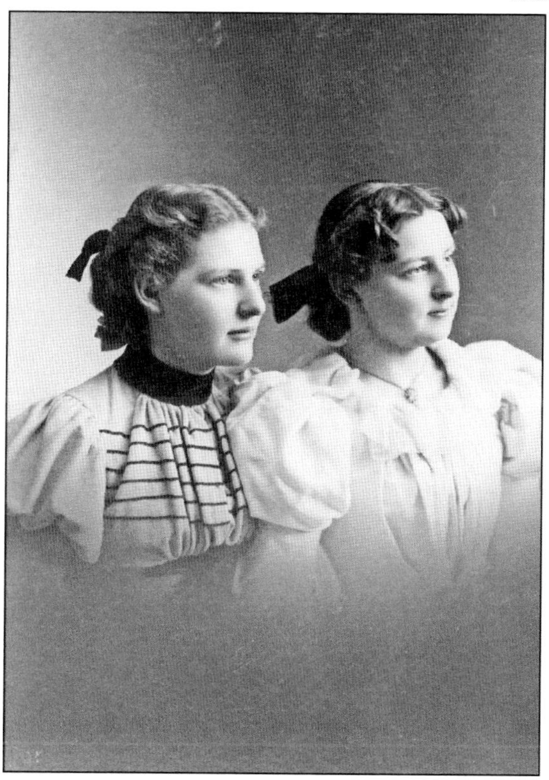

These unidentified sisters posed in "leg-o'-mutton" sleeves ballooning from their blouses elbows. The photograph was taken around 1892 by Harry E. Cutler.

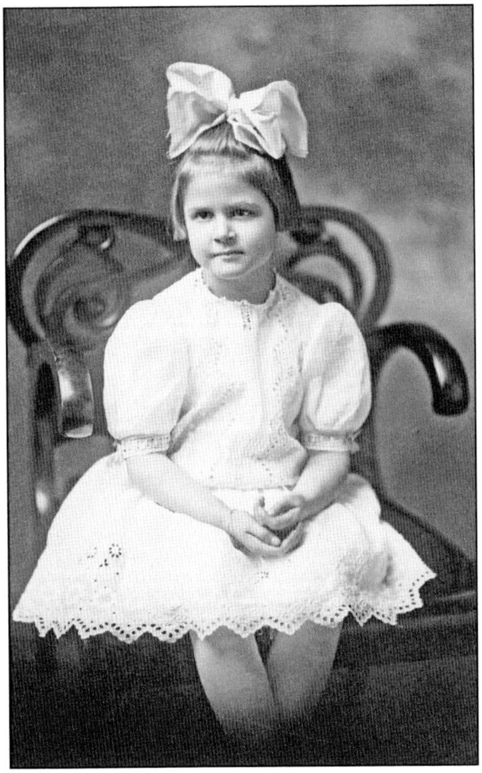

Six-year-old Helen Ruth Ballard posed for her portrait in an ornate and frilly dress with a blouson low waist popular in the late 1800s to early 1900s. She died the next year at age seven. J. Bau Studio did the photography for the Ballards.

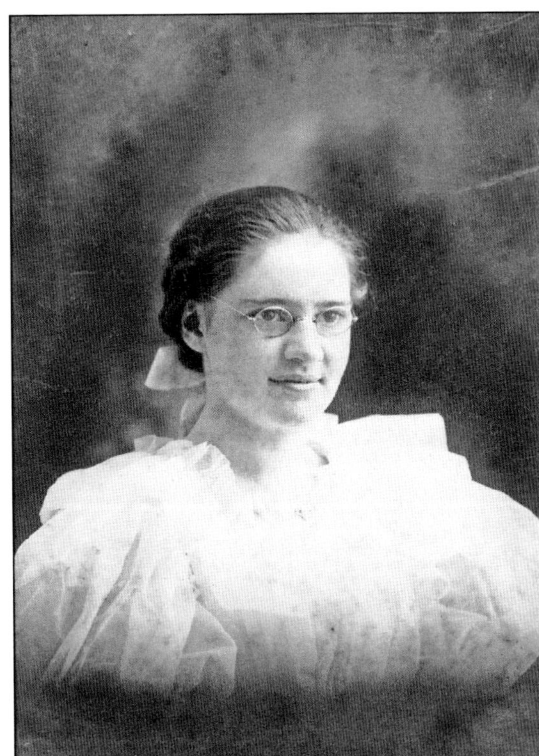

This is a beautiful example, in a Clark photograph, of the popular dress style made of a light material with very full sleeves from the 1890s. The young woman's hair is pulled back with a bow and she is wearing oval-eye spectacles.

This unidentified gentleman posed wearing a matching three-piece suit, a white shirt with a high collar with tips pressed down into wings, and a white tie. The Clark image was taken between 1860 and the early 1900s.

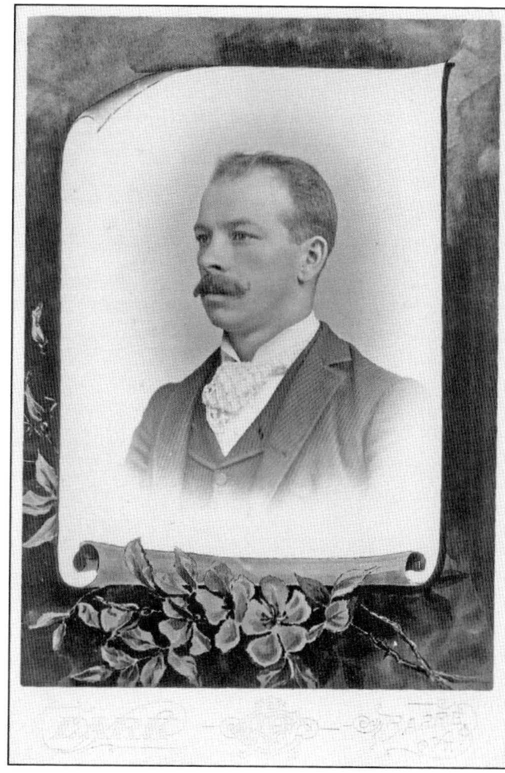

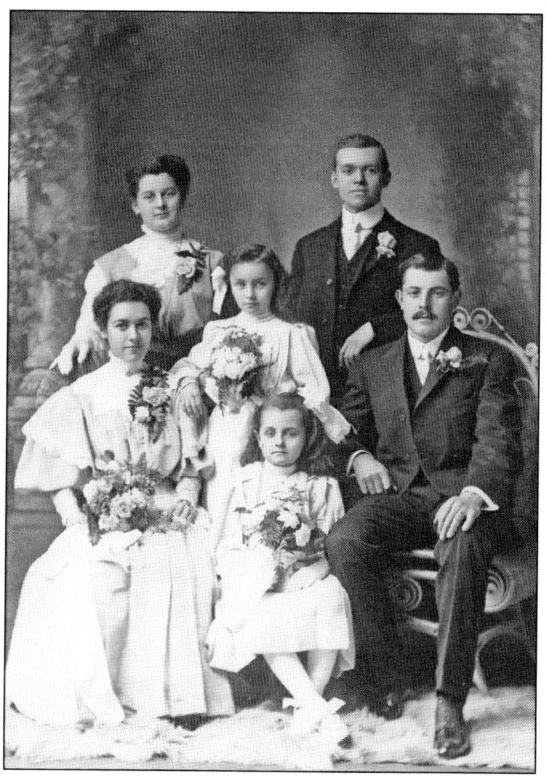

An animal-hide rug is visible in this 1886 cabinet card featuring a photo by Charles Bau's studio. The French named the era from 1871 to 1914 as La Belle Époque or "Beautiful Era." The dress style emphasized a ladylike figure complemented by a tiny waist and full upper body. The skirt flared out all round to balance the massive sleeve heads.

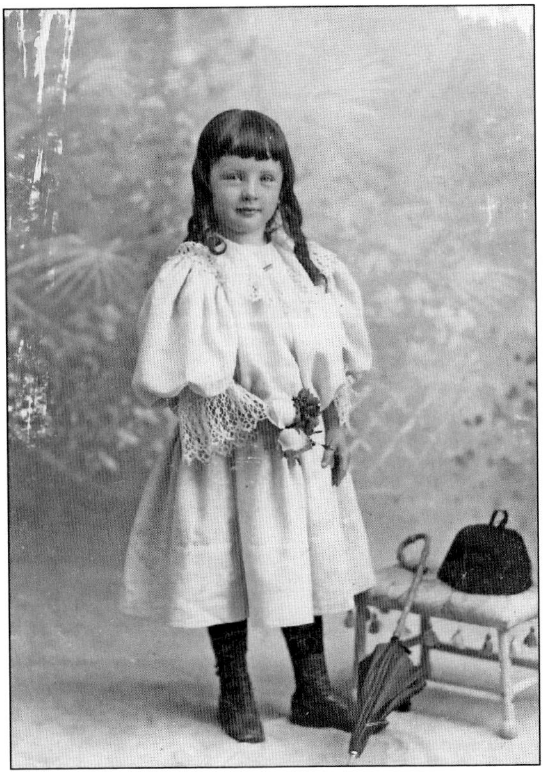

An unidentified young girl is clutching a small bouquet of flowers. She posed for Harry E. Cutler with her little parasol and purse, and her dress had long sleeves with flared cuffs embellished with bobbin lace. During this time period (1880–1893) it was fashionable to wear shoulder length hair with bangs. (Courtesy Bob Somaini.)

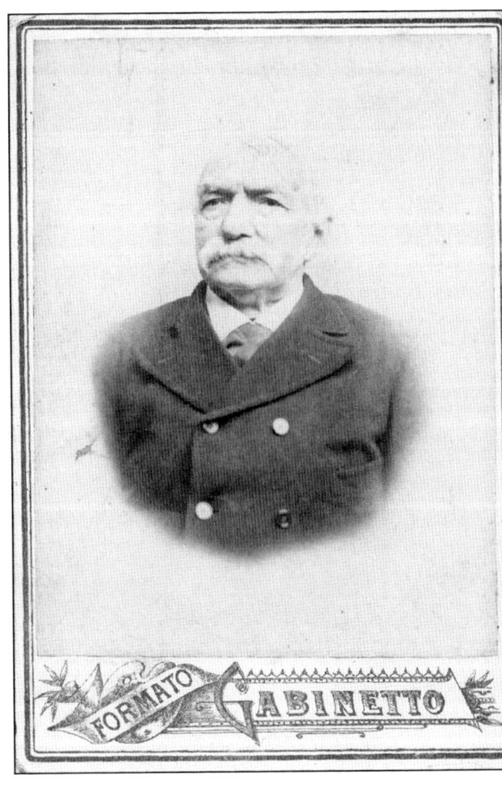

This Italian gentleman worked in the granite industry. He wore a double-breasted jacket, which has four or six buttons. The bottom of the image says "Formato Gabinetto," which is Italian for cabinet size. Cabinet-size card photographs were introduced between the 1880s and the1890s. (Courtesy of the Vermont Granite Museum.)

This c. 1910 photograph by J. Bau Studio illustrates the simple and practical fashion of the time.

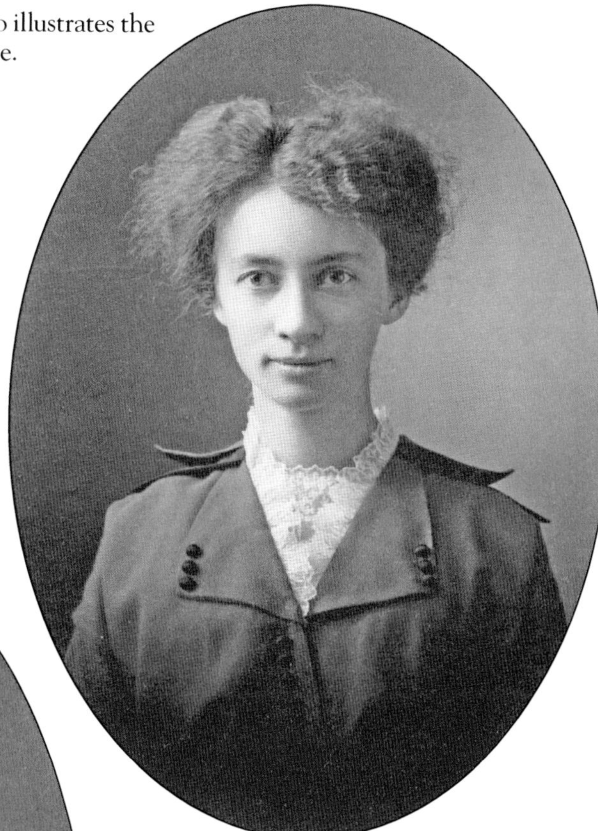

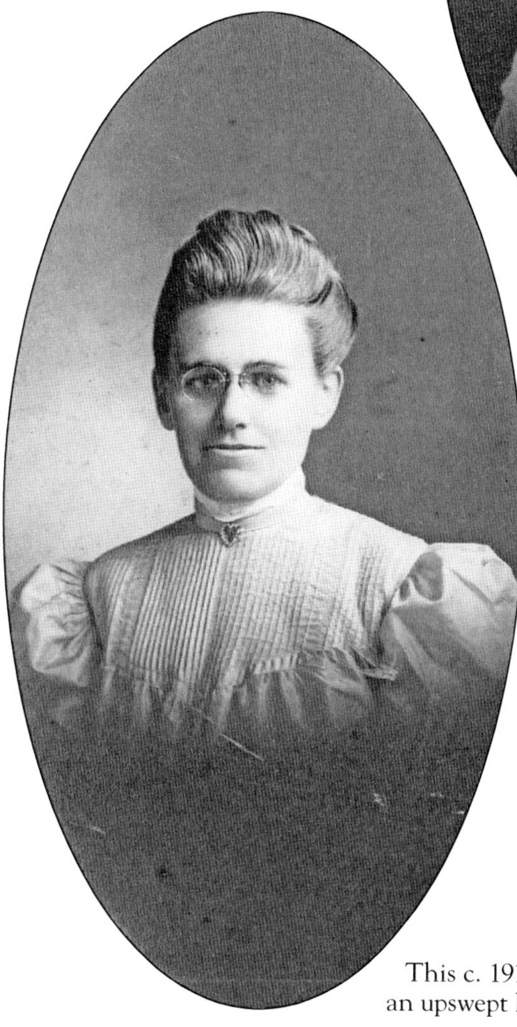

This c. 1910 J. Bau Studio image shows a woman wearing an upswept hairstyle and a simple high-neck blouse.

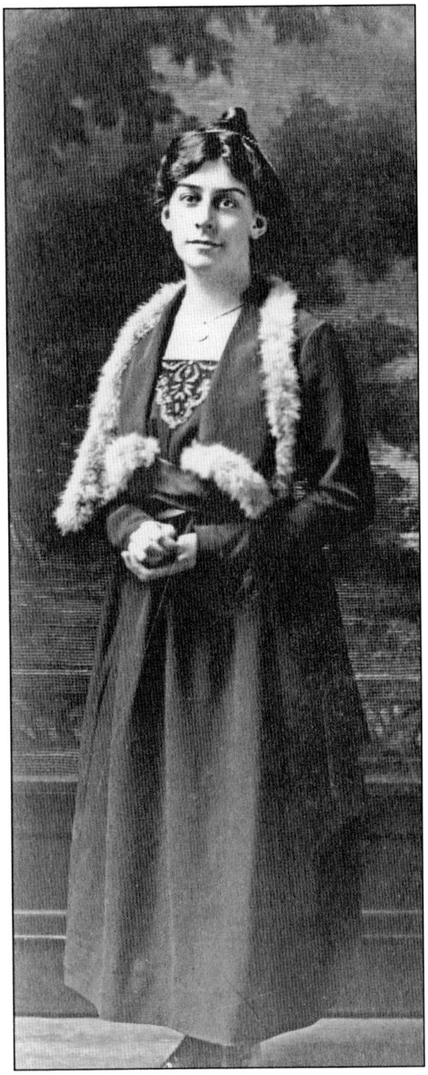

In 1912, fashionable women wore striking hats and fur stoles. The high lace collars were on their way to being out of fashion as shown in this natural neckline with lace insert. The unidentified woman had her hair styled in a loose bun at the nape of the neck, while the hair on top was parted in the center in this Rockward photograph.

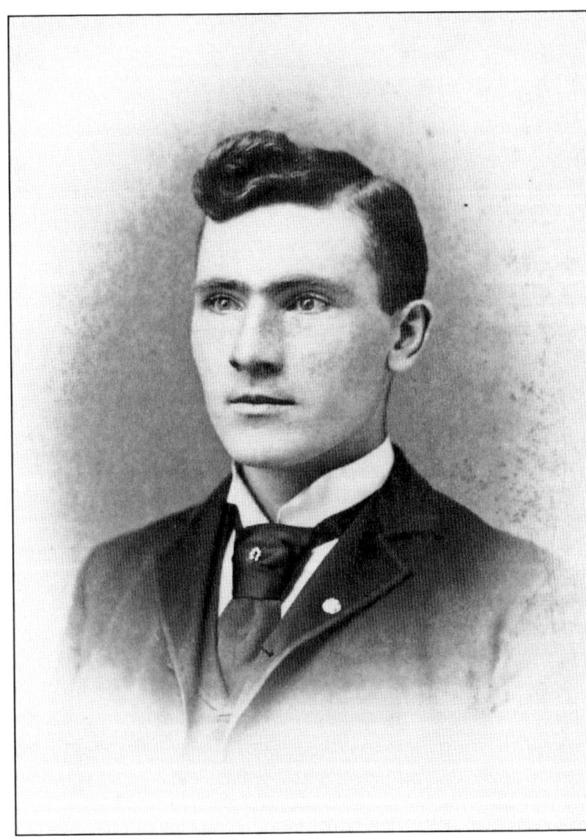

A 1900s Clark image of an unidentified man with a white shirt featuring a high collar with tips pressed down into wings and a black tie with a stickpin. The very short hairstyle is typical of the period.

This image of Felmar Augusta Cordick was taken in the 1900s by Harry E. Cutler, a professional photographer. Harry and his family lived on South Warren Street in Barre.

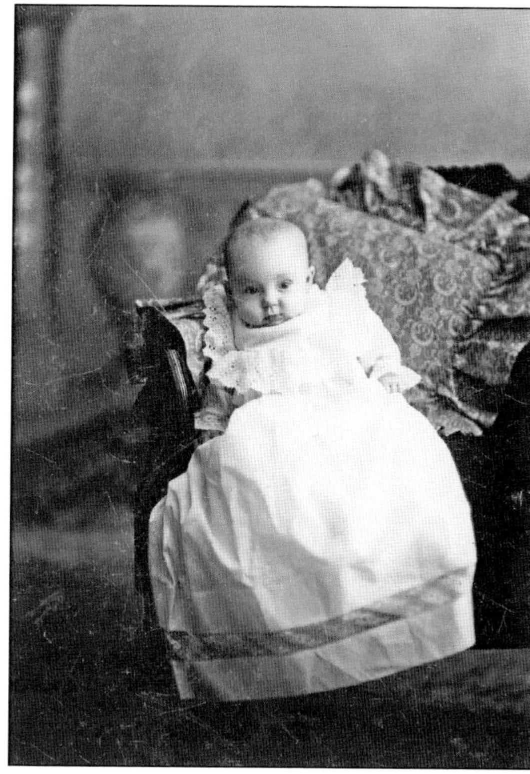

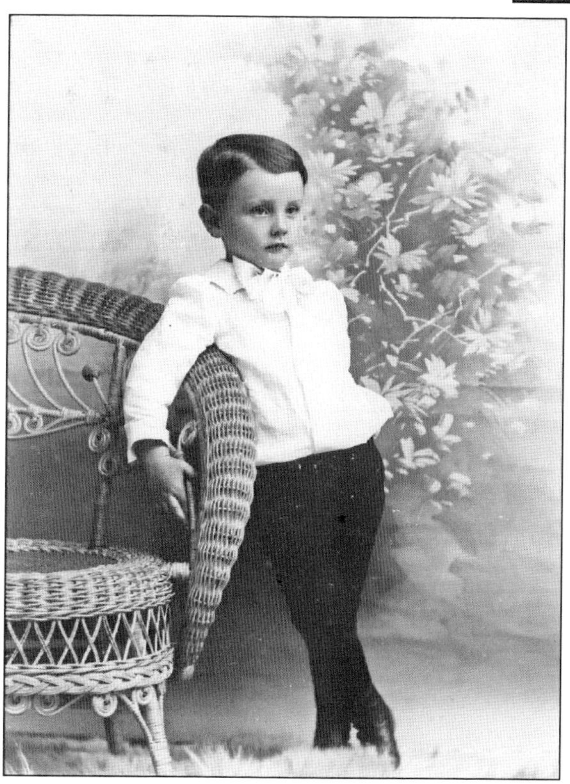

Clark produced this cabinet-card image of a young boy posing near a wicker chair. The image was taken in the 1900s.

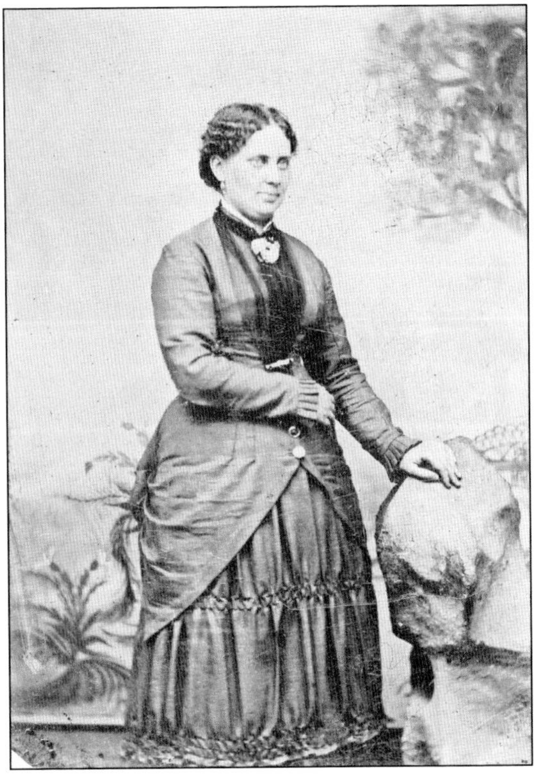

This charming c. 1885 carte de visite photograph of an unidentified Italian woman received expert coloring after it was developed. The scene includes a background painting of a tree and flowers and a papier-mâché studio prop. Fashion in the 1880s was characterized by the bustle, which is a type of framework used to expand the fullness or support the drapery of the back of a woman's dress. (Courtesy Ettore Bonazzi and the Vermont Granite Museum.)

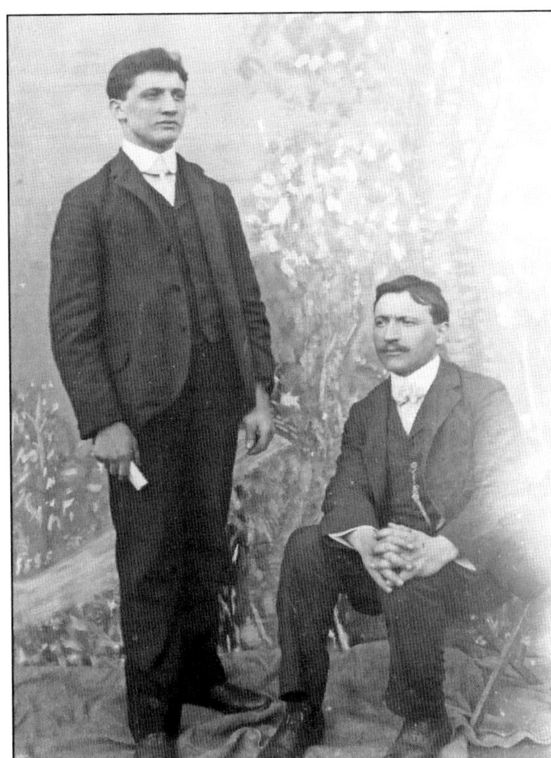

The 1862–1890s cabinet photographs were commonly found to have painted backgrounds. This image shows two unidentified Italian men that worked in the Barre granite industry. They have rounded banker collars, and there is a pocket watch with a chain on the gentleman on the right side. (Courtesy of the Vermont Granite Museum.)

Three unidentified members of the Del Monte family stopped to pose for this photograph. The newsboy cap is worn by a granite worker (left), and a straw hat with a gambler crown and a wide curled brim is worn by both the gentleman with a bowtie (right) and the little girl with a big smile on her face. (Courtesy Frank Del Monte and the Vermont Granite Museum.)

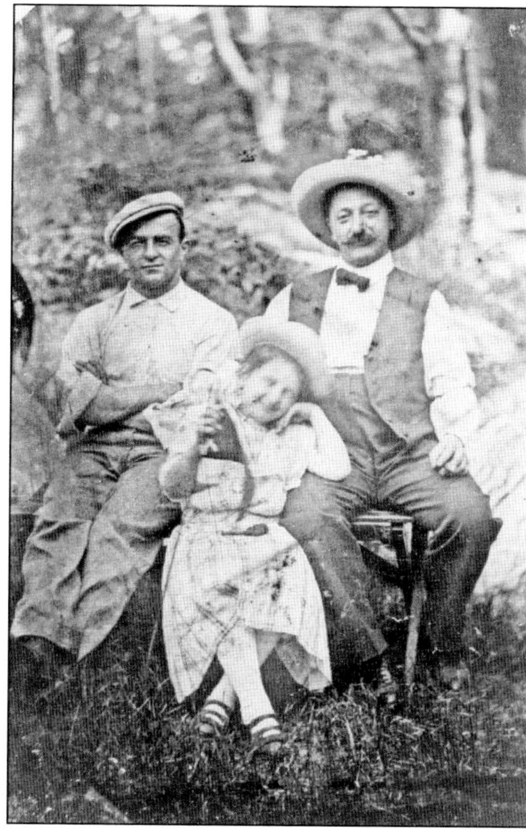

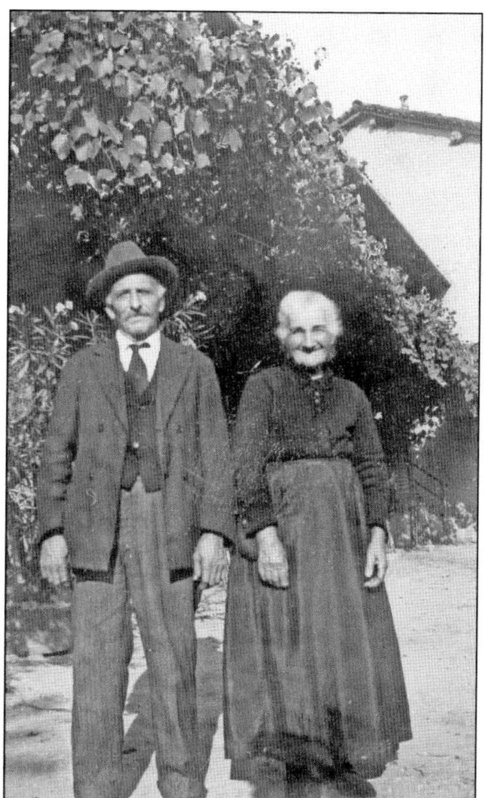

Early-1890s dresses consisted of a tight bodice with a skirt that gathered at the waist and fell naturally over the hips. (Courtesy of the Vermont Granite Museum.)

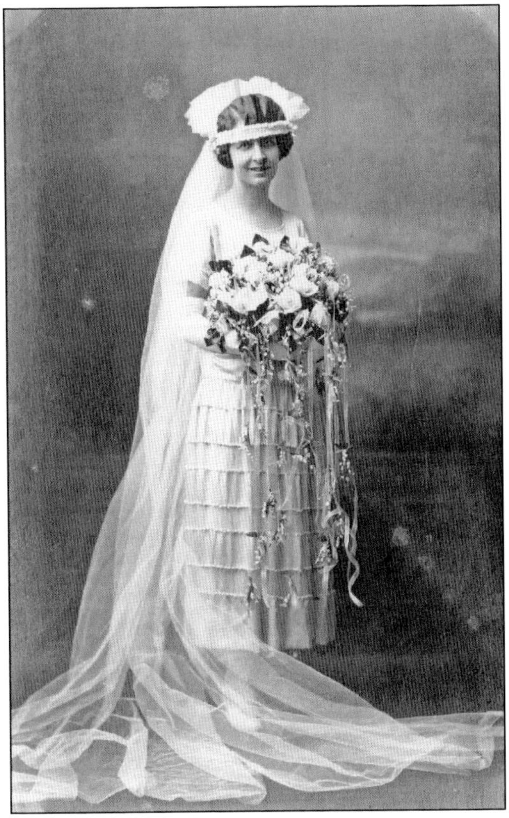

The women's rights movement had a strong effect on women's fashions. Women in the 1920s broke traditions and abandoned the constrictive corset fashions from the previous decade. Here is an unidentified woman in her new-fashion wedding dress and a tulle headdress with a pie-crust-fan edge in 1922. Short hairstyles also gained popularity during this time.

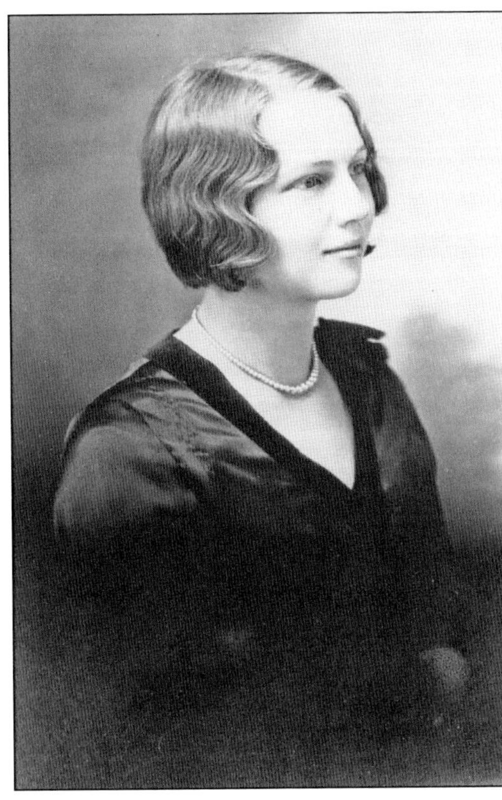

Soft curls and short hair were common in the 1930s. Betty Lane of Barre, Vermont posed for her picture wearing a single set of pearls and a black V-neck dress (photograph by Shores).

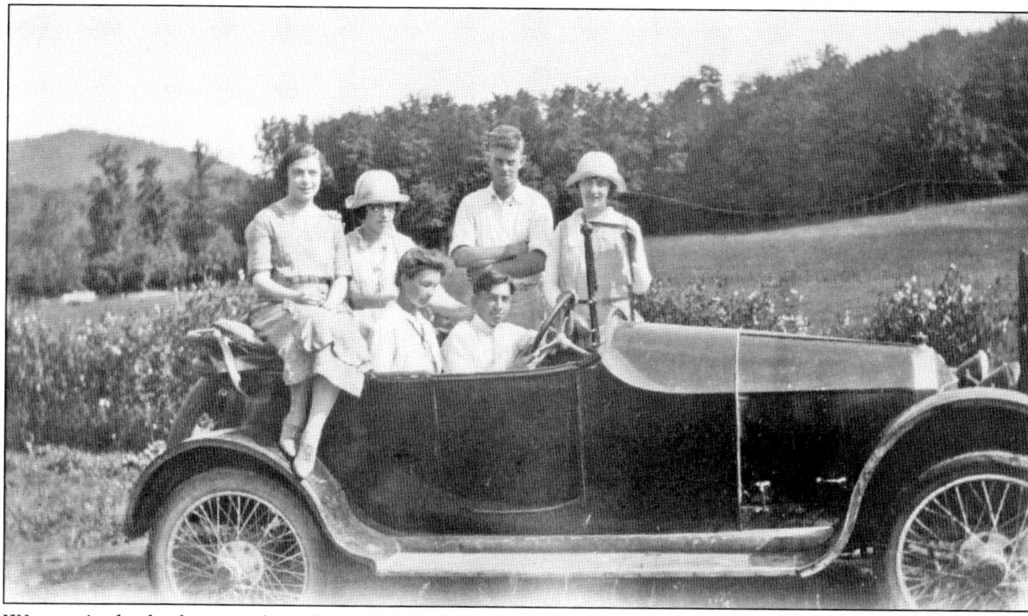

Women's cloche hats and roadsters (a kind of vehicle) were popular in 1932. Traditionally, roadsters did not have windows and sometimes did not have doors. Earlier vehicles had soft roll down roofs, and they were the sports vehicles at the time. The open car seating could accommodate two or three people with additional seating in the rear deck—known as a rumble seat or a dickey seat.

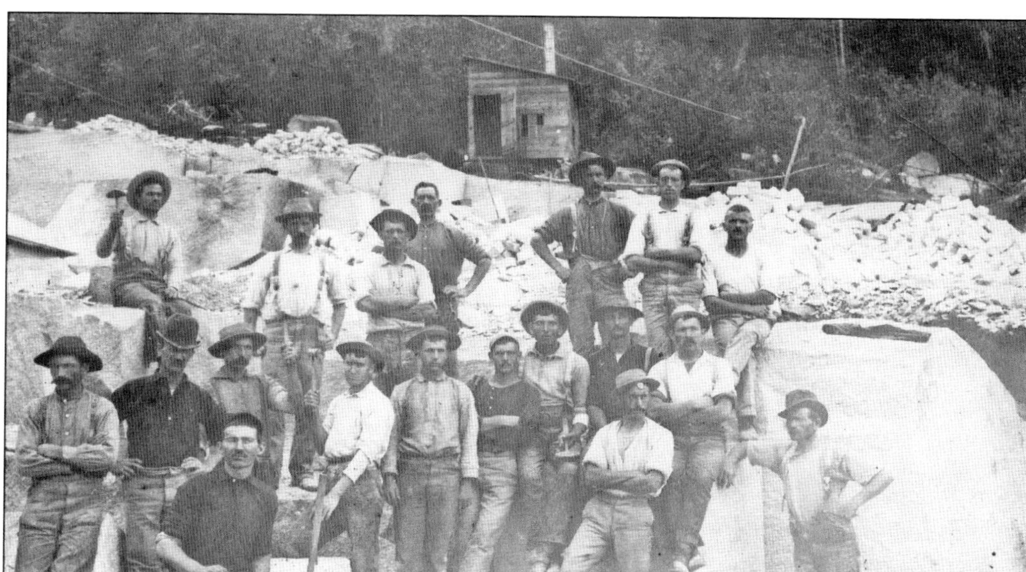

A group of quarry workers are wearing typical quarry worker clothes. The men are in suspenders, and some are holding their tools of the trade. (Courtesy of the Vermont Granite Museum.)

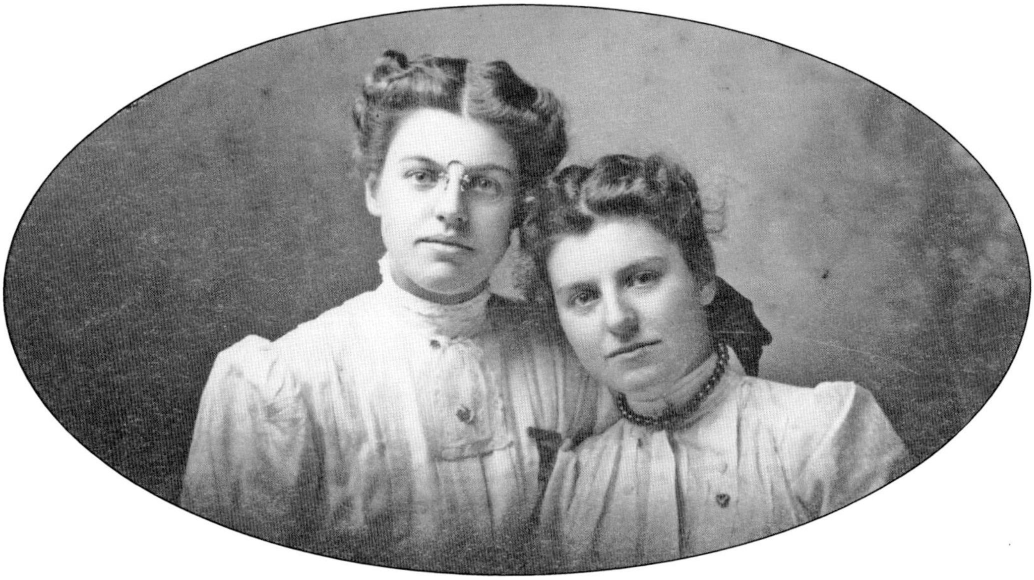

The woman on the left in this image is wearing eyeglasses popular in 1910–1911; sometimes individuals with perfect vision wore them because it made them look distinguished, or because it was fun. Blouses had higher necklines and lace collars. J. Bau's Studio took this photograph.

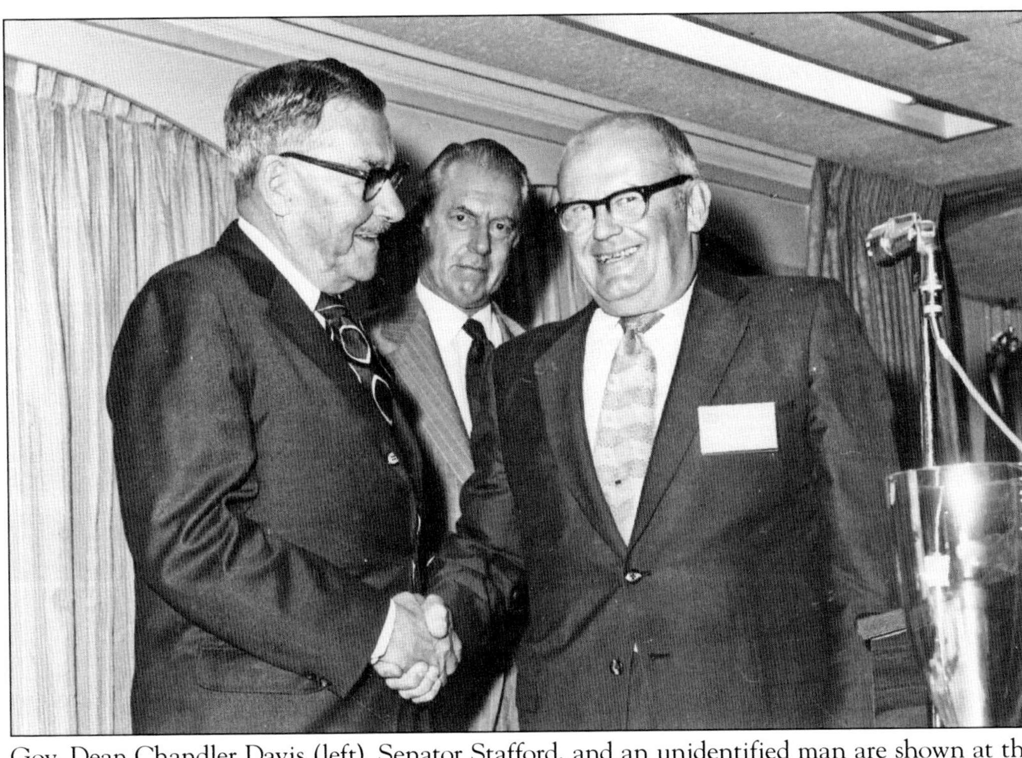

Gov. Dean Chandler Davis (left), Senator Stafford, and an unidentified man are shown at the Capitol Plaza in Montpelier. Davis was born in East Barre (1900–1990), and he worked as a lawyer, judge, insurance executive, and author. At age 69, he ran for governor and won, serving two terms. He was also the president of the Morgan Horse Club.

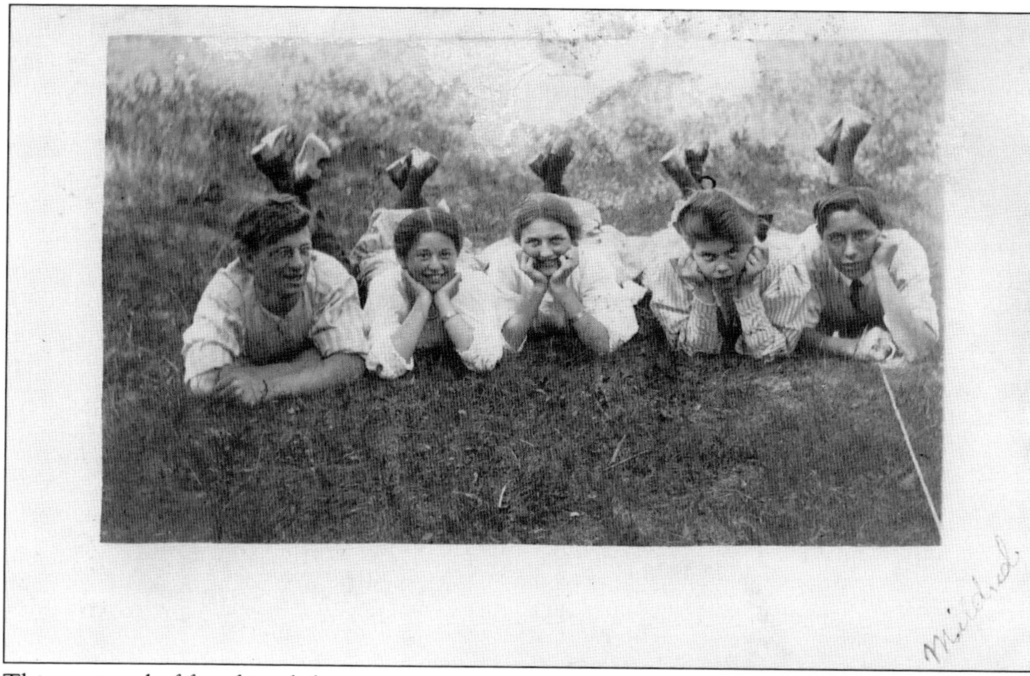

This postcard of five friends has an undivided back with no message permitted, dating the image as being produced before 1907. In this era, private citizens began to take black-and-white photographs and have them printed on paper with postcard backs. "Mildred" is scrawled at the bottom right of image with a white line pointing to her.

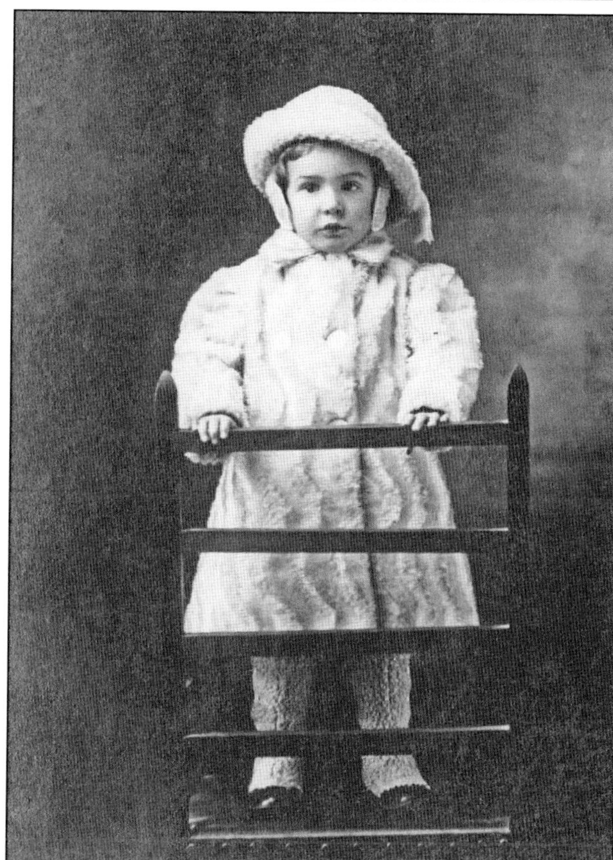

This child wears a fashionable knee-length, plush, fake-fur, big-buttoned down coat (1912–1913). She is getting ready for winter in her little black shoes and woolen stockings. The opposite side of the photograph says, "To aunt Nellie, from Paul."